SHACKLETON

Antarctic Odyssey

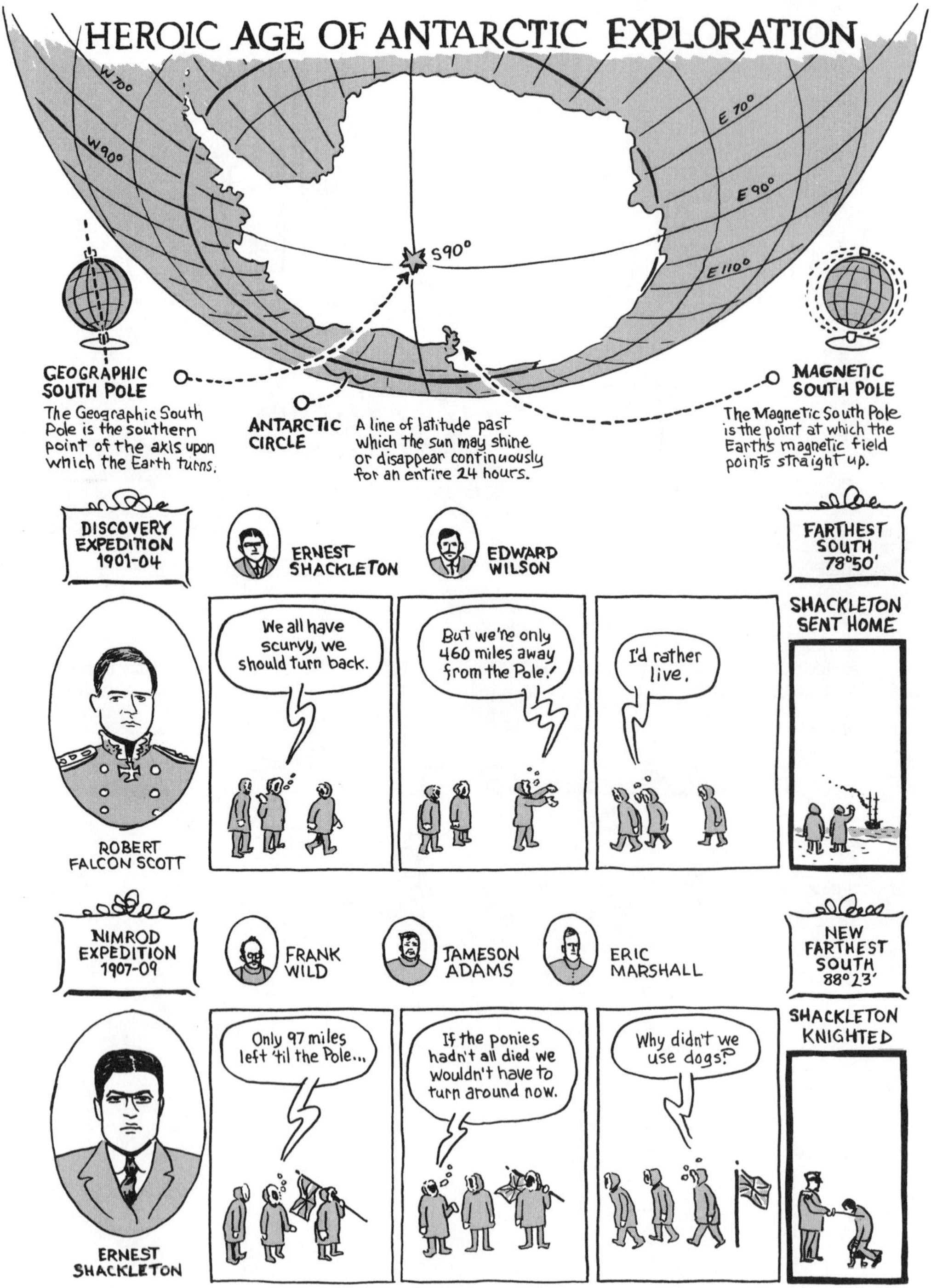
HEROIC AGE OF ANTARCTIC EXPLORATION
W 70°
W 90°
E 70°
E 90°
S 90°
E 110°
GEOGRAPHIC SOUTH POLE
The Geographic South Pole is the southern point of the axis upon which the Earth turns.
ANTARCTIC CIRCLE
A line of latitude past which the sun may shine or disappear continuously for an entire 24 hours.
MAGNETIC SOUTH POLE
The Magnetic South Pole is the point at which the Earth's magnetic field points straight up.
DISCOVERY EXPEDITION 1901-04
ERNEST SHACKLETON
EDWARD WILSON
FARTHEST SOUTH 78°50'
ROBERT FALCON SCOTT
We all have scurvy, we should turn back.
But we're only 460 miles away from the Pole!
I'd rather live.
SHACKLETON SENT HOME
NIMROD EXPEDITION 1907-09
FRANK WILD
JAMESON ADAMS
ERIC MARSHALL
NEW FARTHEST SOUTH 88°23'
ERNEST SHACKLETON
Only 97 miles left 'til the Pole...
If the ponies hadn't all died we wouldn't have to turn around now.
Why didn't we use dogs?
SHACKLETON KNIGHTED

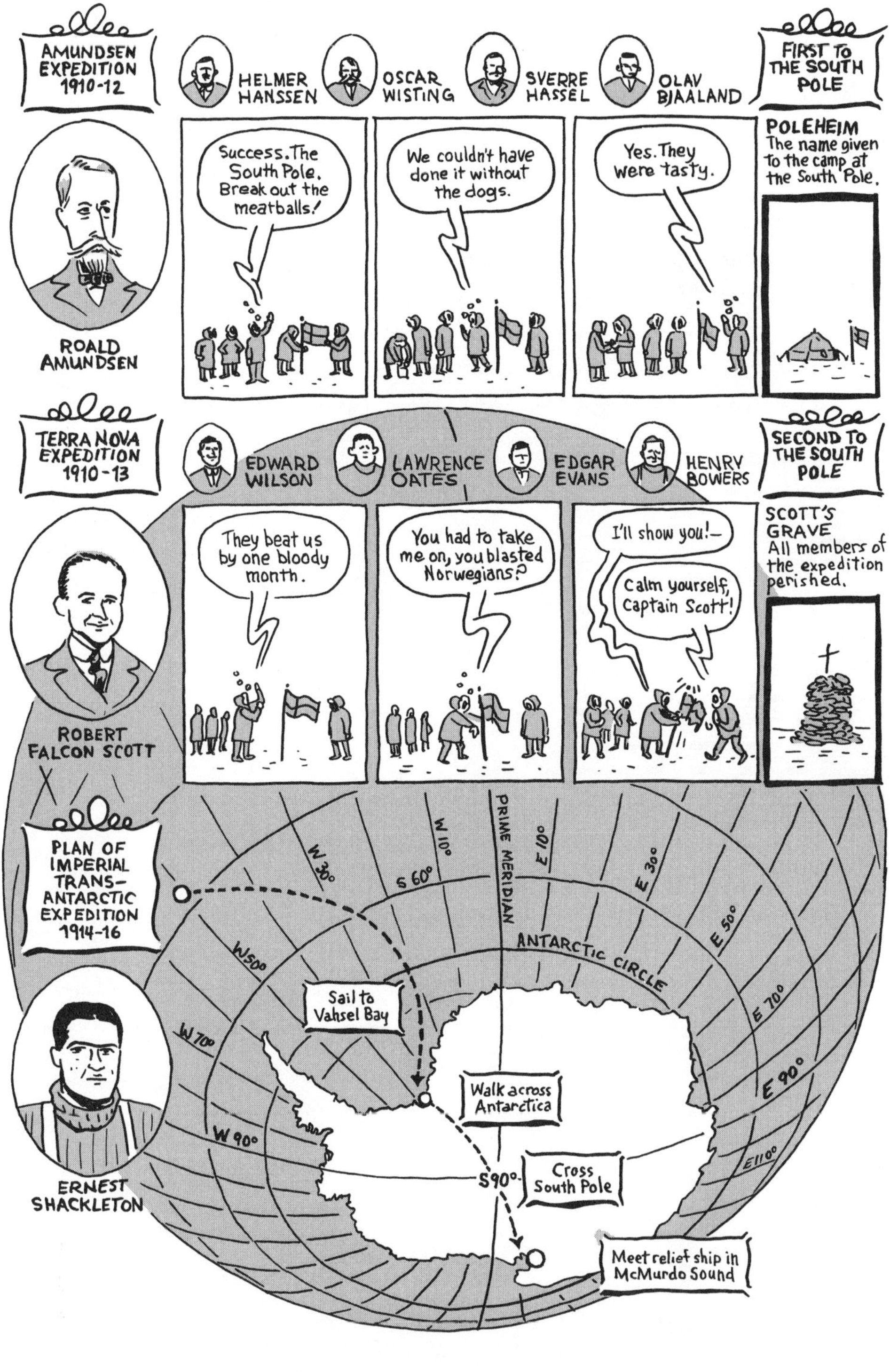
AMUNDSEN EXPEDITION 1910-12
HELMER HANSSEN
OSCAR WISTING
SVERRE HASSEL
OLAV BJAALAND
FIRST TO THE SOUTH POLE
ROALD AMUNDSEN
Success. The South Pole. Break out the meatballs!
We couldn't have done it without the dogs.
Yes. They were tasty.
POLEHEIM
The name given to the camp at the South Pole.
TERRA NOVA EXPEDITION 1910-13
EDWARD WILSON
LAWRENCE OATES
EDGAR EVANS
HENRY BOWERS
SECOND TO THE SOUTH POLE
ROBERT FALCON SCOTT
They beat us by one bloody month.
You had to take me on, you blasted Norwegians!
I'll show you!
Calm yourself, Captain Scott!
SCOTT'S GRAVE
All members of the expedition perished.
PLAN OF IMPERIAL TRANS-ANTARCTIC EXPEDITION 1914-16
ERNEST SHACKLETON
PRIME MERIDIAN
W 10°
W 30°
S 60°
E 10°
E 30°
E 50°
W 50°
ANTARCTIC CIRCLE
E 70°
W 70°
E 90°
W 90°
E 110°
S 90°
Sail to Vahsel Bay
Walk across Antarctica
Cross South Pole
Meet relief ship in McMurdo Sound

While I strove for historical accuracy in this book, there are some details of the story that are compressed for dramatic reasons. This book should have been three hundred pages, but then my hand would have fallen off. For those readers who finish this account eager for more details, there is a great wealth of literature and film about Shackleton and I hope you will devour it as I have.

—Nick Bertozzi

SHACKLETON

Antarctic Odyssey

Nick Bertozzi

:01

First Second
New York

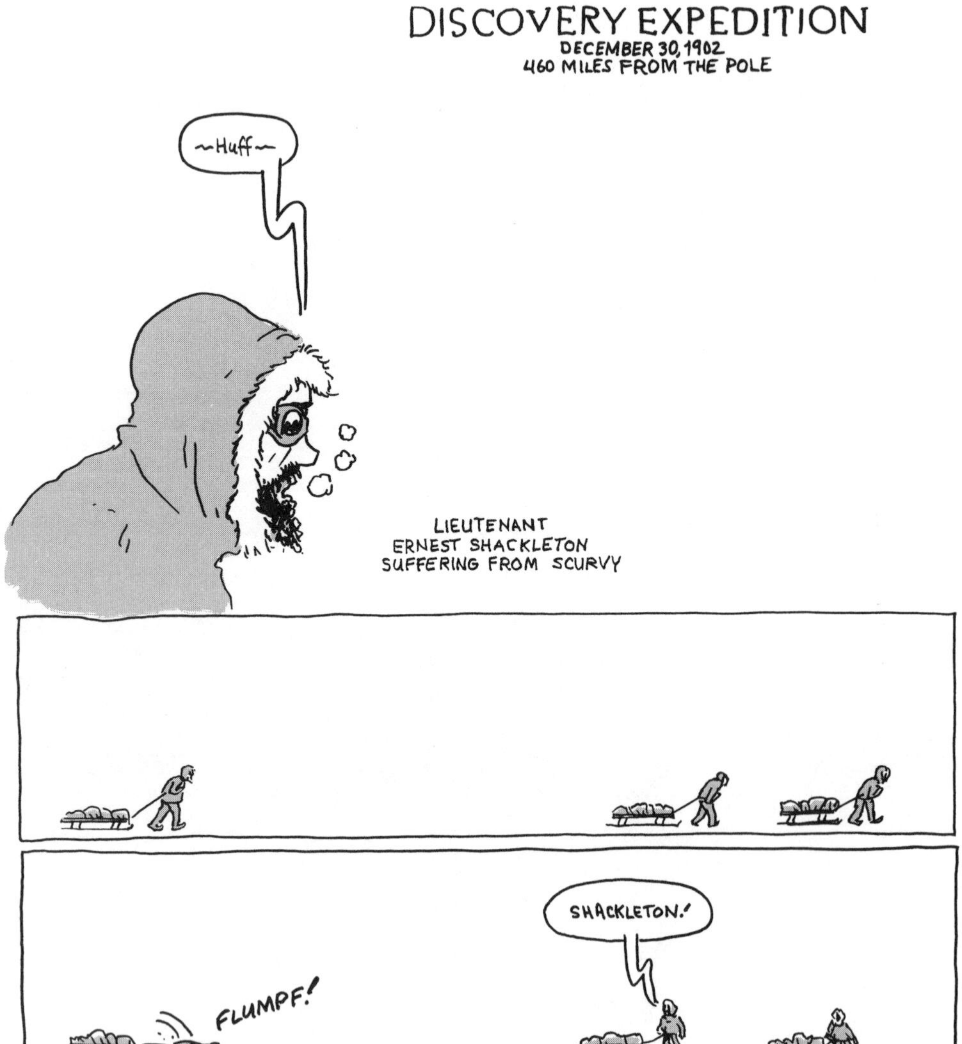
DISCOVERY EXPEDITION
DECEMBER 30, 1902
460 MILES FROM THE POLE
~Huff~
LIEUTENANT ERNEST SHACKLETON SUFFERING FROM SCURVY
FLUMPF!
SHACKLETON!

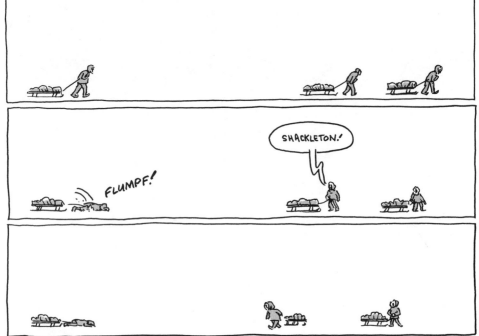

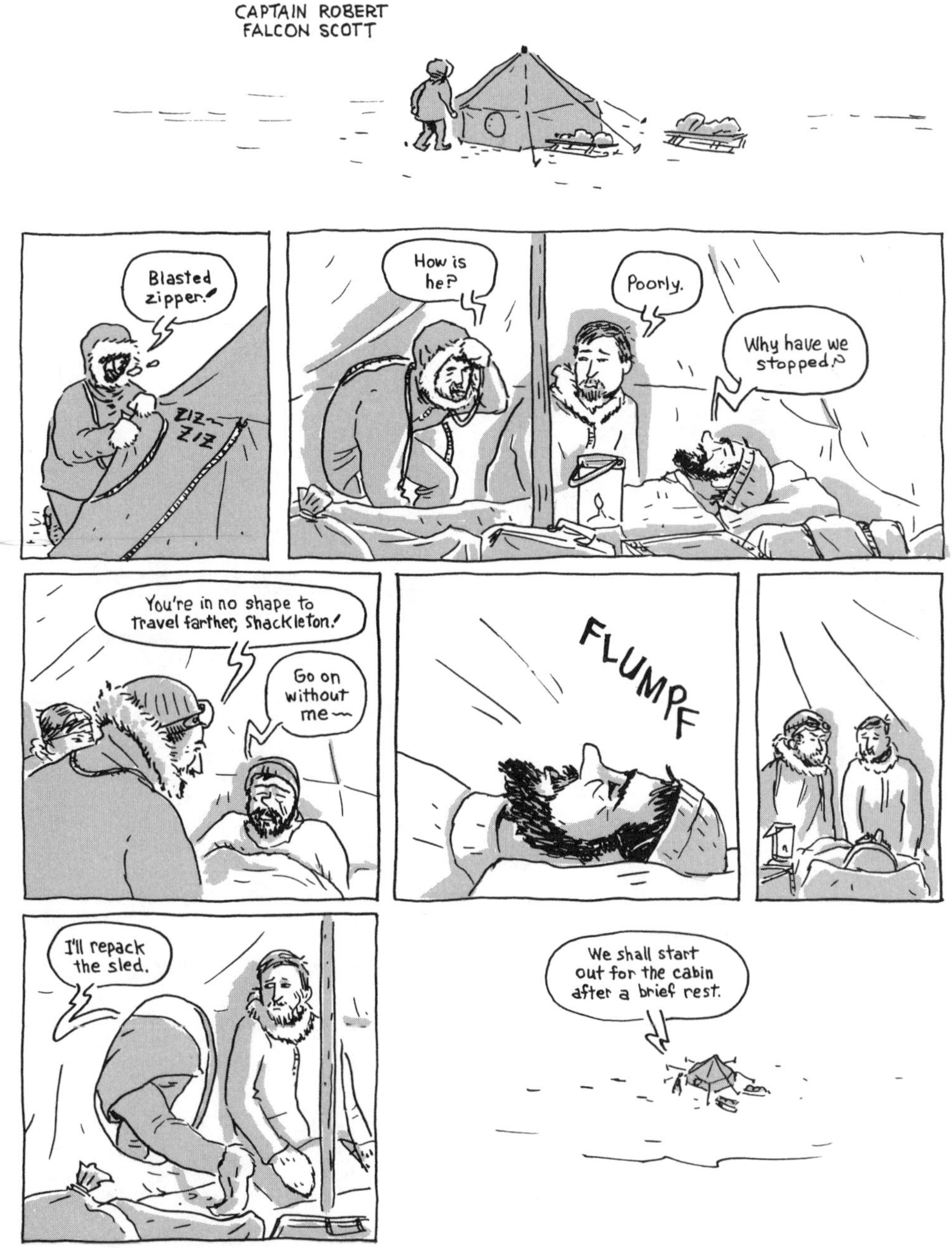
CAPTAIN ROBERT FALCON SCOTT
Blasted zipper.!
ZIZ~ ZIZ
How is he?
Poorly.
Why have we stopped.?
You're in no shape to travel farther, Shackleton.!
Go on without me~
FLUMPF
I'll repack the sled.
We shall start out for the cabin after a brief rest.

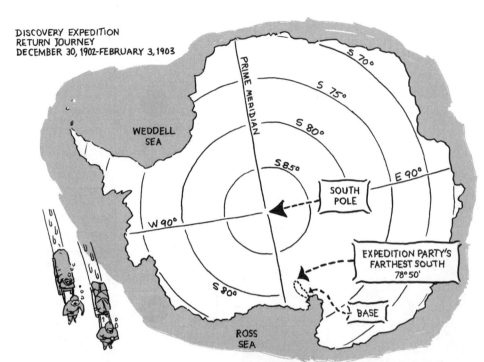

DISCOVERY EXPEDITION
RETURN JOURNEY
DECEMBER 30, 1902-FEBRUARY 3, 1903

PRIME MERIDIAN

S 70°
S 75°
S 80°
S 85°
E 90°

WEDDELL
SEA

W 90°

SOUTH
POLE

EXPEDITION PARTY'S
FARTHEST SOUTH
78° 50'

S 80°

BASE

ROSS
SEA

RETURN TO CAMP

HO!

SEVERAL WEEKS LATER

You wished to see me, Captain Scott, sir?

Due to your ongoing illness I'm relieving you of your post and sending you home.

RELIEF SHIP *MORNING* DEPARTS
MARCH 2, 1903

Ready to head home, Shacks?

No, I'll be back.

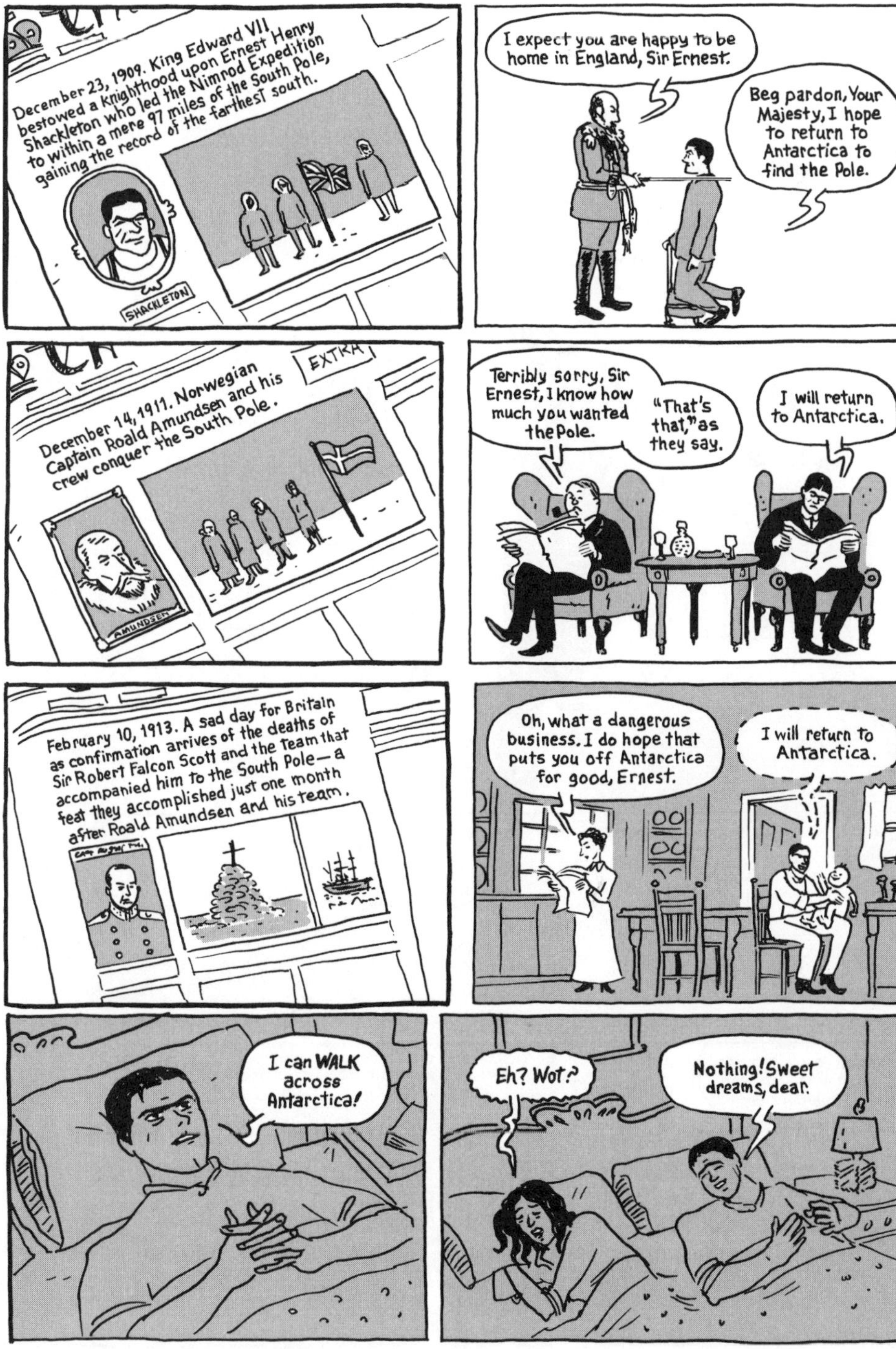
December 23, 1909. King Edward VII bestowed a knighthood upon Ernest Henry Shackleton who led the Nimrod Expedition to within a mere 97 miles of the South Pole, gaining the record of the farthest south.
SHACKLETON
I expect you are happy to be home in England, Sir Ernest.
Beg pardon, Your Majesty, I hope to return to Antarctica to find the Pole.
EXTRA
December 14, 1911. Norwegian Captain Roald Amundsen and his crew conquer the South Pole.
AMUNDSEN
Terribly sorry, Sir Ernest, I know how much you wanted the Pole.
"That's that," as they say.
I will return to Antarctica.
February 10, 1913. A sad day for Britain as confirmation arrives of the deaths of Sir Robert Falcon Scott and the team that accompanied him to the South Pole—a feat they accomplished just one month after Roald Amundsen and his team.
Oh, what a dangerous business. I do hope that puts you off Antarctica for good, Ernest.
I will return to Antarctica.
I can WALK across Antarctica!
Eh? Wot?
Nothing! Sweet dreams, dear.

HYDE PARK, LONDON
SEPTEMBER, 1913

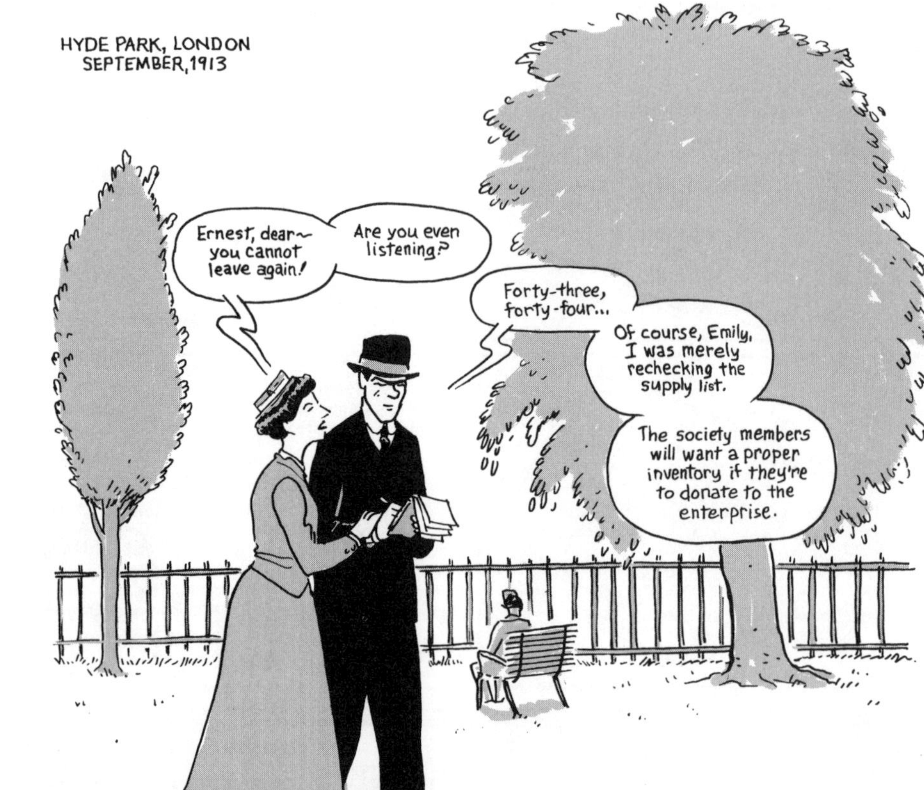
Ernest, dear~ you cannot leave again!
Are you even listening?
Forty-three, forty-four...
Of course, Emily, I was merely rechecking the supply list.
The society members will want a proper inventory if they're to donate to the enterprise.

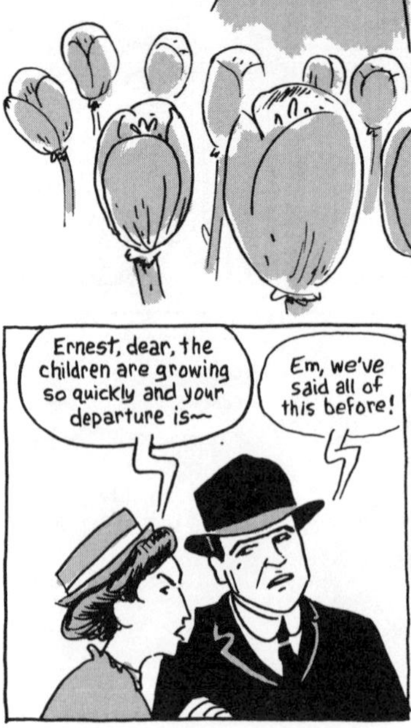
Ernest, dear, the children are growing so quickly and your departure is~
Em, we've said all of this before!

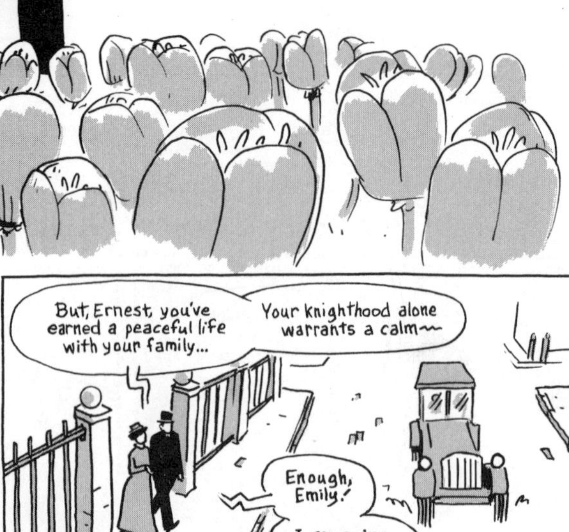
But, Ernest, you've earned a peaceful life with your family...
Your knighthood alone warrants a calm~
Enough, Emily!
I am going to the Pole!

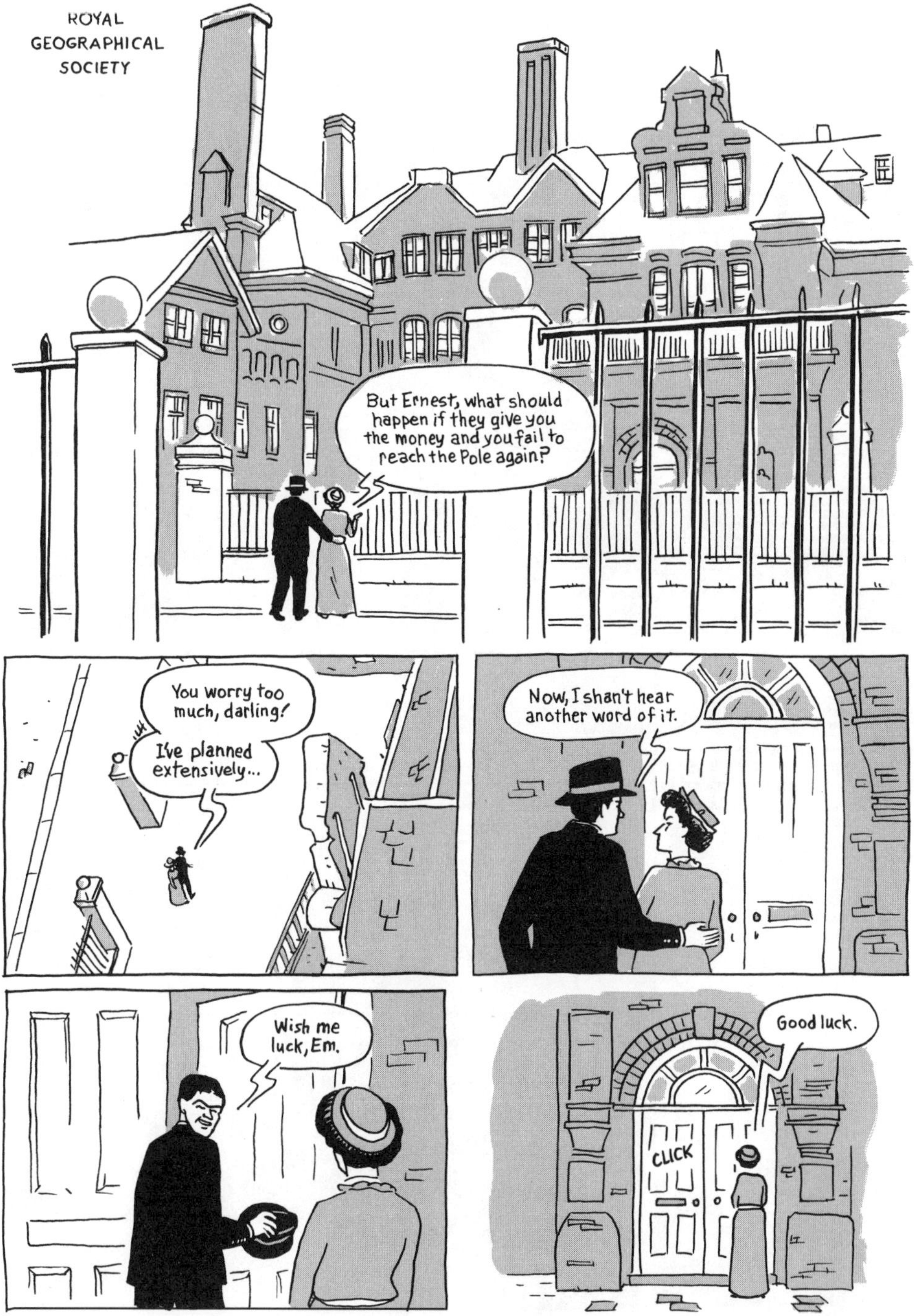
ROYAL GEOGRAPHICAL SOCIETY
But Ernest, what should happen if they give you the money and you fail to reach the Pole again?
You worry too much, darling!
I've planned extensively...
Now, I shan't hear another word of it.
Wish me luck, Em.
Good luck.
CLICK

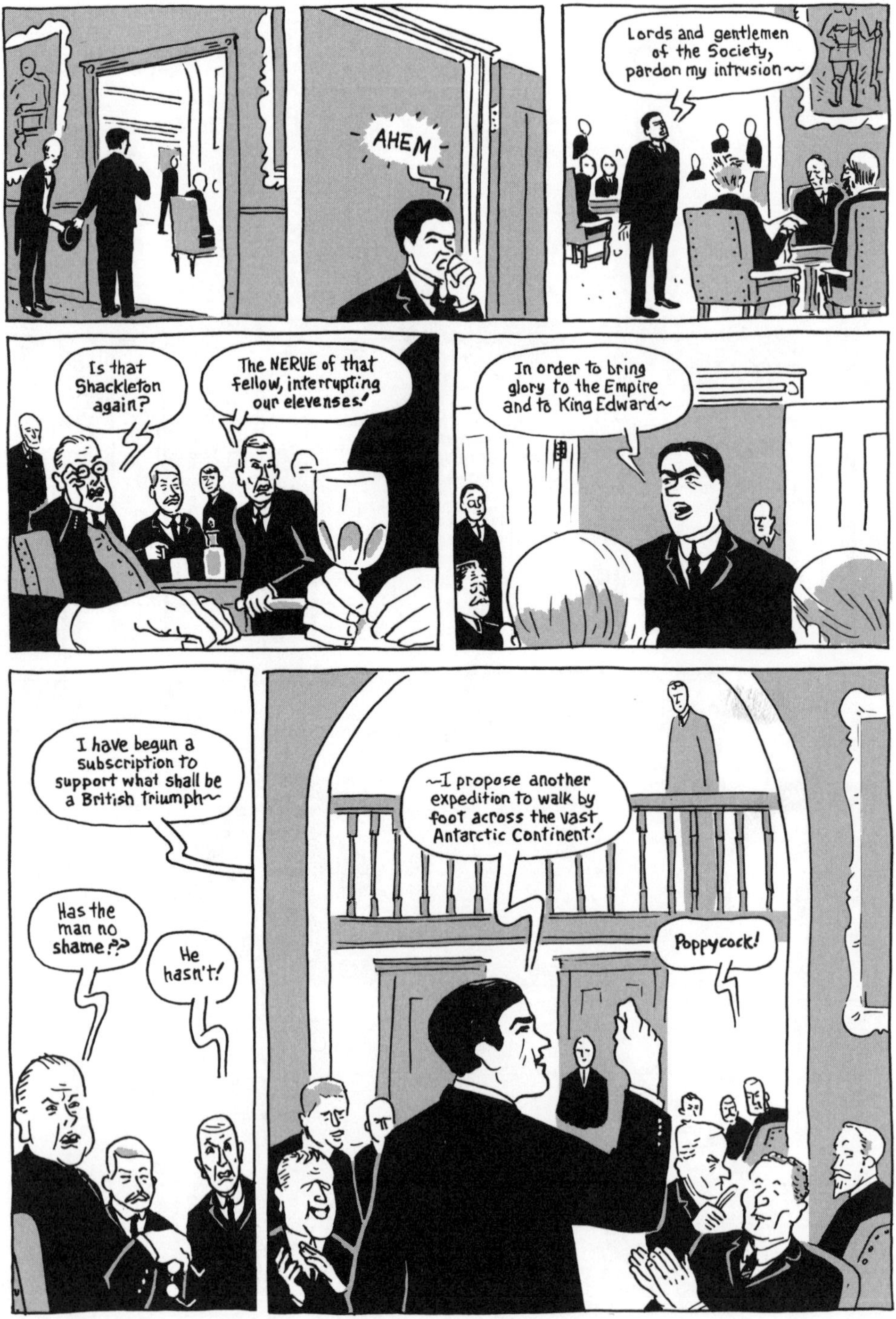
AHEM
Lords and gentlemen of the Society, pardon my intrusion~~
Is that Shackleton again?
The NERVE of that fellow, interrupting our elevenses!
In order to bring glory to the Empire and to King Edward~
I have begun a subscription to support what shall be a British triumph~
~I propose another expedition to walk by foot across the vast Antarctic Continent!
Has the man no shame?!?
He hasn't!
Poppycock!

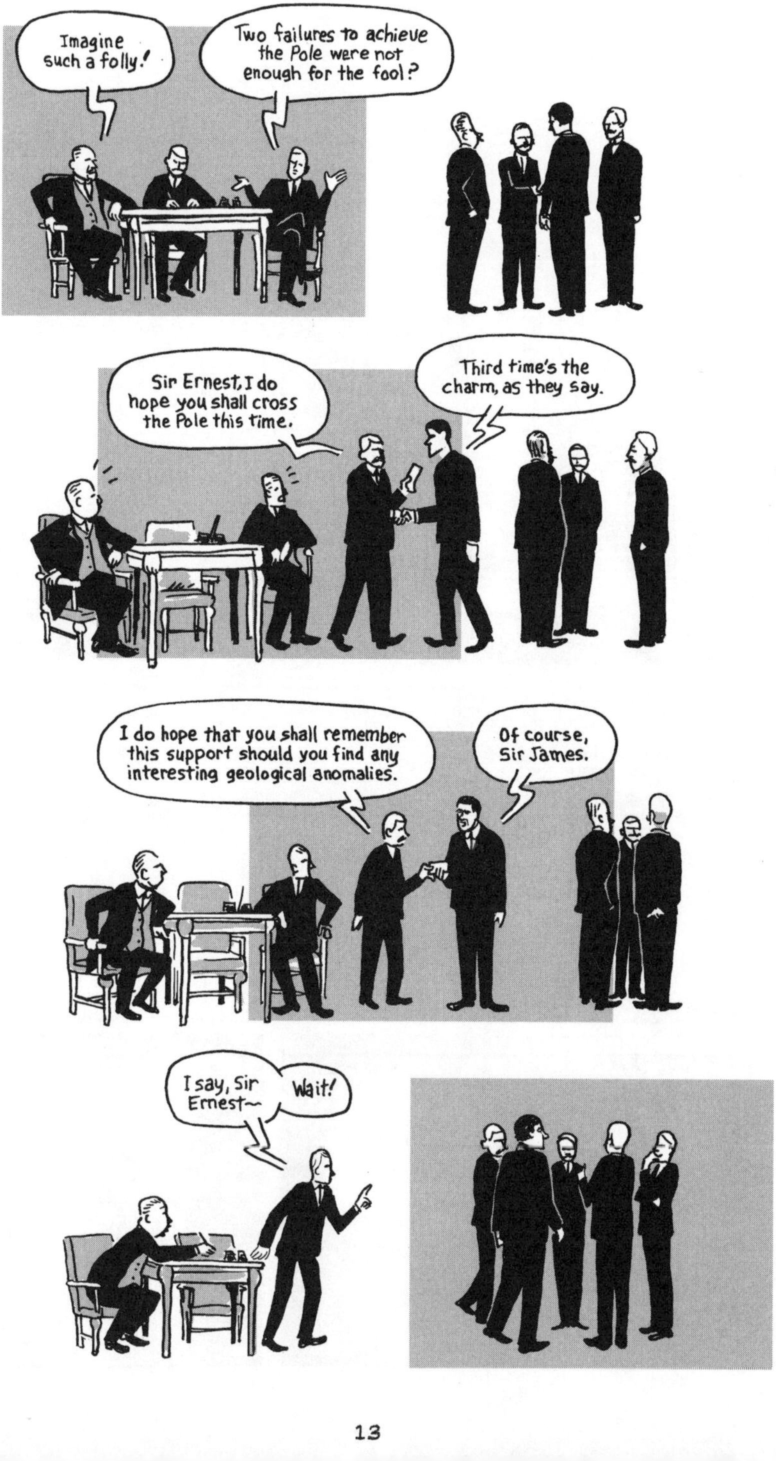
Imagine such a folly!
Two failures to achieve the Pole were not enough for the fool?
Sir Ernest, I do hope you shall cross the Pole this time.
Third time's the charm, as they say.
I do hope that you shall remember this support should you find any interesting geological anomalies.
Of course, Sir James.
I say, Sir Ernest~
Wait!

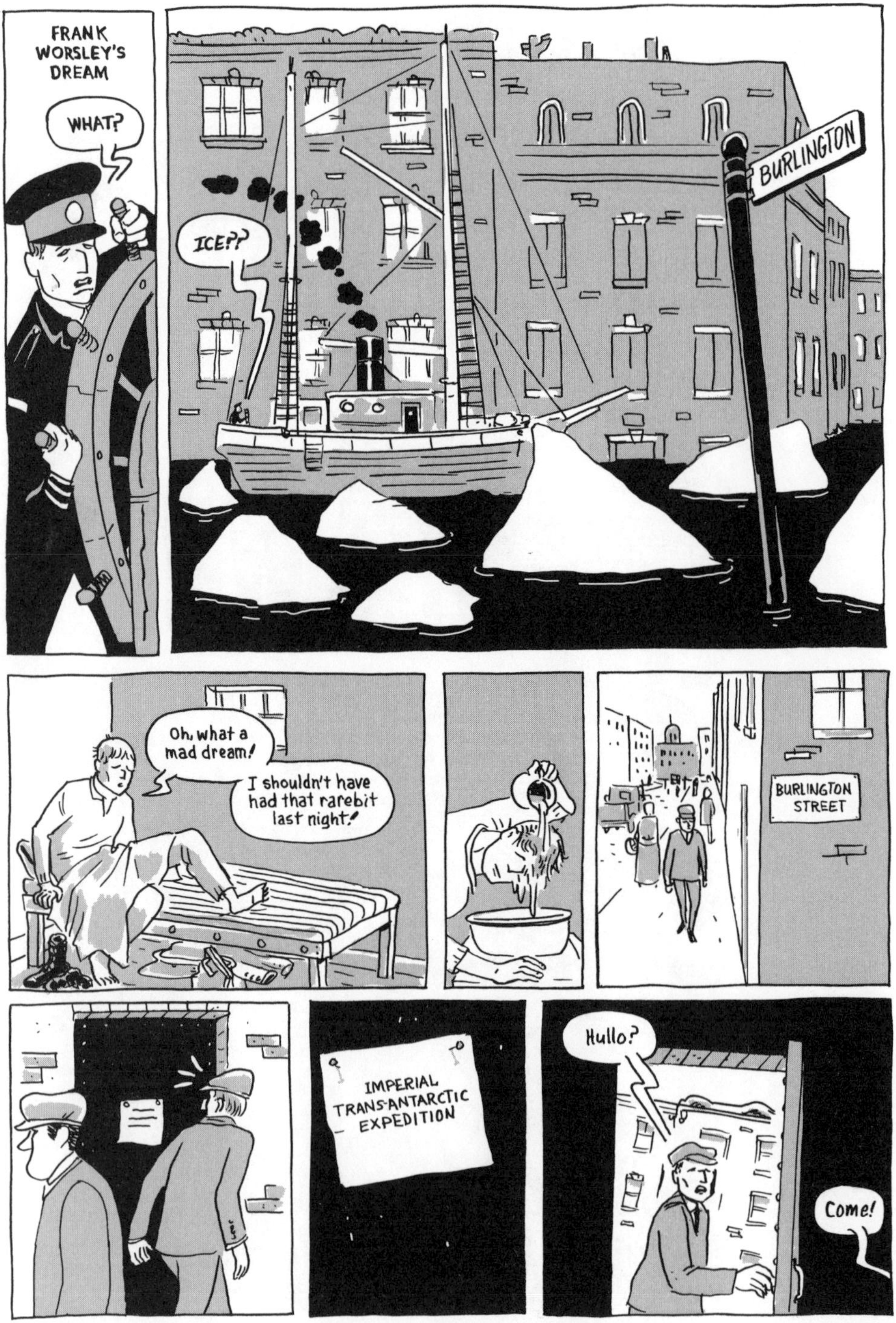

FRANK WORSLEY'S DREAM
WHAT?
ICE??
BURLINGTON
Oh, what a mad dream!
I shouldn't have had that rarebit last night!
BURLINGTON STREET
IMPERIAL TRANS-ANTARCTIC EXPEDITION
Hullo?
Come!

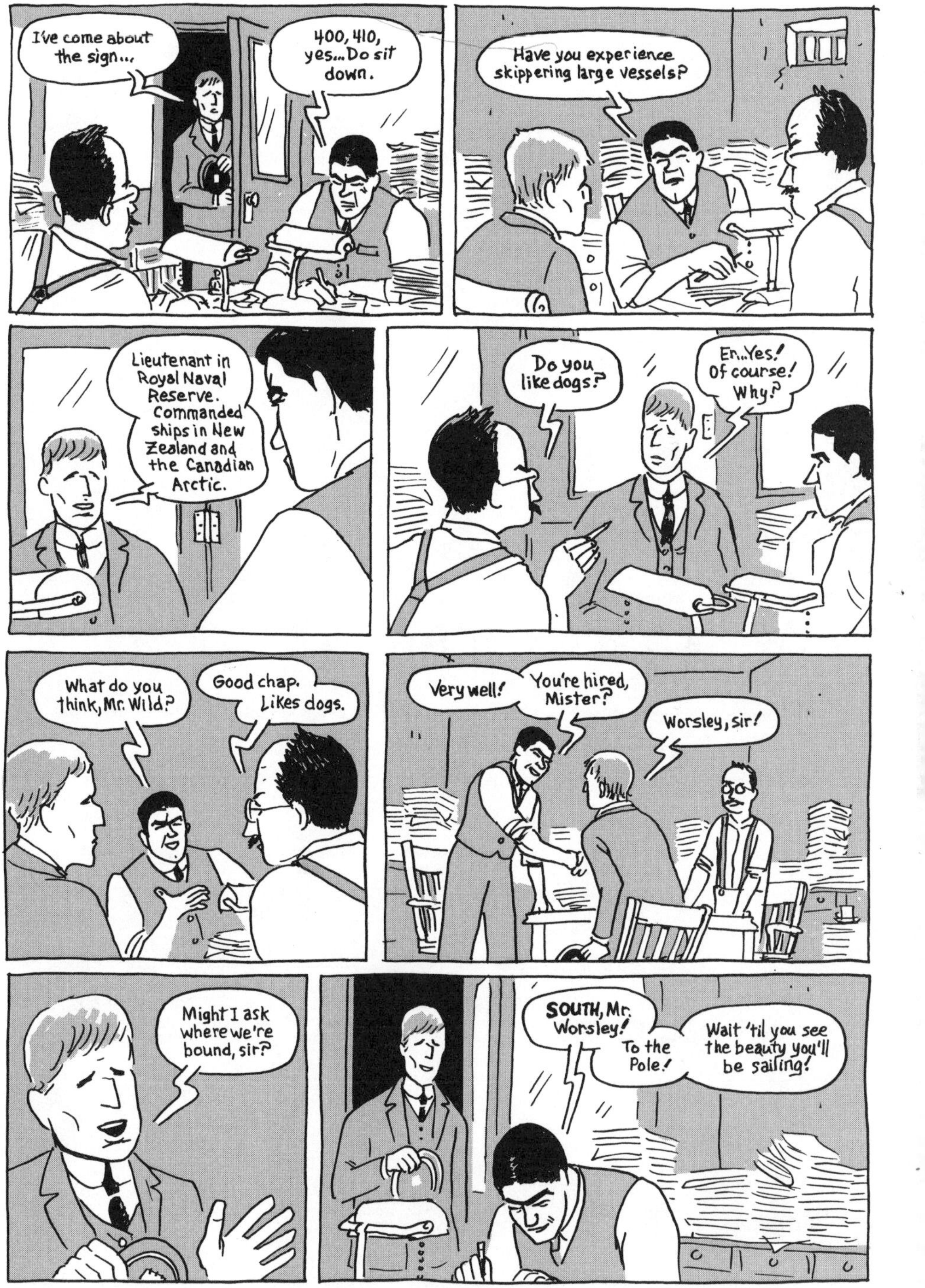
I've come about the sign...
400, 410, yes... Do sit down.
Have you experience skippering large vessels?
Lieutenant in Royal Naval Reserve. Commanded ships in New Zealand and the Canadian Arctic.
Do you like dogs?
Er... Yes! Of course! Why?
What do you think, Mr. Wild?
Good chap. Likes dogs.
Very well!
You're hired, Mister?
Worsley, sir!
Might I ask where we're bound, sir?
SOUTH, Mr. Worsley! To the Pole!
Wait 'til you see the beauty you'll be sailing!

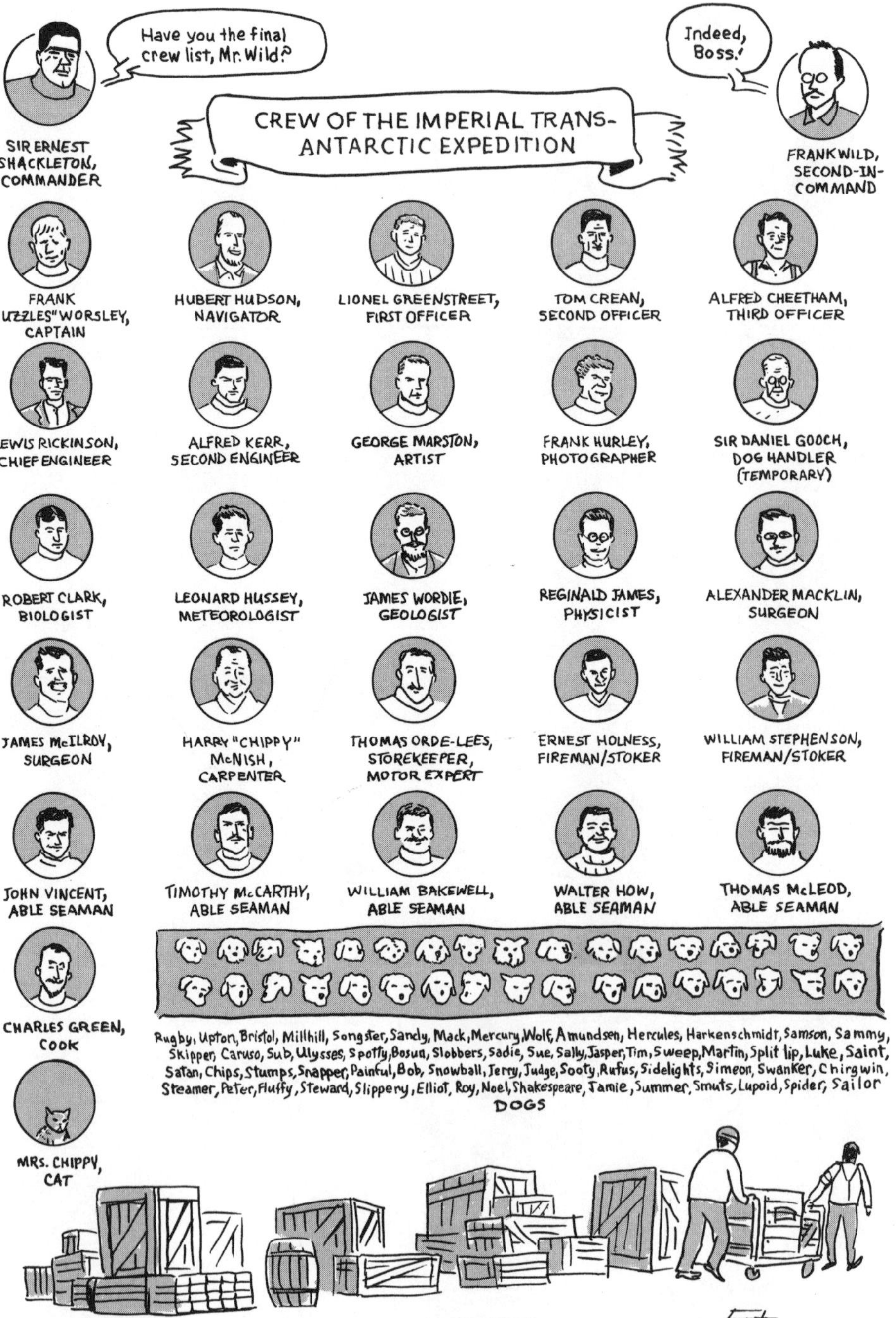
Have you the final crew list, Mr. Wild?
Indeed, Boss!
CREW OF THE IMPERIAL TRANS-ANTARCTIC EXPEDITION
SIR ERNEST SHACKLETON, COMMANDER
FRANK WILD, SECOND-IN-COMMAND
FRANK "WUZZLES" WORSLEY, CAPTAIN
HUBERT HUDSON, NAVIGATOR
LIONEL GREENSTREET, FIRST OFFICER
TOM CREAN, SECOND OFFICER
ALFRED CHEETHAM, THIRD OFFICER
LEWIS RICKINSON, CHIEF ENGINEER
ALFRED KERR, SECOND ENGINEER
GEORGE MARSTON, ARTIST
FRANK HURLEY, PHOTOGRAPHER
SIR DANIEL GOOCH, DOG HANDLER (TEMPORARY)
ROBERT CLARK, BIOLOGIST
LEONARD HUSSEY, METEOROLOGIST
JAMES WORDIE, GEOLOGIST
REGINALD JAMES, PHYSICIST
ALEXANDER MACKLIN, SURGEON
JAMES McILROY, SURGEON
HARRY "CHIPPY" McNISH, CARPENTER
THOMAS ORDE-LEES, STOREKEEPER, MOTOR EXPERT
ERNEST HOLNESS, FIREMAN/STOKER
WILLIAM STEPHENSON, FIREMAN/STOKER
JOHN VINCENT, ABLE SEAMAN
TIMOTHY McCARTHY, ABLE SEAMAN
WILLIAM BAKEWELL, ABLE SEAMAN
WALTER HOW, ABLE SEAMAN
THOMAS McLEOD, ABLE SEAMAN
CHARLES GREEN, COOK
Rugby, Upton, Bristol, Millhill, Songster, Sandy, Mack, Mercury, Wolf, Amundsen, Hercules, Harkenschmidt, Samson, Sammy, Skipper, Caruso, Sub, Ulysses, Spotty, Bosun, Slobbers, Sadie, Sue, Sally, Jasper, Tim, Sweep, Martin, Split lip, Luke, Saint, Satan, Chips, Stumps, Snapper, Painful, Bob, Snowball, Jerry, Judge, Sooty, Rufus, Sidelights, Simeon, Swanker, Chirgwin, Steamer, Peter, Fluffy, Steward, Slippery, Elliot, Roy, Noel, Shakespeare, Jamie, Summer, Smuts, Lupoid, Spider, Sailor
DOGS
MRS. CHIPPY, CAT

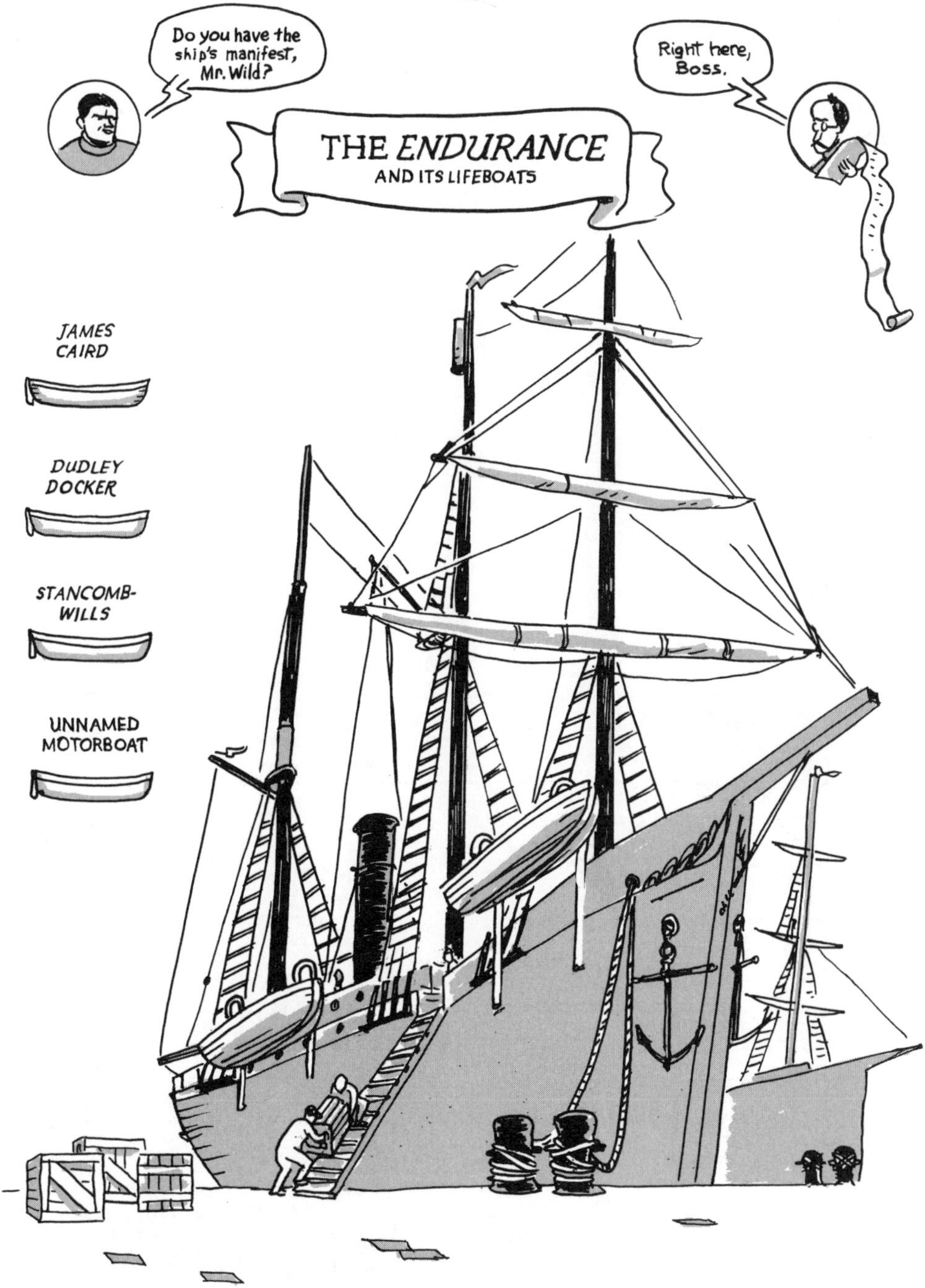
Do you have the ship's manifest, Mr. Wild?
Right here, Boss.
THE *ENDURANCE*
AND ITS LIFEBOATS
JAMES CAIRD
DUDLEY DOCKER
STANCOMB-WILLS
UNNAMED MOTORBOAT

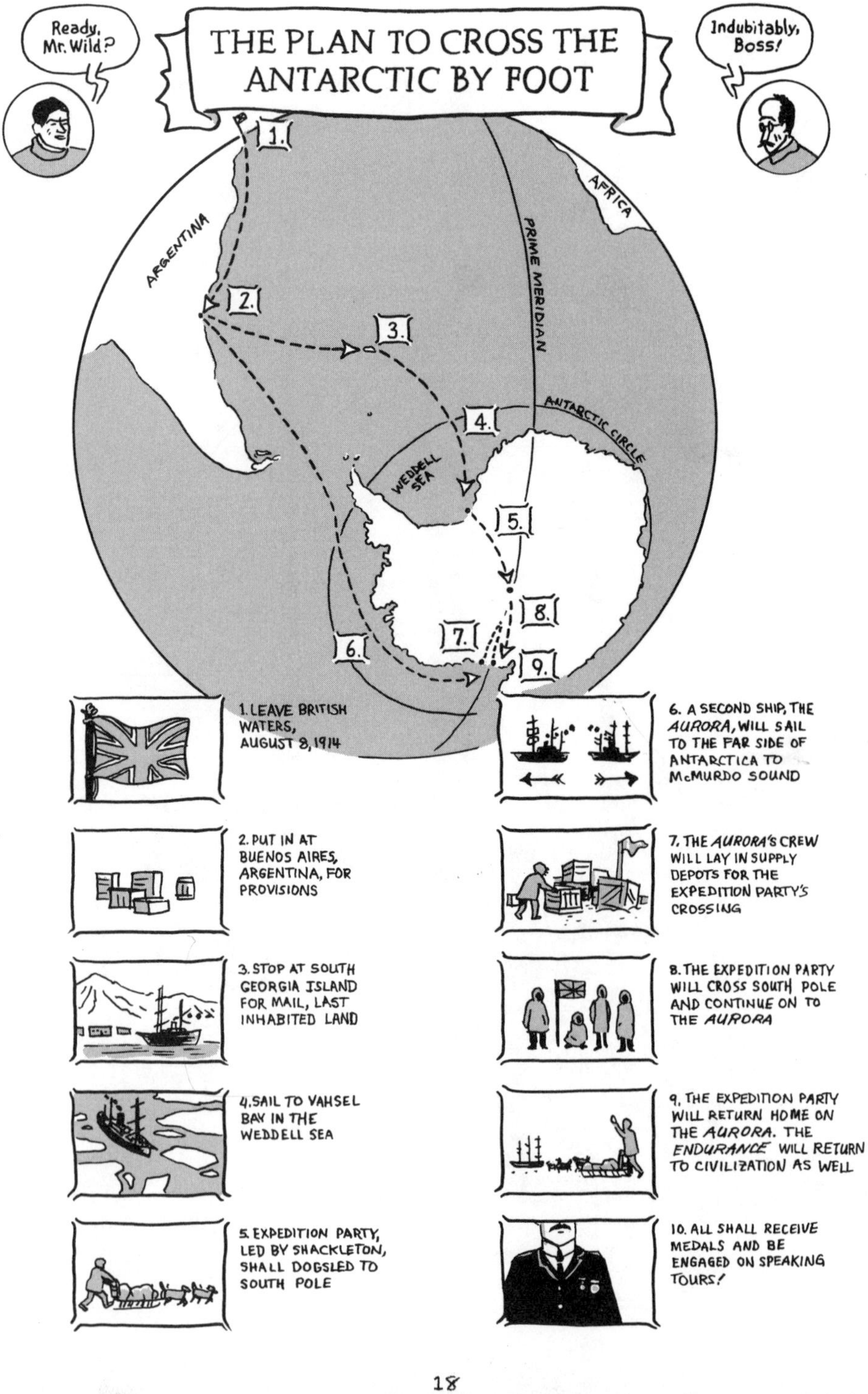
Ready, Mr. Wild?
THE PLAN TO CROSS THE ANTARCTIC BY FOOT
Indubitably, Boss!
1.
ARGENTINA
AFRICA
PRIME MERIDIAN
2.
3.
4.
ANTARCTIC CIRCLE
WEDDELL SEA
5.
8.
7.
6.
9.
1. LEAVE BRITISH WATERS, AUGUST 8, 1914
2. PUT IN AT BUENOS AIRES, ARGENTINA, FOR PROVISIONS
3. STOP AT SOUTH GEORGIA ISLAND FOR MAIL, LAST INHABITED LAND
4. SAIL TO VAHSEL BAY IN THE WEDDELL SEA
5. EXPEDITION PARTY, LED BY SHACKLETON, SHALL DOGSLED TO SOUTH POLE
6. A SECOND SHIP, THE AURORA, WILL SAIL TO THE FAR SIDE OF ANTARCTICA TO McMURDO SOUND
7. THE AURORA'S CREW WILL LAY IN SUPPLY DEPOTS FOR THE EXPEDITION PARTY'S CROSSING
8. THE EXPEDITION PARTY WILL CROSS SOUTH POLE AND CONTINUE ON TO THE AURORA
9. THE EXPEDITION PARTY WILL RETURN HOME ON THE AURORA. THE ENDURANCE WILL RETURN TO CIVILIZATION AS WELL
10. ALL SHALL RECEIVE MEDALS AND BE ENGAGED ON SPEAKING TOURS!

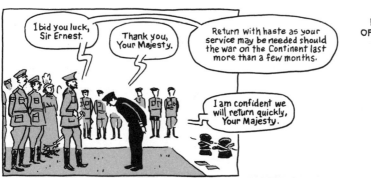

ROYAL SEND-OFF
OF THE *ENDURANCE*
AUGUST 1, 1914

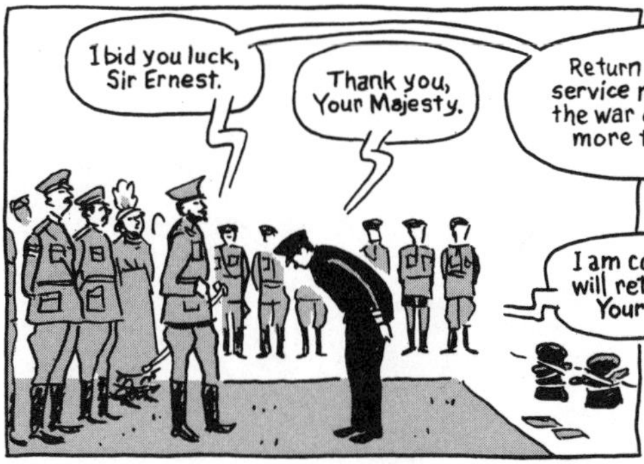
I bid you luck, Sir Ernest.
Thank you, Your Majesty.
Return with haste as your service may be needed should the war on the Continent last more than a few months.
I am confident we will return quickly, Your Majesty.

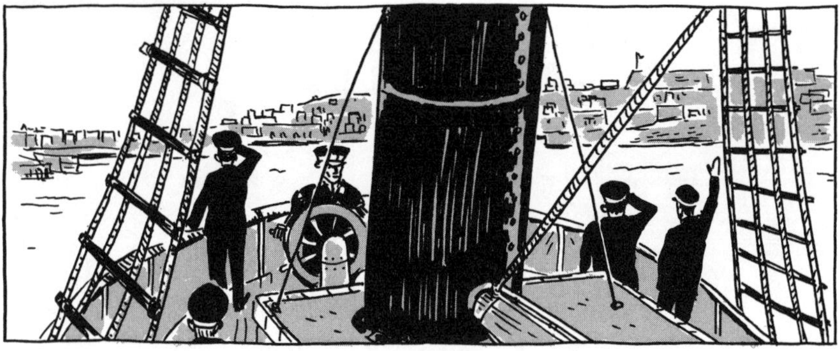

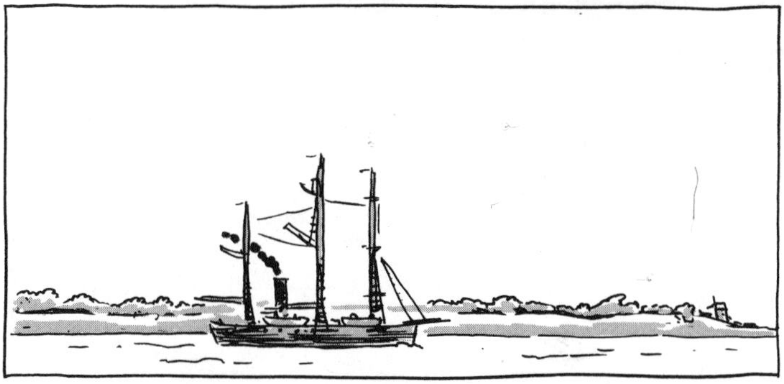

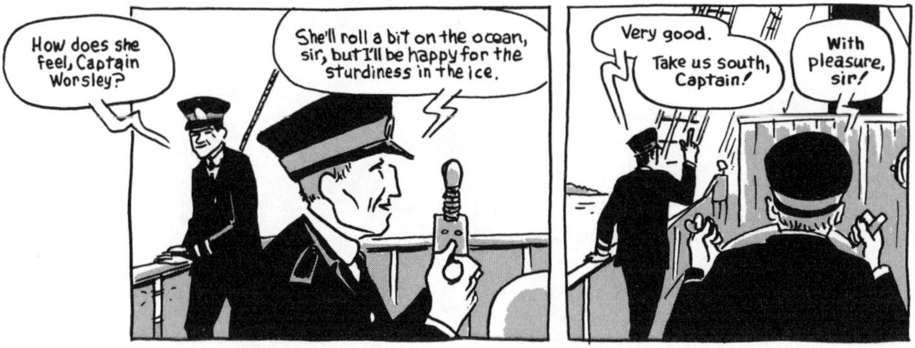
How does she feel, Captain Worsley?
She'll roll a bit on the ocean, sir, but I'll be happy for the sturdiness in the ice.
Very good.
Take us south, Captain!
With pleasure, sir!

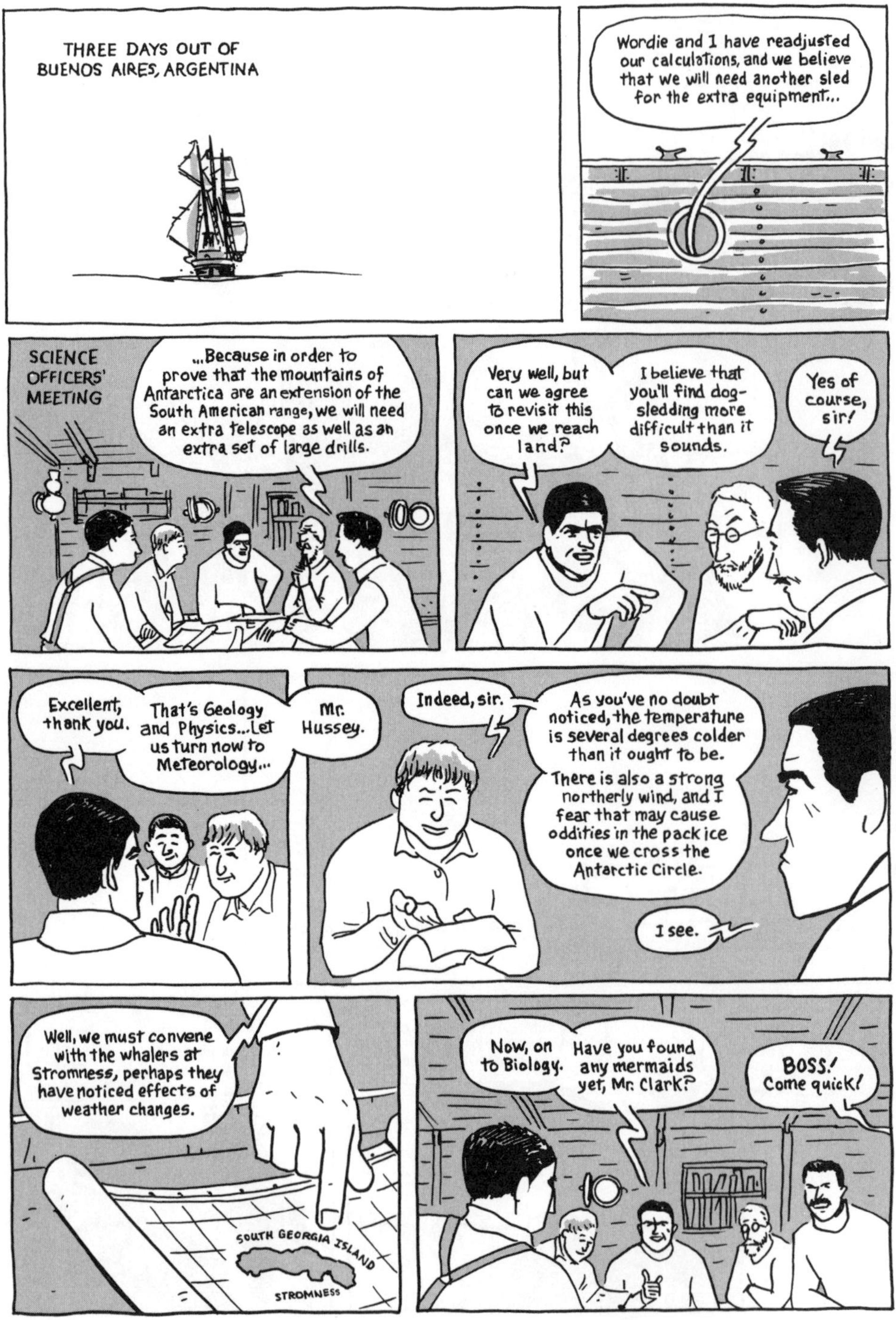

THREE DAYS OUT OF BUENOS AIRES, ARGENTINA
Wordie and I have readjusted our calculations, and we believe that we will need another sled for the extra equipment...
SCIENCE OFFICERS' MEETING
...Because in order to prove that the mountains of Antarctica are an extension of the South American range, we will need an extra telescope as well as an extra set of large drills.
Very well, but can we agree to revisit this once we reach land?
I believe that you'll find dog-sledding more difficult than it sounds.
Yes of course, sir!
Excellent, thank you.
That's Geology and Physics...Let us turn now to Meteorology...
Mr. Hussey.
Indeed, sir.
As you've no doubt noticed, the temperature is several degrees colder than it ought to be.
There is also a strong northerly wind, and I fear that may cause oddities in the pack ice once we cross the Antarctic Circle.
I see.
Well, we must convene with the whalers at Stromness, perhaps they have noticed effects of weather changes.
SOUTH GEORGIA ISLAND
STROMNESS
Now, on to Biology.
Have you found any mermaids yet, Mr. Clark?
BOSS! Come quick!

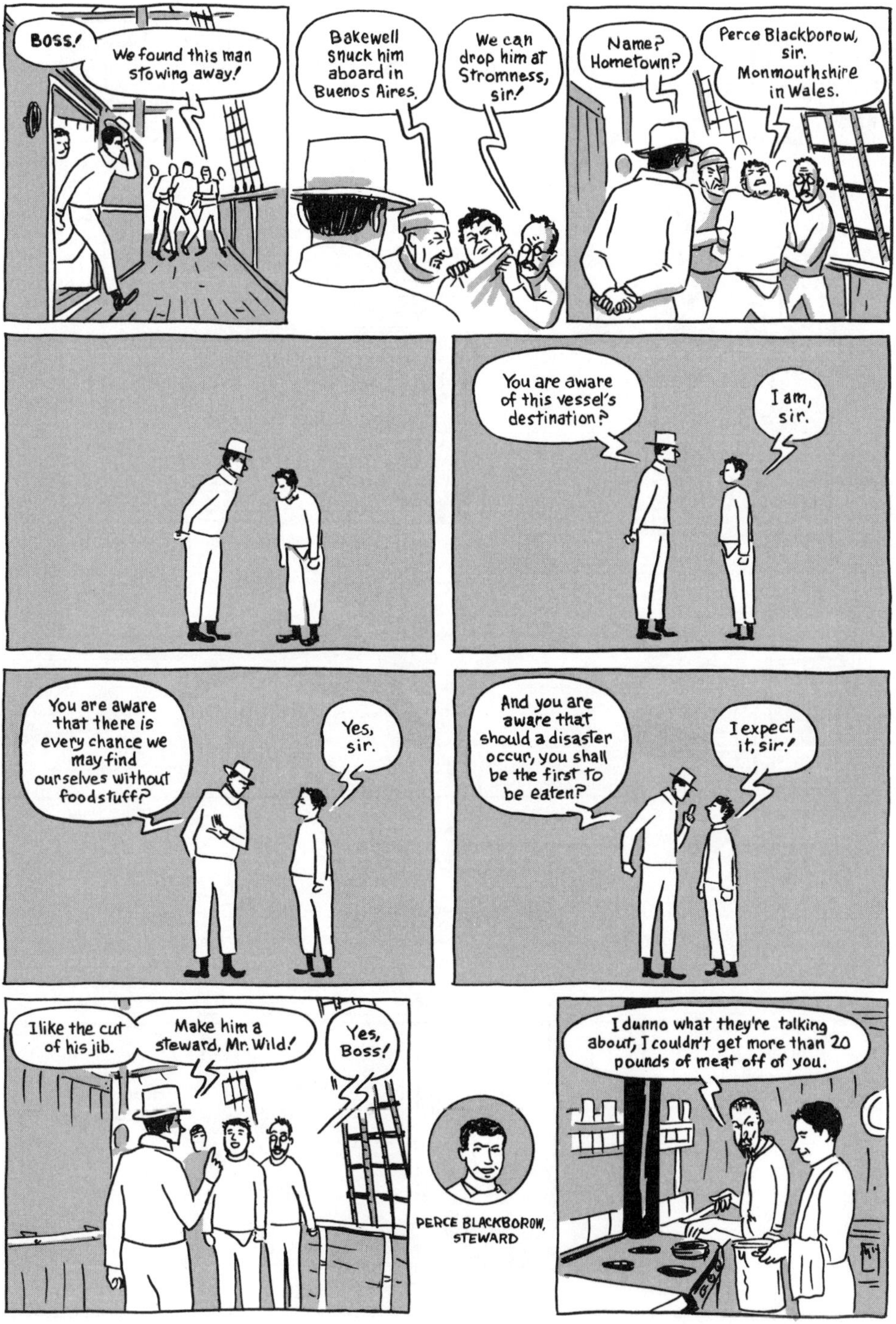
BOSS!
We found this man stowing away!
Bakewell snuck him aboard in Buenos Aires.
We can drop him at Stromness, sir!
Name? Hometown?
Perce Blackborow, sir. Monmouthshire in Wales.
You are aware of this vessel's destination?
I am, sir.
You are aware that there is every chance we may find ourselves without foodstuff?
Yes, sir.
And you are aware that should a disaster occur, you shall be the first to be eaten?
I expect it, sir!
I like the cut of his jib.
Make him a steward, Mr. Wild!
Yes, Boss!
PERCE BLACKBOROW, STEWARD
I dunno what they're talking about, I couldn't get more than 20 pounds of meat off of you.

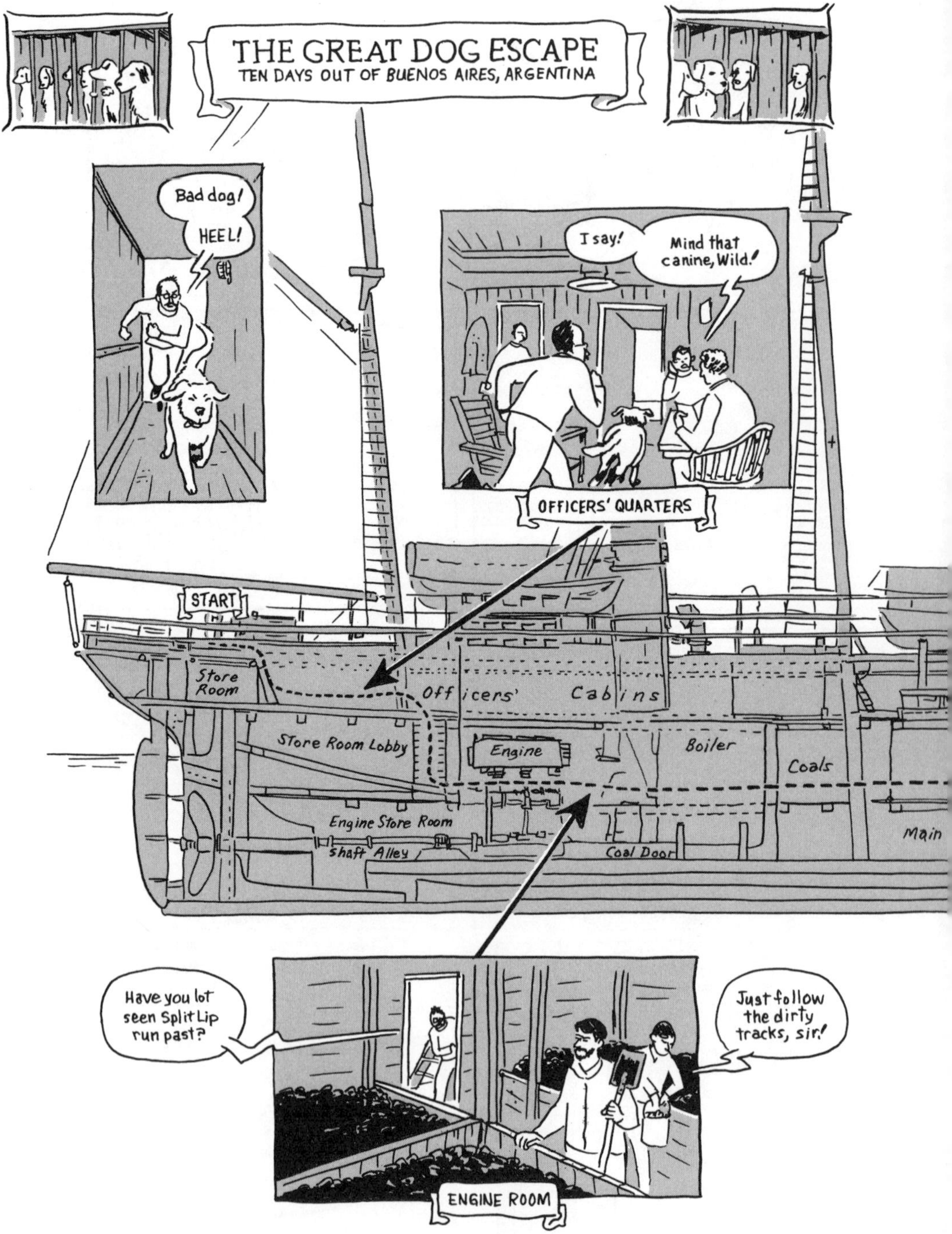
THE GREAT DOG ESCAPE
TEN DAYS OUT OF BUENOS AIRES, ARGENTINA
Bad dog!
HEEL!
I say!
Mind that canine, Wild!
OFFICERS' QUARTERS
START
Store Room
Officers' Cabins
Store Room Lobby
Engine
Boiler
Coals
Engine Store Room
Shaft Alley
Coal Door
Main
Have you lot seen Split Lip run past?
Just follow the dirty tracks, sir!
ENGINE ROOM

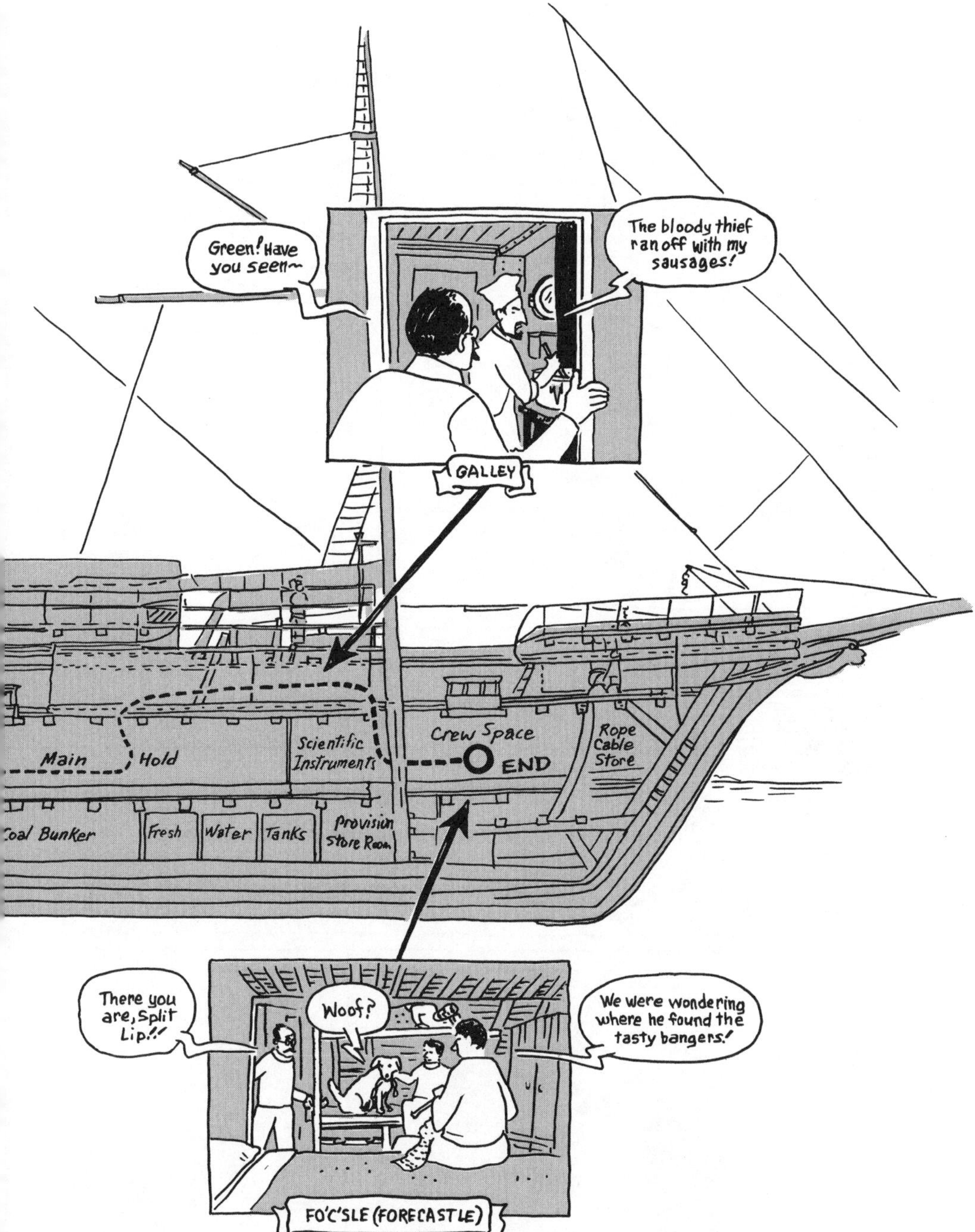

Green! Have you seen~
The bloody thief ran off with my sausages!
GALLEY
Main Hold
Scientific Instruments
Crew Space
END
Rope Cable Store
Coal Bunker
Fresh Water Tanks
Provision Store Room
There you are, Split Lip!!
Woof?
We were wondering where he found the tasty bangers!
FO'C'SLE (FORECASTLE)

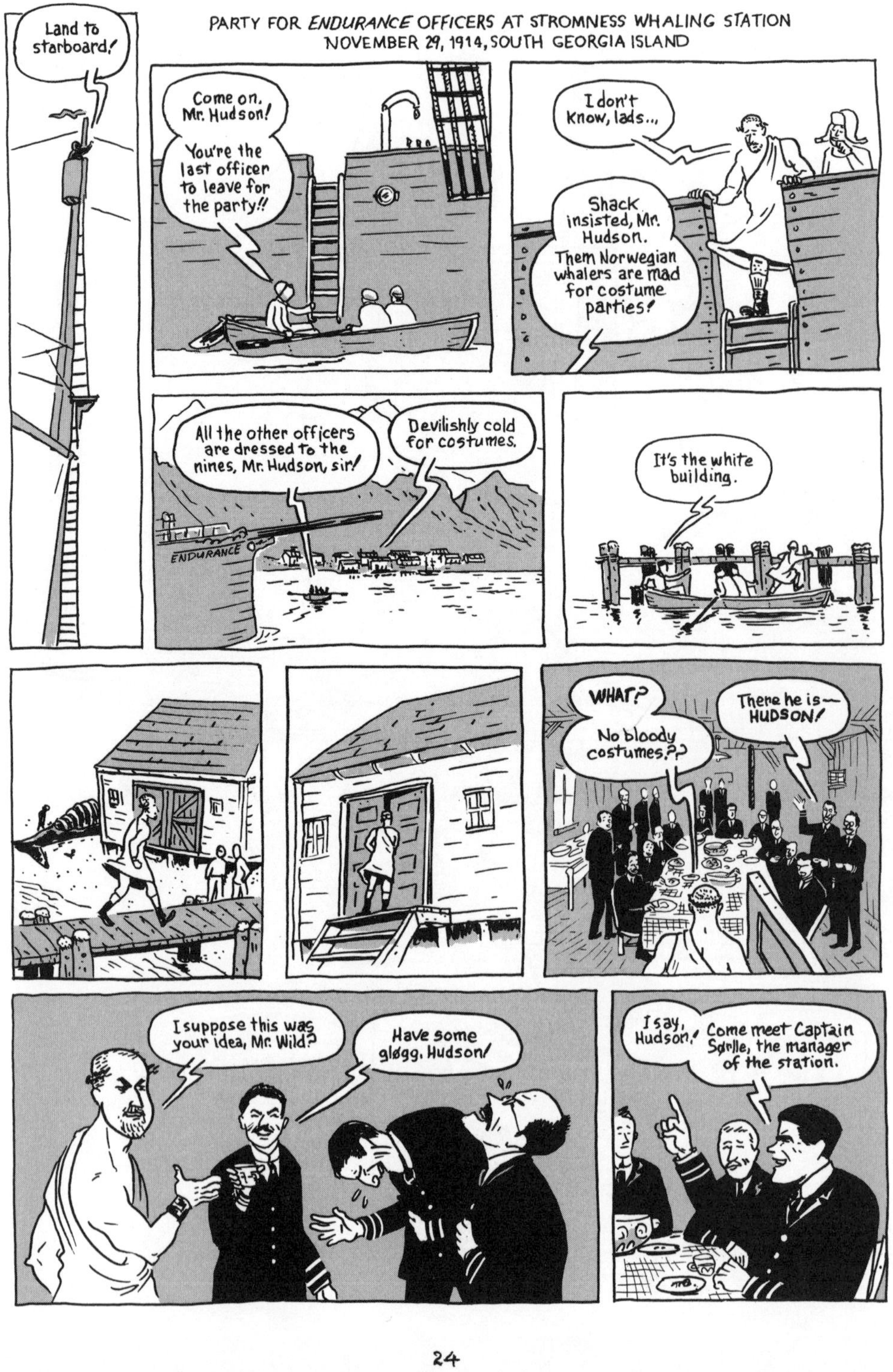
Land to starboard!
PARTY FOR *ENDURANCE* OFFICERS AT STROMNESS WHALING STATION
NOVEMBER 29, 1914, SOUTH GEORGIA ISLAND
Come on, Mr. Hudson!
You're the last officer to leave for the party!!
I don't know, lads...
Shack insisted, Mr. Hudson. Them Norwegian whalers are mad for costume parties!
All the other officers are dressed to the nines, Mr. Hudson, sir!
Devilishly cold for costumes.
ENDURANCE
It's the white building.
WHAT?
No bloody costumes?!?
There he is— HUDSON!
I suppose this was your idea, Mr. Wild?
Have some gløgg, Hudson!
I say, Hudson!
Come meet Captain Sørlle, the manager of the station.

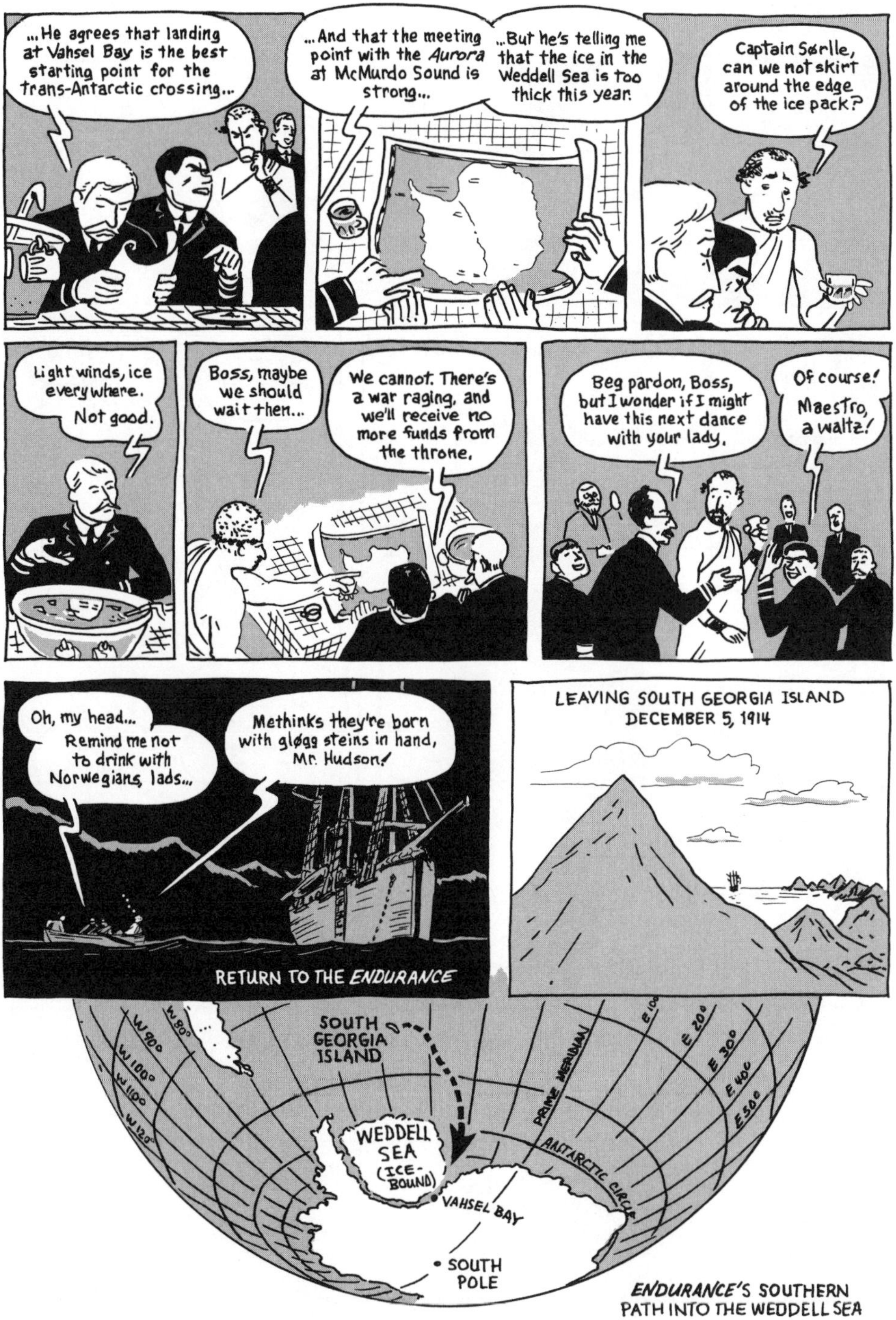

...He agrees that landing at Vahsel Bay is the best starting point for the trans-Antarctic crossing...
...And that the meeting point with the *Aurora* at McMurdo Sound is strong...
...But he's telling me that the ice in the Weddell Sea is too thick this year.
Captain Sørlle, can we not skirt around the edge of the ice pack?
Light winds, ice everywhere. Not good.
Boss, maybe we should wait then...
We cannot. There's a war raging, and we'll receive no more funds from the throne.
Beg pardon, Boss, but I wonder if I might have this next dance with your lady.
Of course! Maestro, a waltz!
Oh, my head... Remind me not to drink with Norwegians, lads...
Methinks they're born with gløgg steins in hand, Mr. Hudson!
RETURN TO THE *ENDURANCE*
LEAVING SOUTH GEORGIA ISLAND
DECEMBER 5, 1914
W 80°
W 90°
W 100°
W 110°
W 120°
SOUTH GEORGIA ISLAND
PRIME MERIDIAN
E 10°
E 20°
E 30°
E 40°
E 50°
WEDDELL SEA (ICE-BOUND)
ANTARCTIC CIRCLE
VAHSEL BAY
SOUTH POLE

ENDURANCE'S SOUTHERN PATH INTO THE WEDDELL SEA

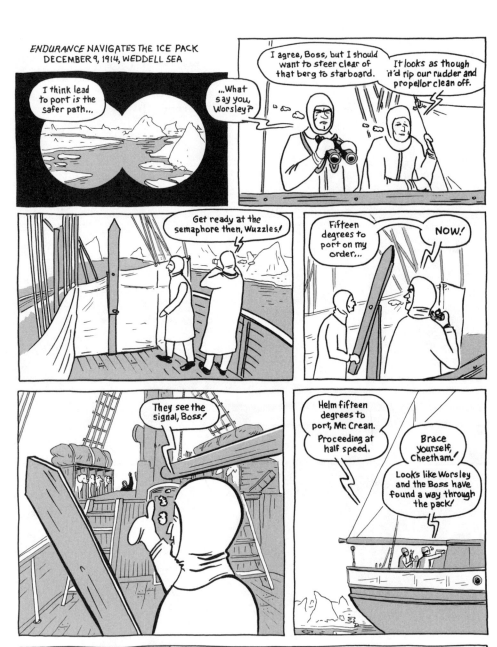

ENDURANCE NAVIGATES THE ICE PACK
DECEMBER 9, 1914, WEDDELL SEA

I think lead to port is the safer path...

...What say you, Worsley?

I agree, Boss, but I should want to steer clear of that berg to starboard.

It looks as though it'd rip our rudder and propellor clean off.

Get ready at the semaphore then, Wuzzles!

Fifteen degrees to port on my order...

NOW!

They see the signal, Boss!

Helm fifteen degrees to port, Mr. Crean. Proceeding at half speed.

Brace yourself, Cheetham!

Looks like Worsley and the Boss have found a way through the pack!

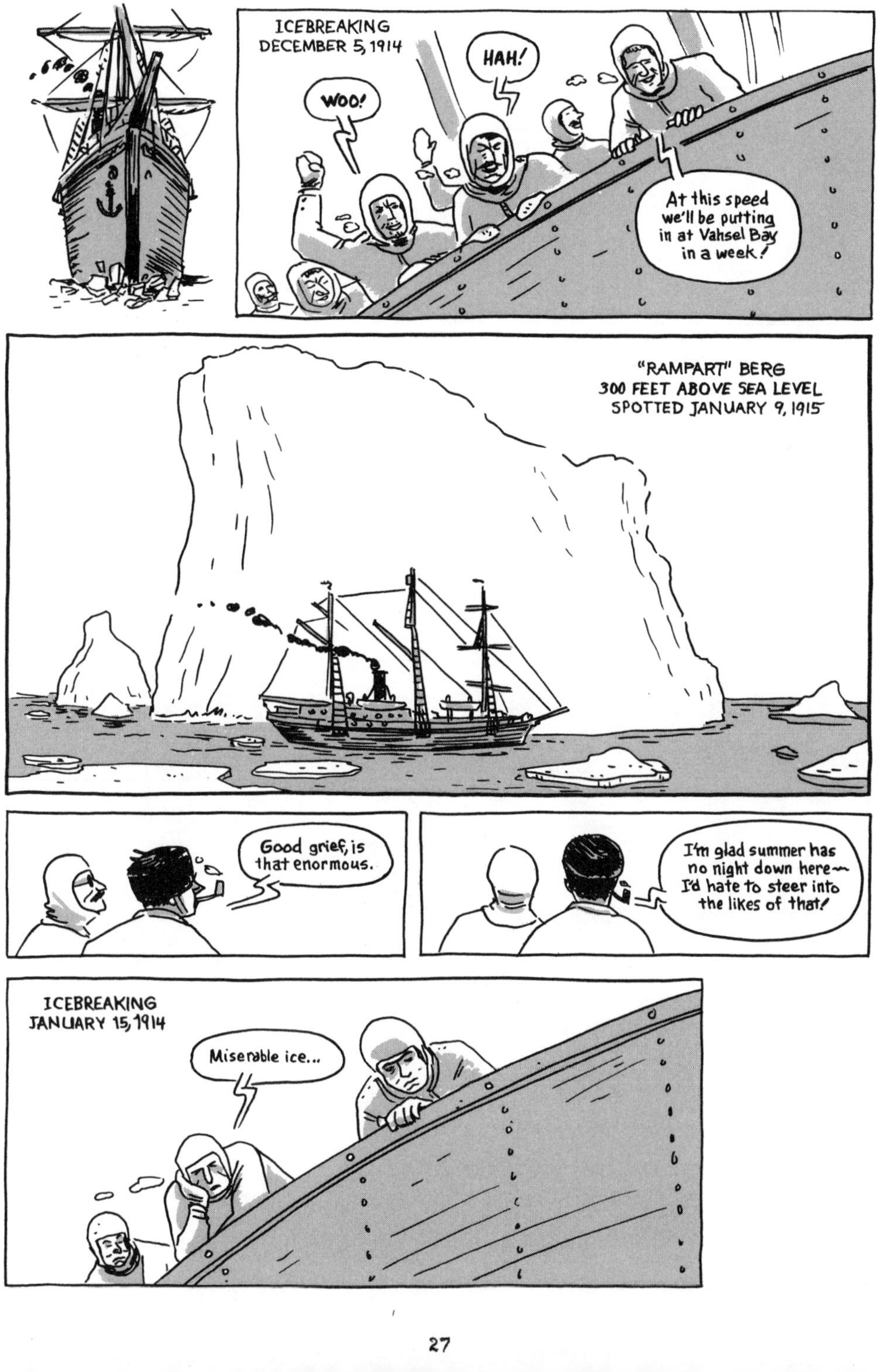
ICEBREAKING
DECEMBER 5, 1914
WOO!
HAH!
At this speed we'll be putting in at Vahsel Bay in a week!
"RAMPART" BERG
300 FEET ABOVE SEA LEVEL
SPOTTED JANUARY 9, 1915
Good grief, is that enormous.
I'm glad summer has no night down here~ I'd hate to steer into the likes of that!
ICEBREAKING
JANUARY 15, 1914
Miserable ice...

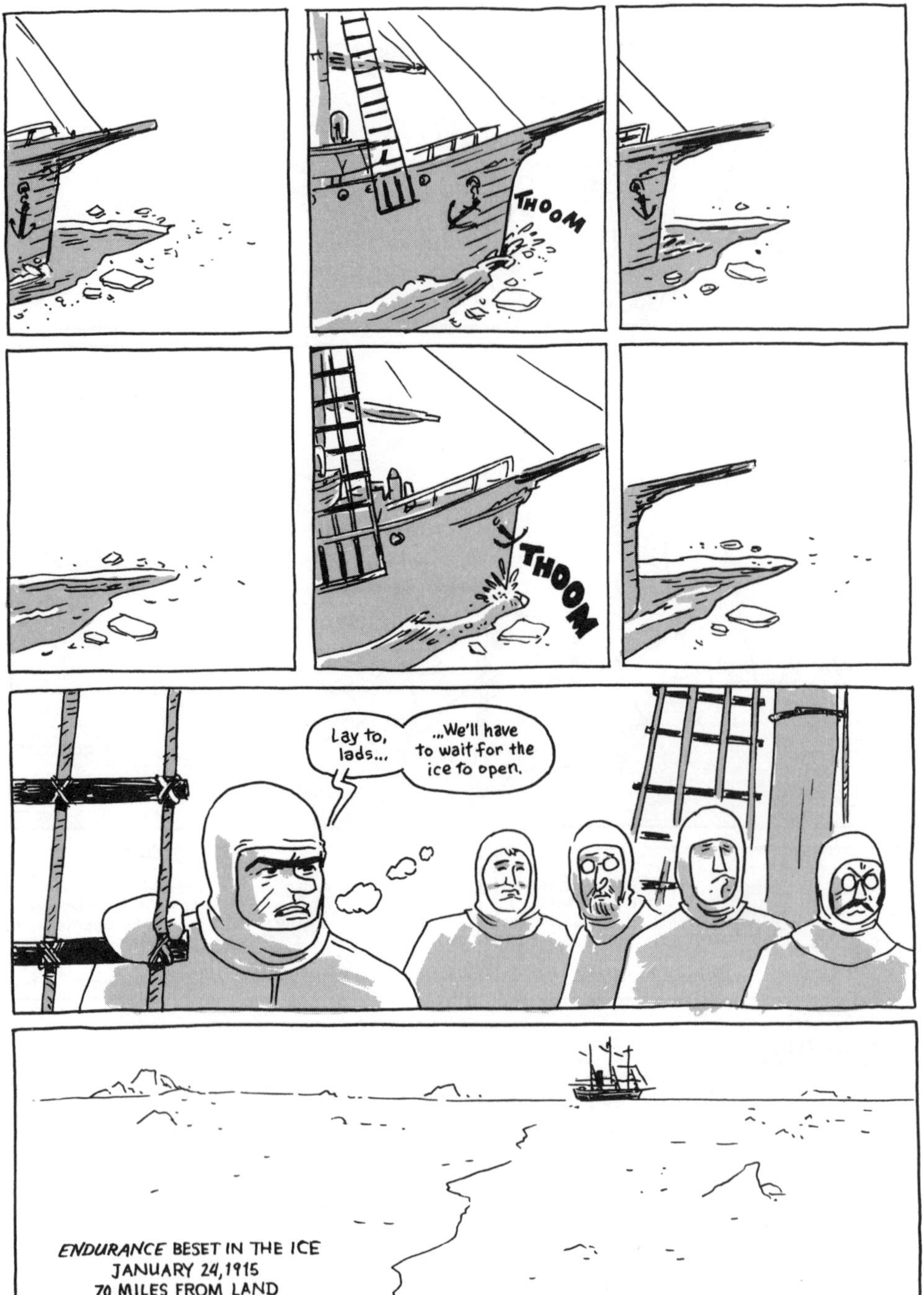
THOOM
THOOM
Lay to, lads...
...We'll have to wait for the ice to open.
ENDURANCE BESET IN THE ICE
JANUARY 24, 1915
70 MILES FROM LAND

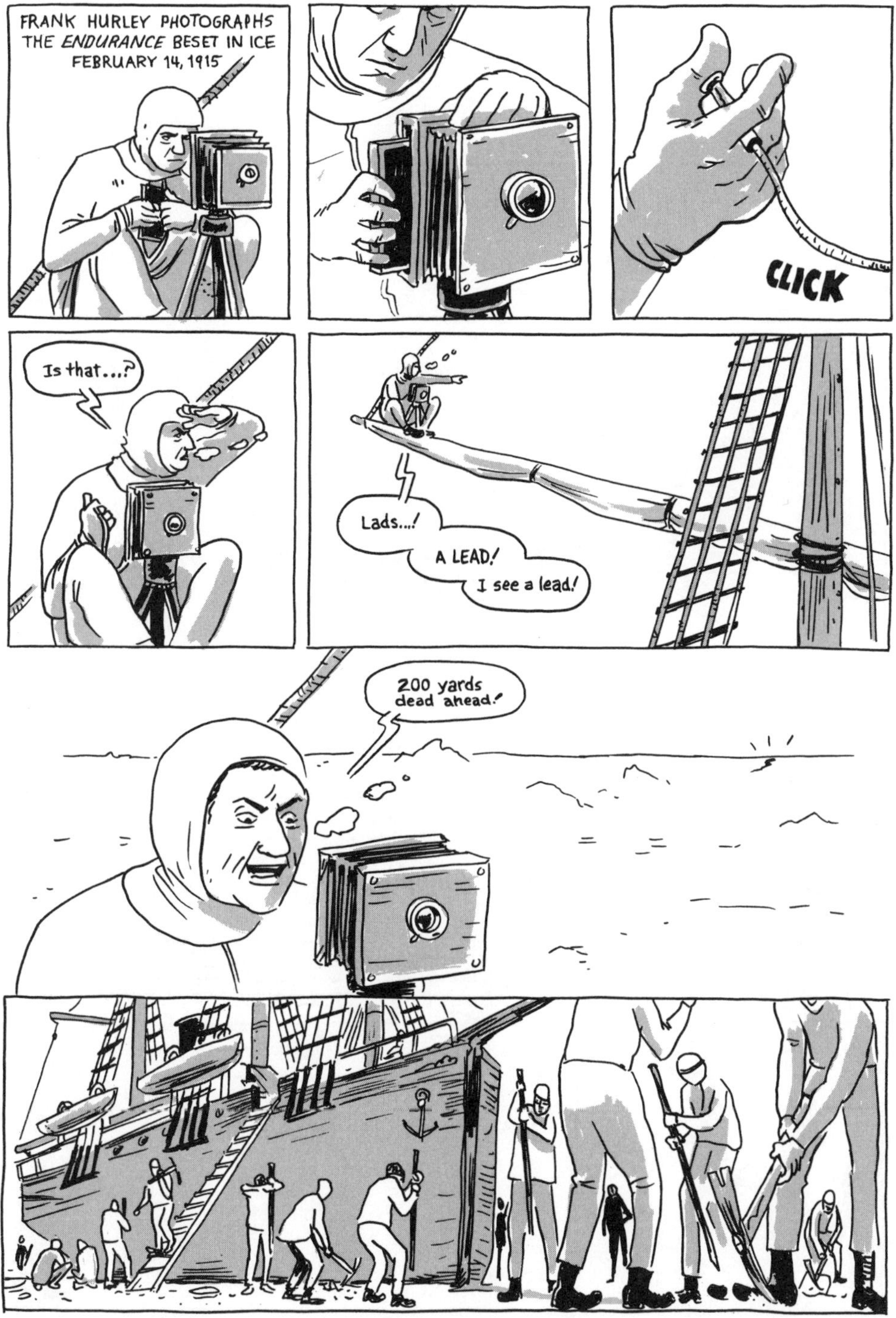
FRANK HURLEY PHOTOGRAPHS THE *ENDURANCE* BESET IN ICE FEBRUARY 14, 1915
CLICK
Is that...?
Lads...!
A LEAD!
I see a lead!
200 yards dead ahead!

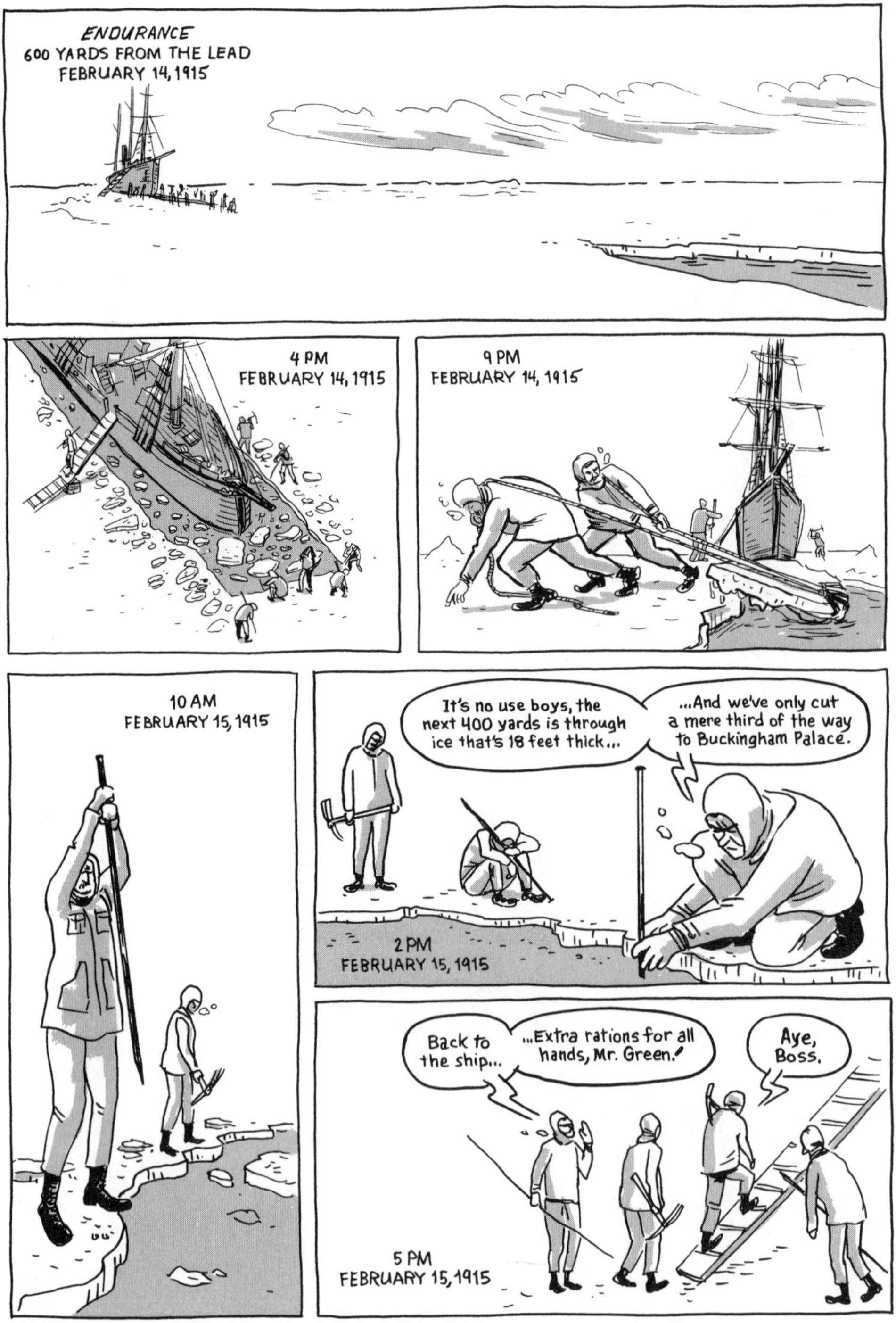
ENDURANCE
600 YARDS FROM THE LEAD
FEBRUARY 14, 1915
4 PM
FEBRUARY 14, 1915
9 PM
FEBRUARY 14, 1915
10 AM
FEBRUARY 15, 1915
It's no use boys, the next 400 yards is through ice that's 18 feet thick...
...And we've only cut a mere third of the way to Buckingham Palace.
2 PM
FEBRUARY 15, 1915
Back to the ship...
...Extra rations for all hands, Mr. Green.
Aye, Boss.
5 PM
FEBRUARY 15, 1915

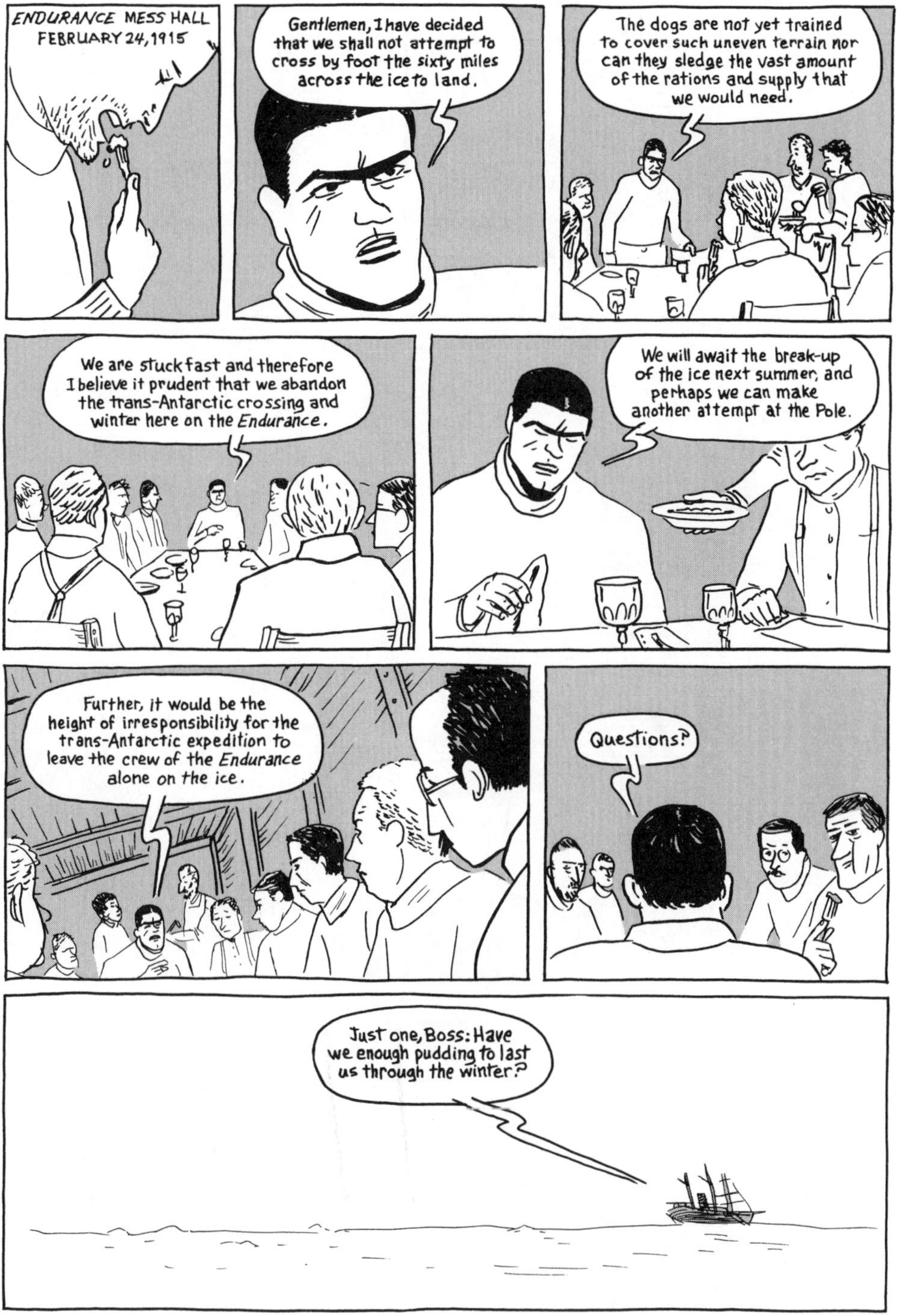
ENDURANCE MESS HALL FEBRUARY 24, 1915
Gentlemen, I have decided that we shall not attempt to cross by foot the sixty miles across the ice to land.
The dogs are not yet trained to cover such uneven terrain nor can they sledge the vast amount of the rations and supply that we would need.
We are stuck fast and therefore I believe it prudent that we abandon the trans-Antarctic crossing and winter here on the Endurance.
We will await the break-up of the ice next summer, and perhaps we can make another attempr at the Pole.
Further, it would be the height of irresponsibility for the trans-Antarctic expedition to leave the crew of the Endurance alone on the ice.
Questions?
Just one, Boss: Have we enough pudding to last us through the winter?

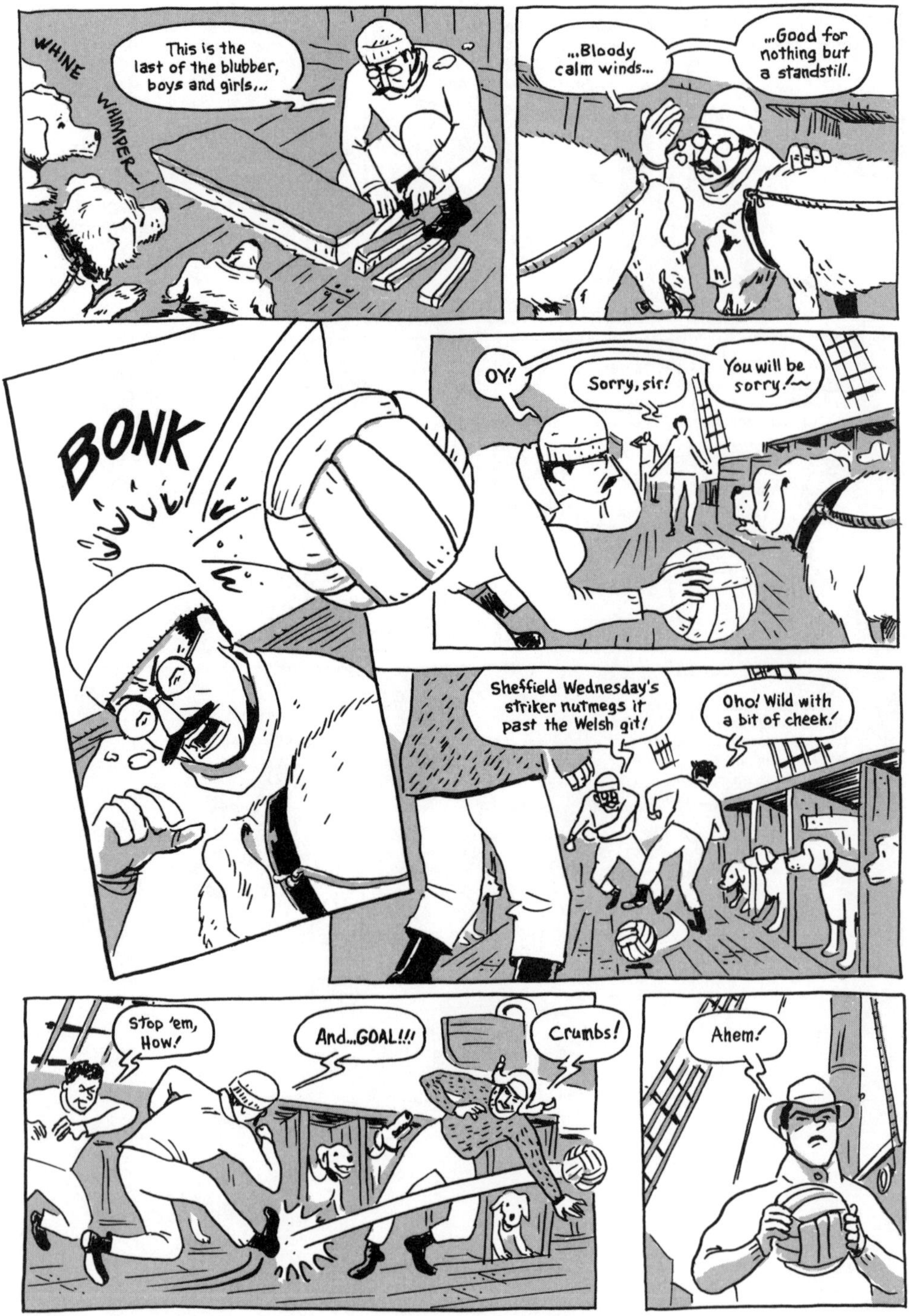
WHINE
WHIMPER
This is the last of the blubber, boys and girls...
...Bloody calm winds...
...Good for nothing but a standstill.
BONK
OY!
Sorry, sir!
You will be sorry!
Sheffield Wednesday's striker nutmegs it past the Welsh git!
Oho! Wild with a bit of cheek!
Stop 'em, How!
And...GOAL!!!
Crumbs!
Ahem!

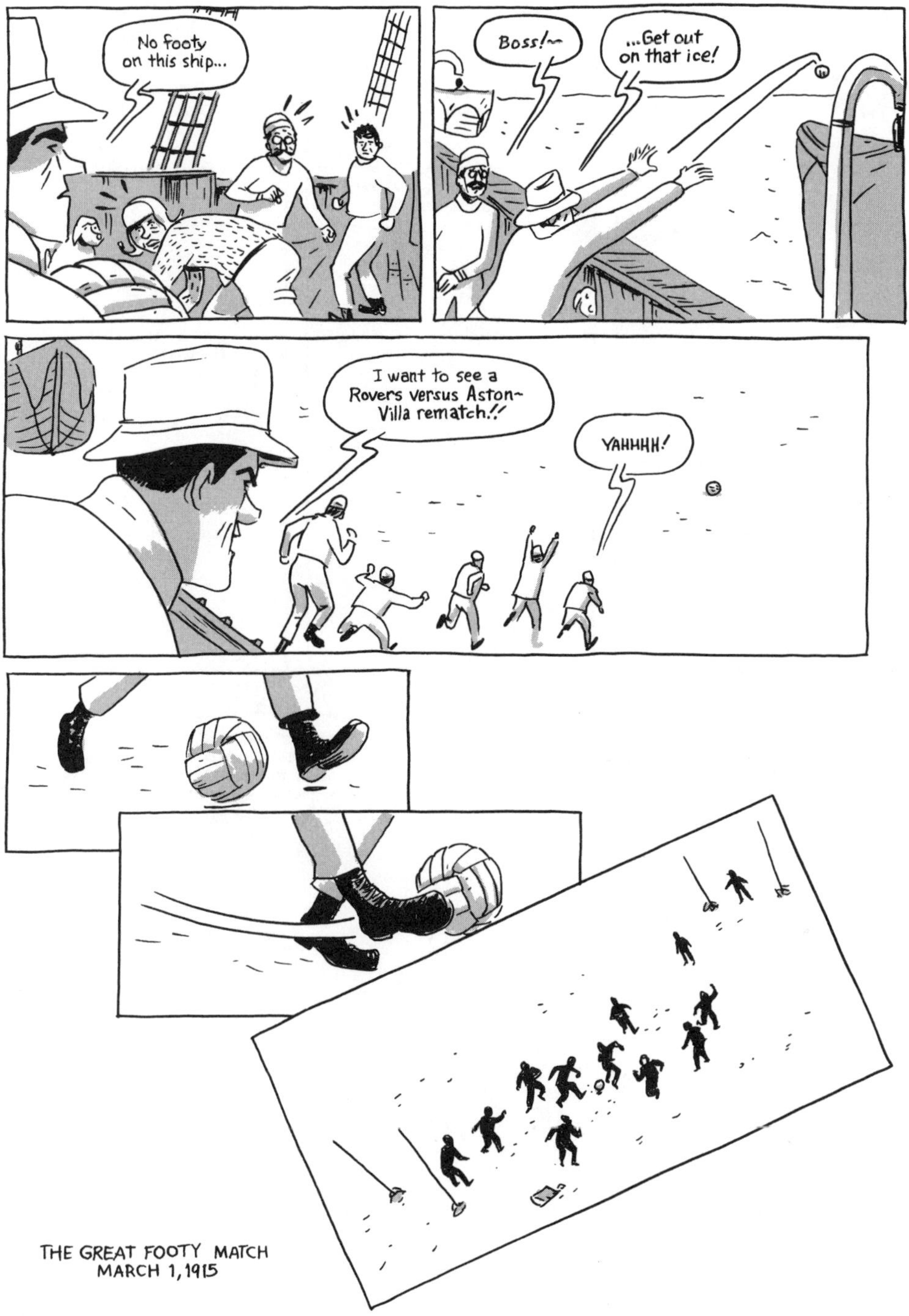
No footy on this ship...
Boss!~
...Get out on that ice!
I want to see a Rovers versus Aston-Villa rematch!!
YAHHHH!
THE GREAT FOOTY MATCH
MARCH 1, 1915

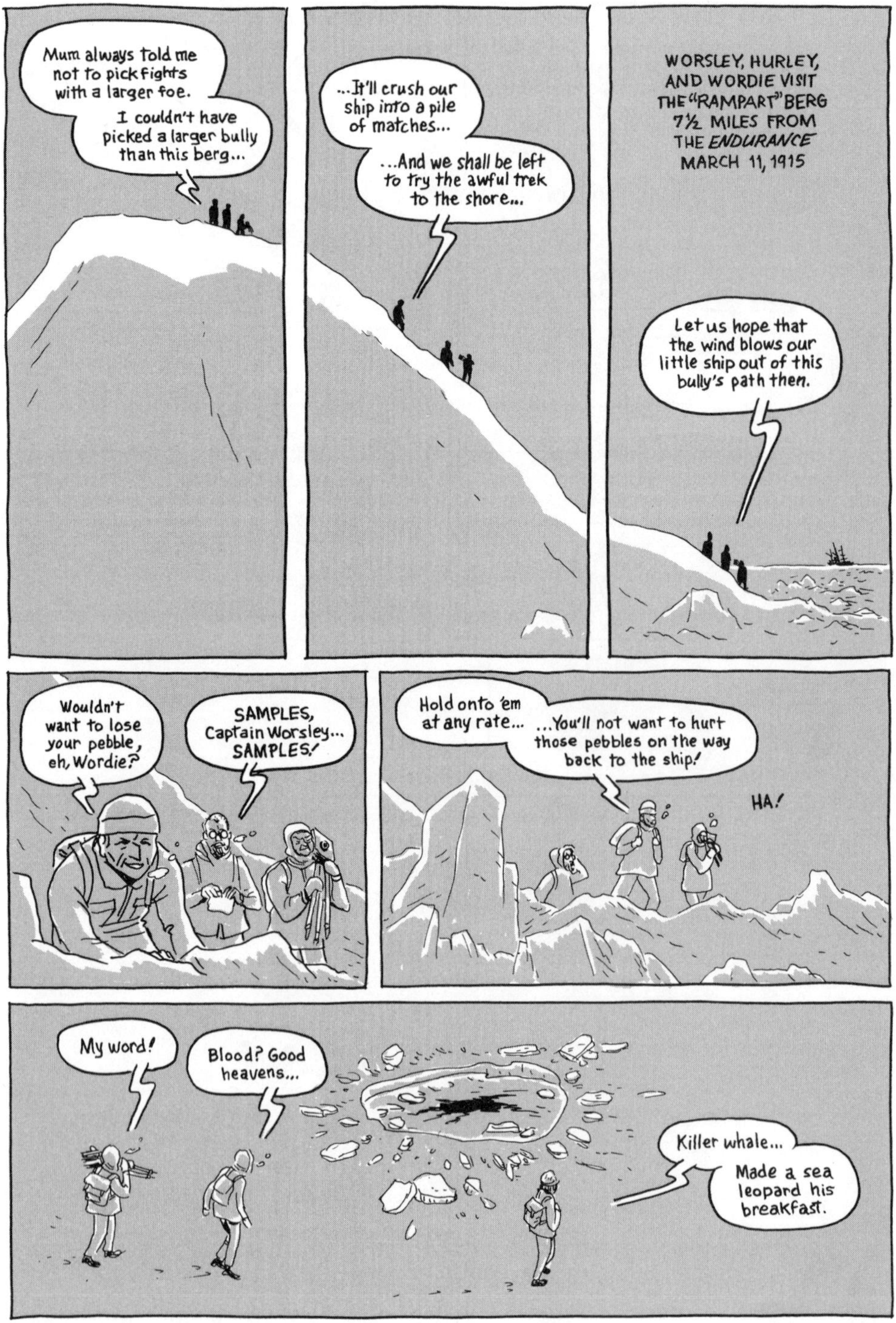
Mum always told me not to pick fights with a larger foe.
I couldn't have picked a larger bully than this berg...
...It'll crush our ship into a pile of matches...
...And we shall be left to try the awful trek to the shore...
WORSLEY, HURLEY, AND WORDIE VISIT THE "RAMPART" BERG 7½ MILES FROM THE *ENDURANCE* MARCH 11, 1915
Let us hope that the wind blows our little ship out of this bully's path then.
Wouldn't want to lose your pebble, eh, Wordie?
SAMPLES, Captain Worsley... SAMPLES!
Hold onto 'em at any rate...
...You'll not want to hurt those pebbles on the way back to the ship!
HA!
My word!
Blood? Good heavens...
Killer whale...
Made a sea leopard his breakfast.

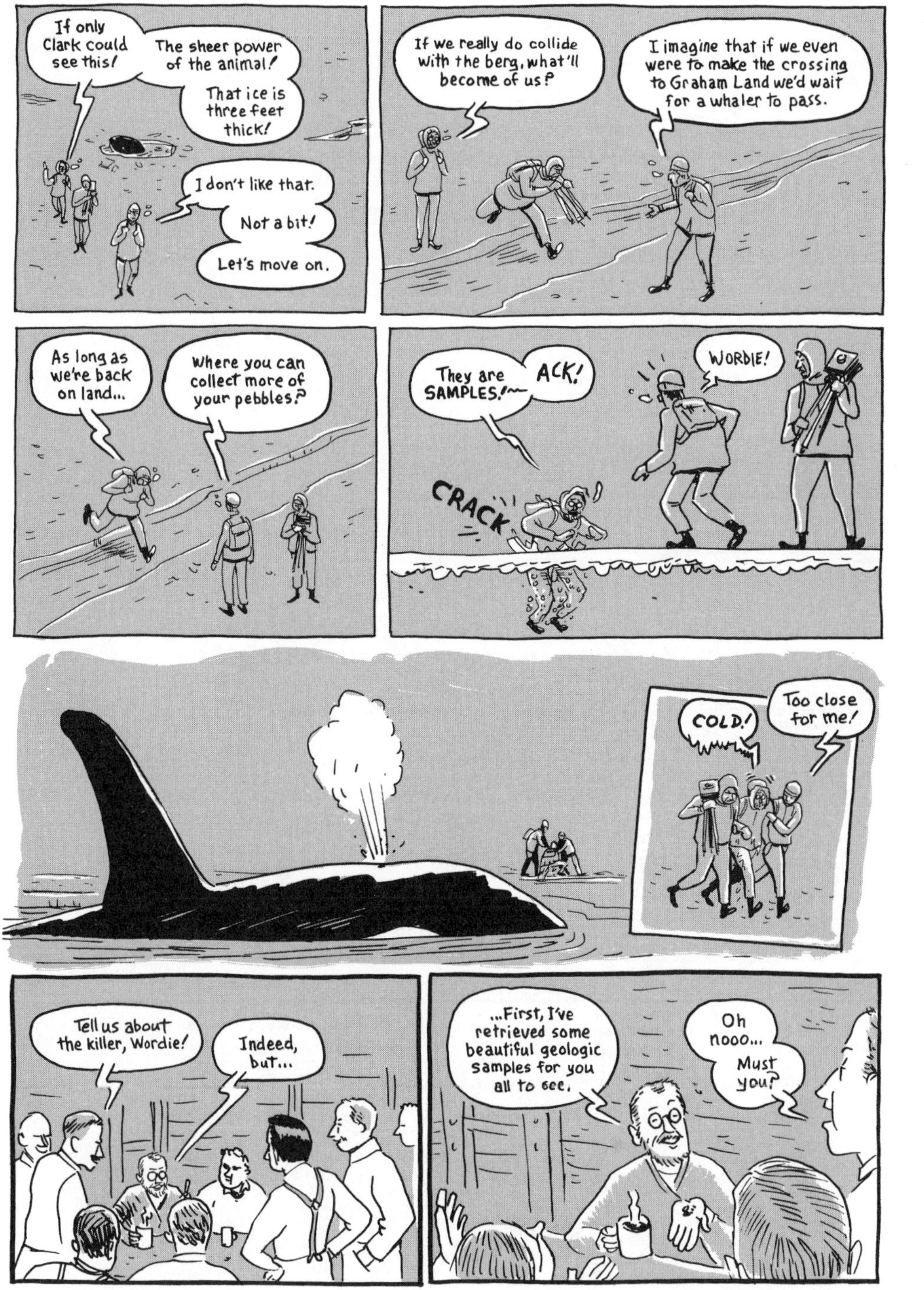
If only Clark could see this!
The sheer power of the animal!
That ice is three feet thick!
I don't like that.
Not a bit!
Let's move on.
If we really do collide with the berg, what'll become of us?
I imagine that if we even were to make the crossing to Graham Land we'd wait for a whaler to pass.
As long as we're back on land...
Where you can collect more of your pebbles?
They are SAMPLES!
ACK!
WORDIE!
CRACK
COLD!
Too close for me!
Tell us about the killer, Wordie!
Indeed, but...
...First, I've retrieved some beautiful geologic samples for you all to see.
Oh nooo...
Must you?

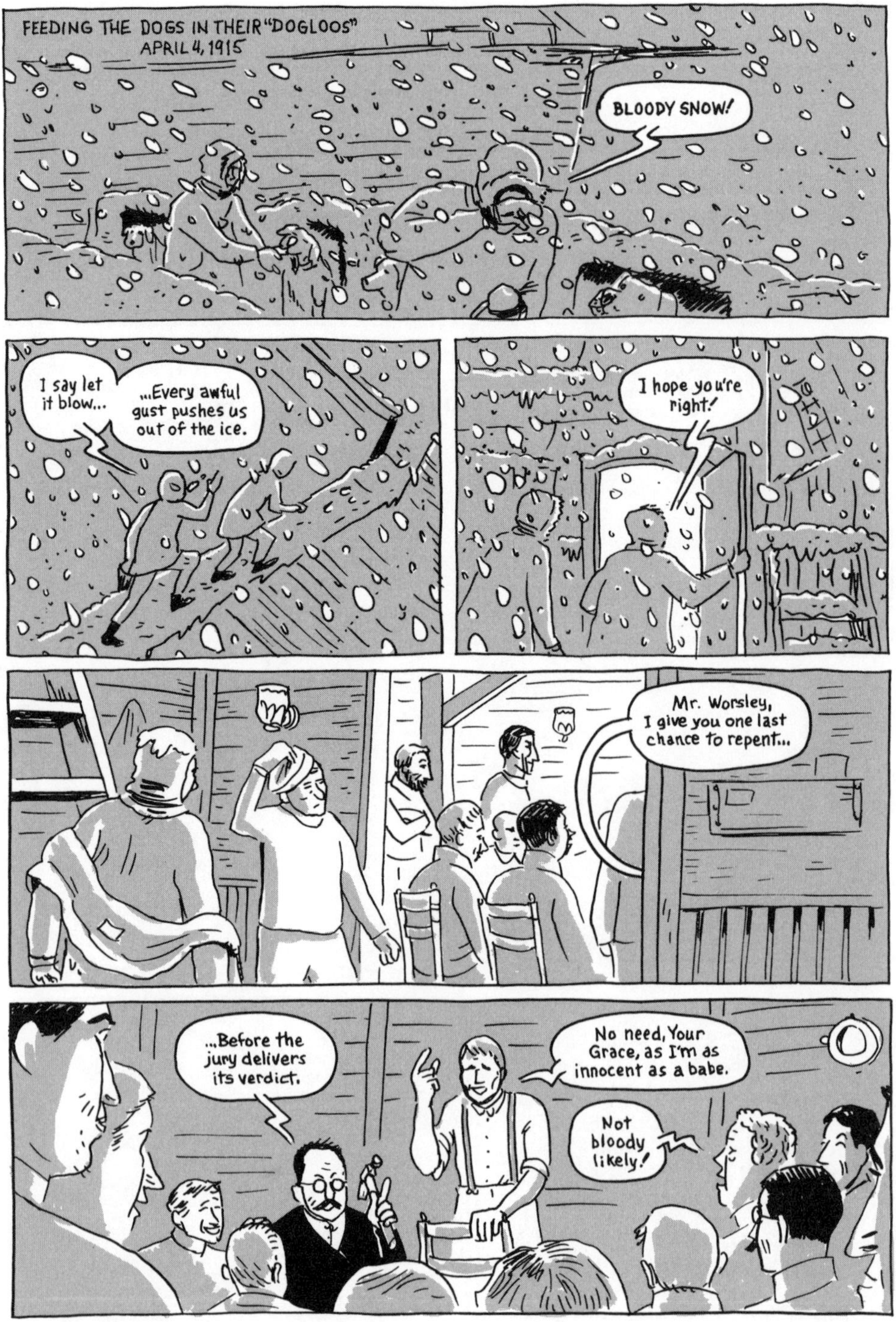
FEEDING THE DOGS IN THEIR "DOGLOOS"
APRIL 4, 1915
BLOODY SNOW!
I say let it blow...
...Every awful gust pushes us out of the ice.
I hope you're right!
Mr. Worsley, I give you one last chance to repent...
...Before the jury delivers its verdict.
No need, Your Grace, as I'm as innocent as a babe.
Not bloody likely!

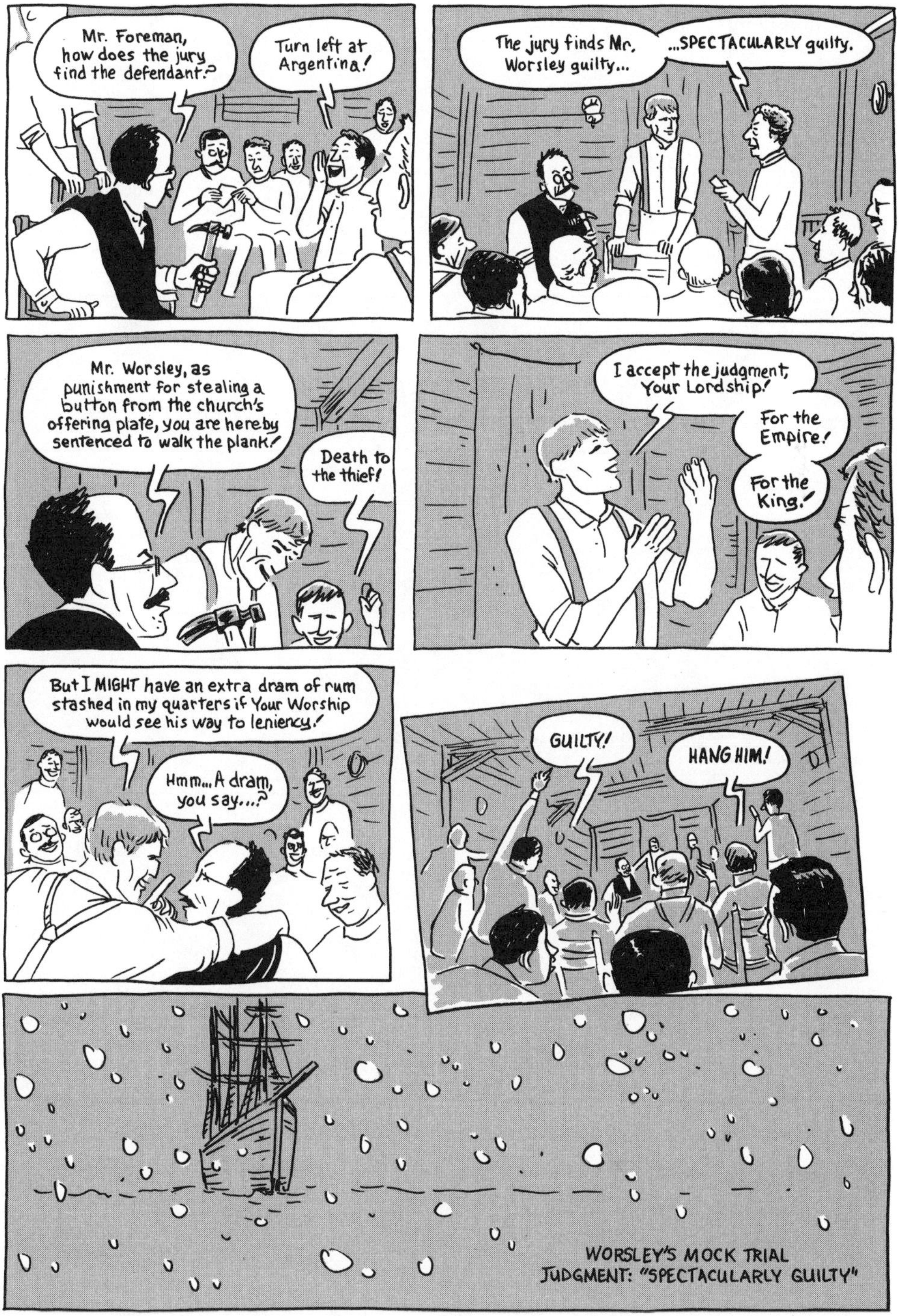
Mr. Foreman, how does the jury find the defendant?
Turn left at Argentina!
The jury finds Mr. Worsley guilty...
...SPECTACULARLY guilty.
Mr. Worsley, as punishment for stealing a button from the church's offering plate, you are hereby sentenced to walk the plank!
Death to the thief!
I accept the judgment, Your Lordship!
For the Empire!
For the King!
But I MIGHT have an extra dram of rum stashed in my quarters if Your Worship would see his way to leniency!
Hmm... A dram, you say...?
GUILTY!
HANG HIM!
WORSLEY'S MOCK TRIAL
JUDGMENT: "SPECTACULARLY GUILTY"

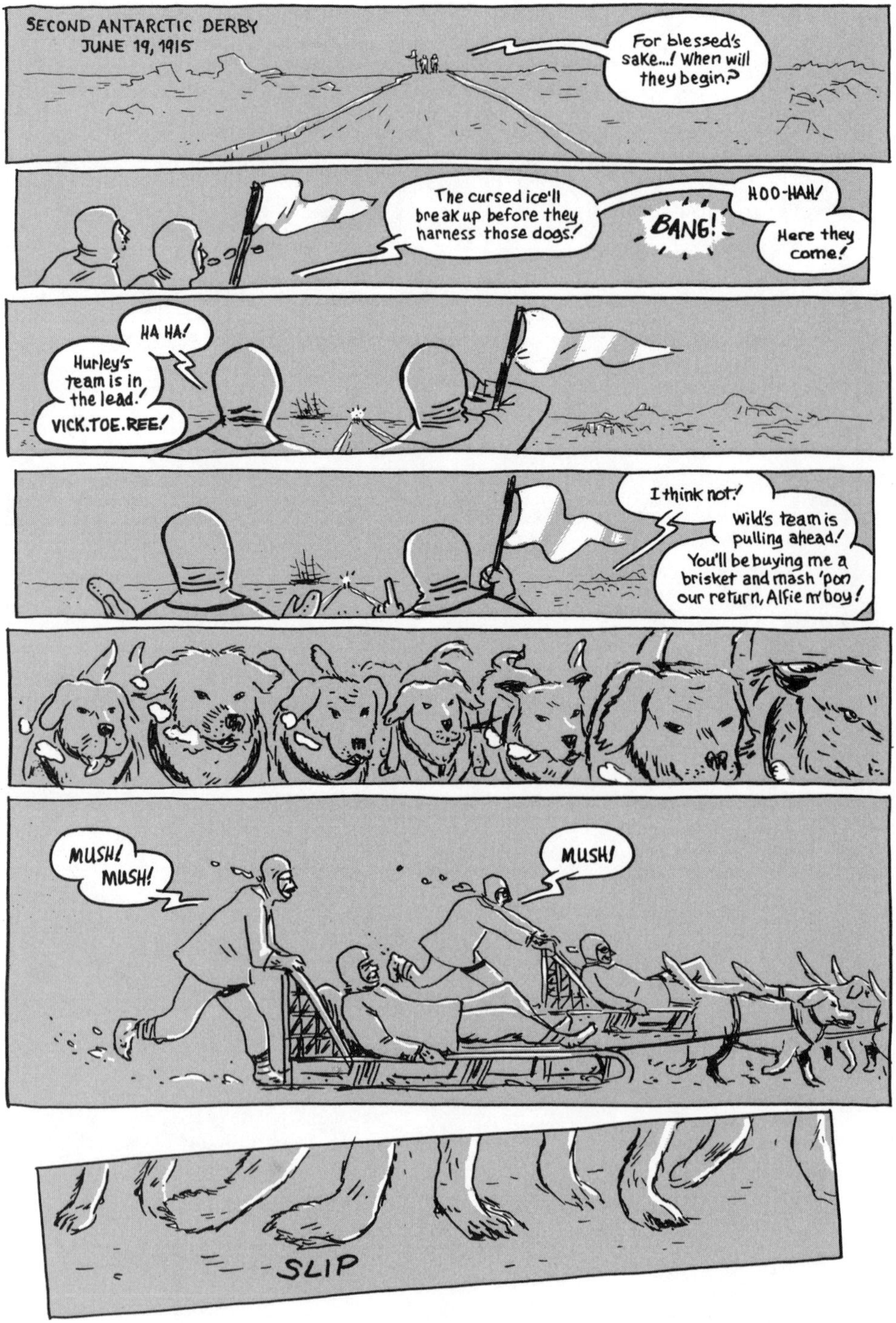
SECOND ANTARCTIC DERBY
JUNE 19, 1915
For blessed's sake...! When will they begin?
The cursed ice'll break up before they harness those dogs!
BANG!
HOO-HAH!
Here they come!
HA HA!
Hurley's team is in the lead!
VICK.TOE.REE!
I think not!
Wild's team is pulling ahead!
You'll be buying me a brisket and mash 'pon our return, Alfie m'boy!
MUSH! MUSH!
MUSH!
SLIP

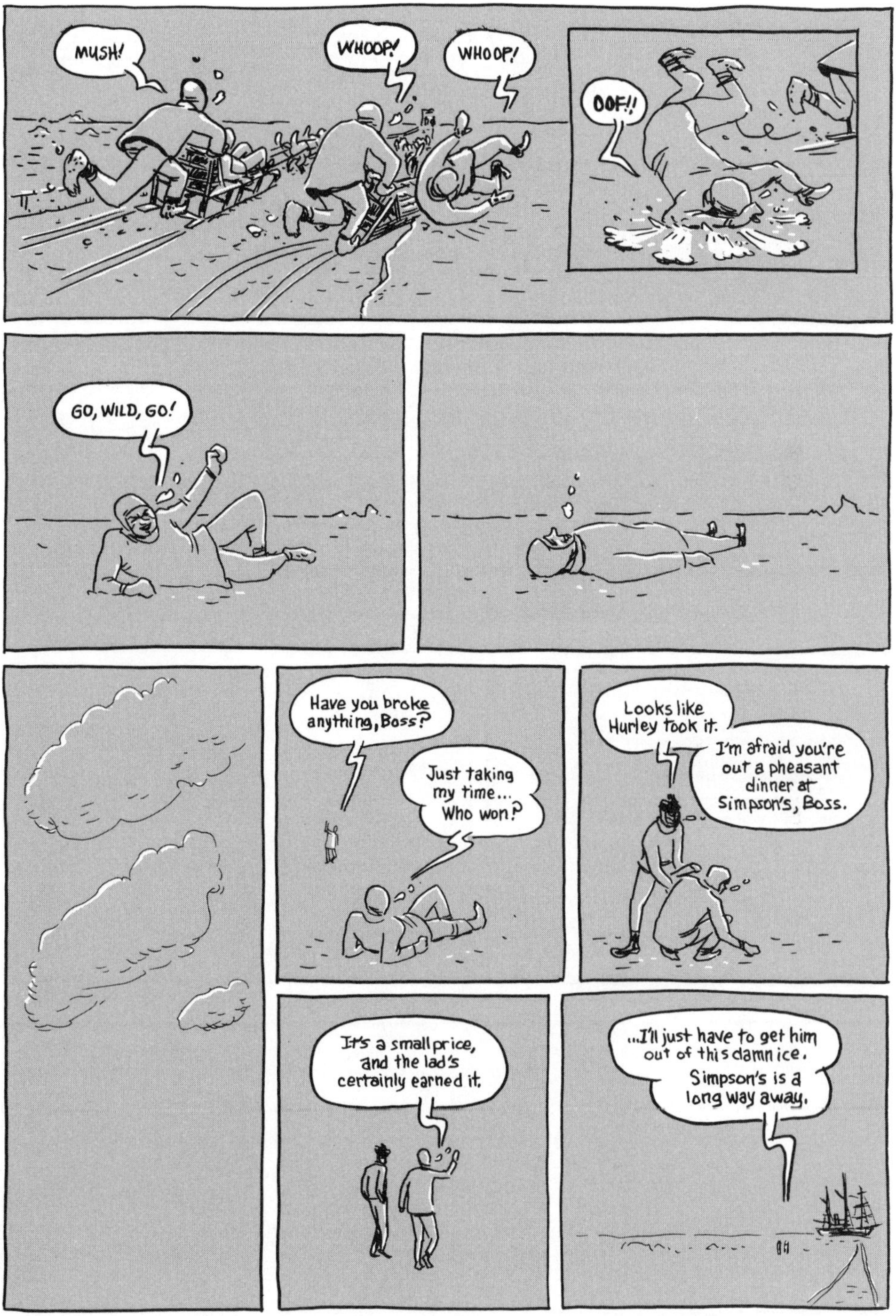
MUSH!
WHOOP!
WHOOP!
OOF!!
GO, WILD, GO!
Have you broke anything, Boss?
Just taking my time... Who won?
Looks like Hurley took it.
I'm afraid you're out a pheasant dinner at Simpson's, Boss.
It's a small price, and the lad's certainly earned it.
...I'll just have to get him out of this damn ice.
Simpson's is a long way away.

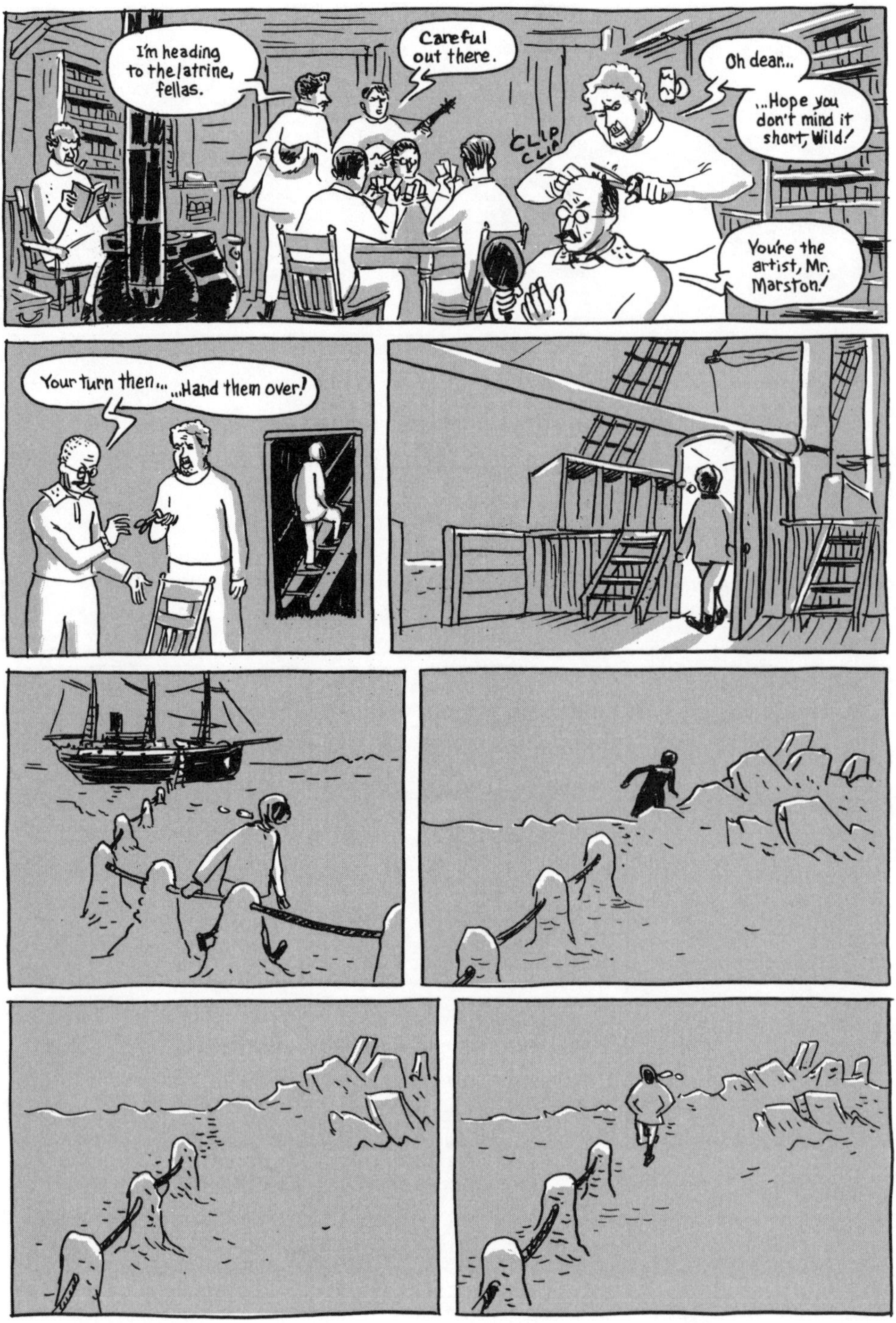
I'm heading to the latrine, fellas.
Careful out there.
Oh dear...
...Hope you don't mind it short, Wild!
CLIP CLIP
You're the artist, Mr. Marston!
Your turn then...
...Hand them over!

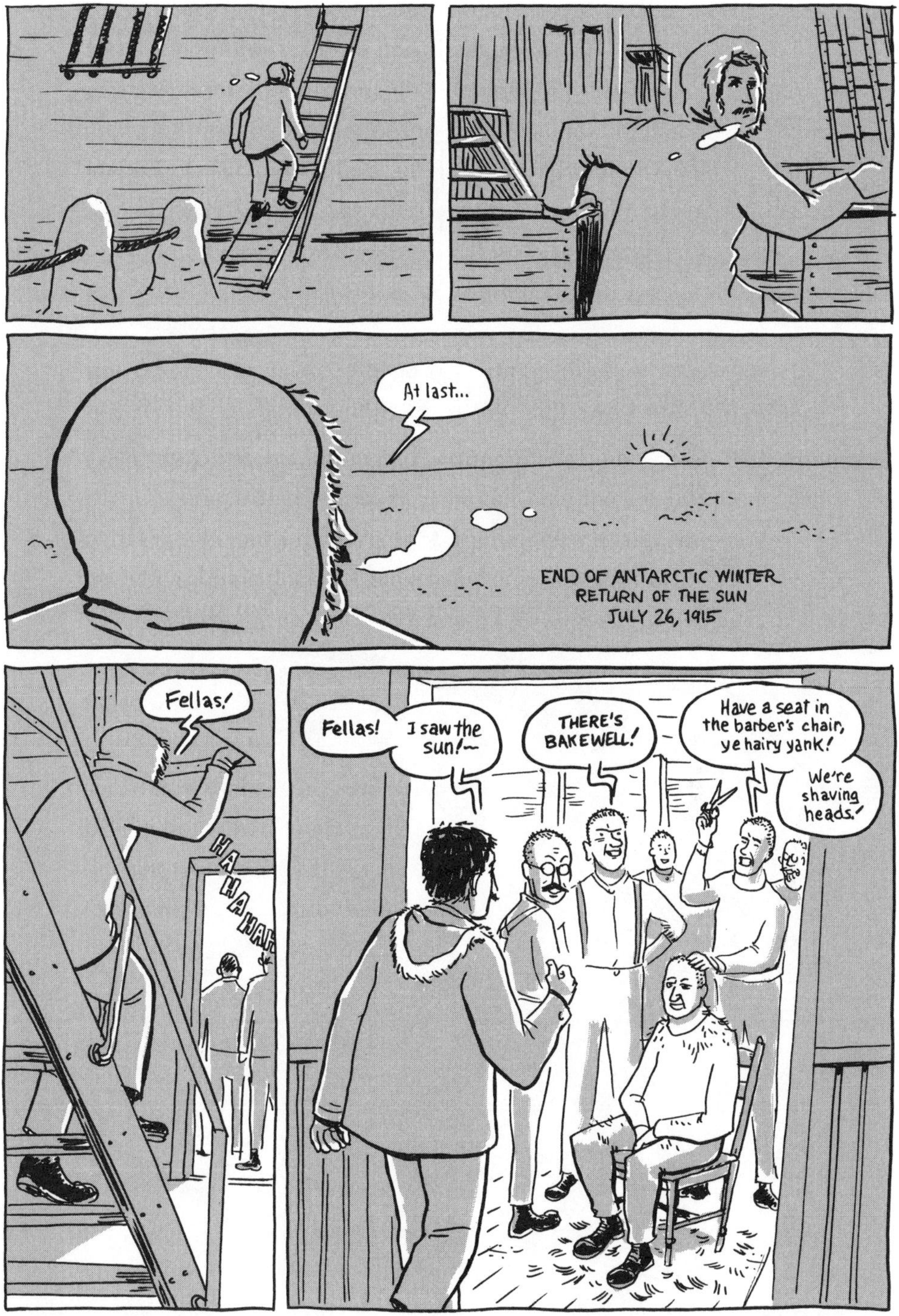
At last...
END OF ANTARCTIC WINTER
RETURN OF THE SUN
JULY 26, 1915
Fellas!
HAHAHAHAH
Fellas!
I saw the sun!
THERE'S BAKEWELL!
Have a seat in the barber's chair, ye hairy yank!
We're shaving heads!

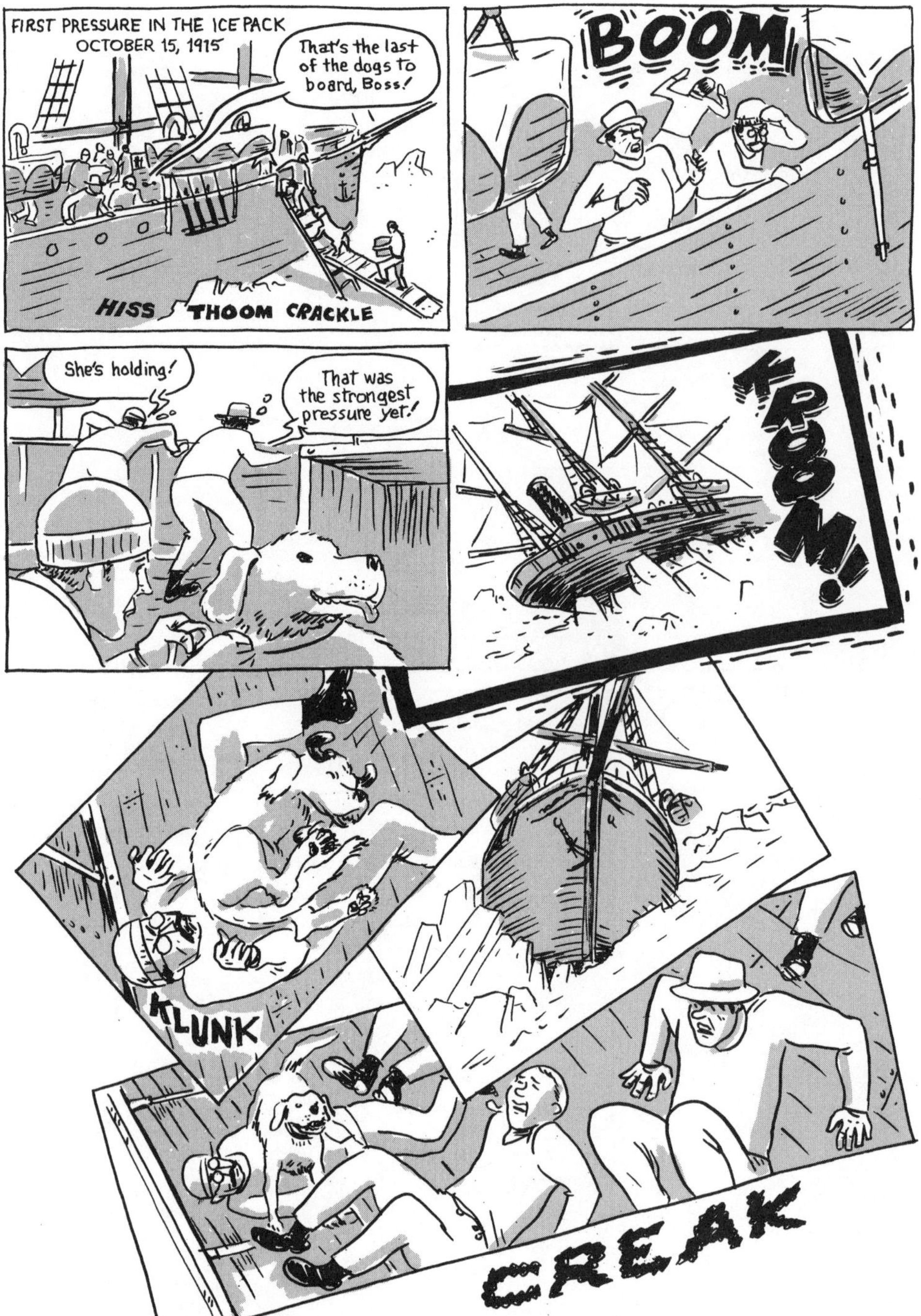
FIRST PRESSURE IN THE ICE PACK
OCTOBER 15, 1915
That's the last of the dogs to board, Boss!
HISS THOOM CRACKLE
BOOM
She's holding!
That was the strongest pressure yet!
KROOM!
KLUNK
CREAK

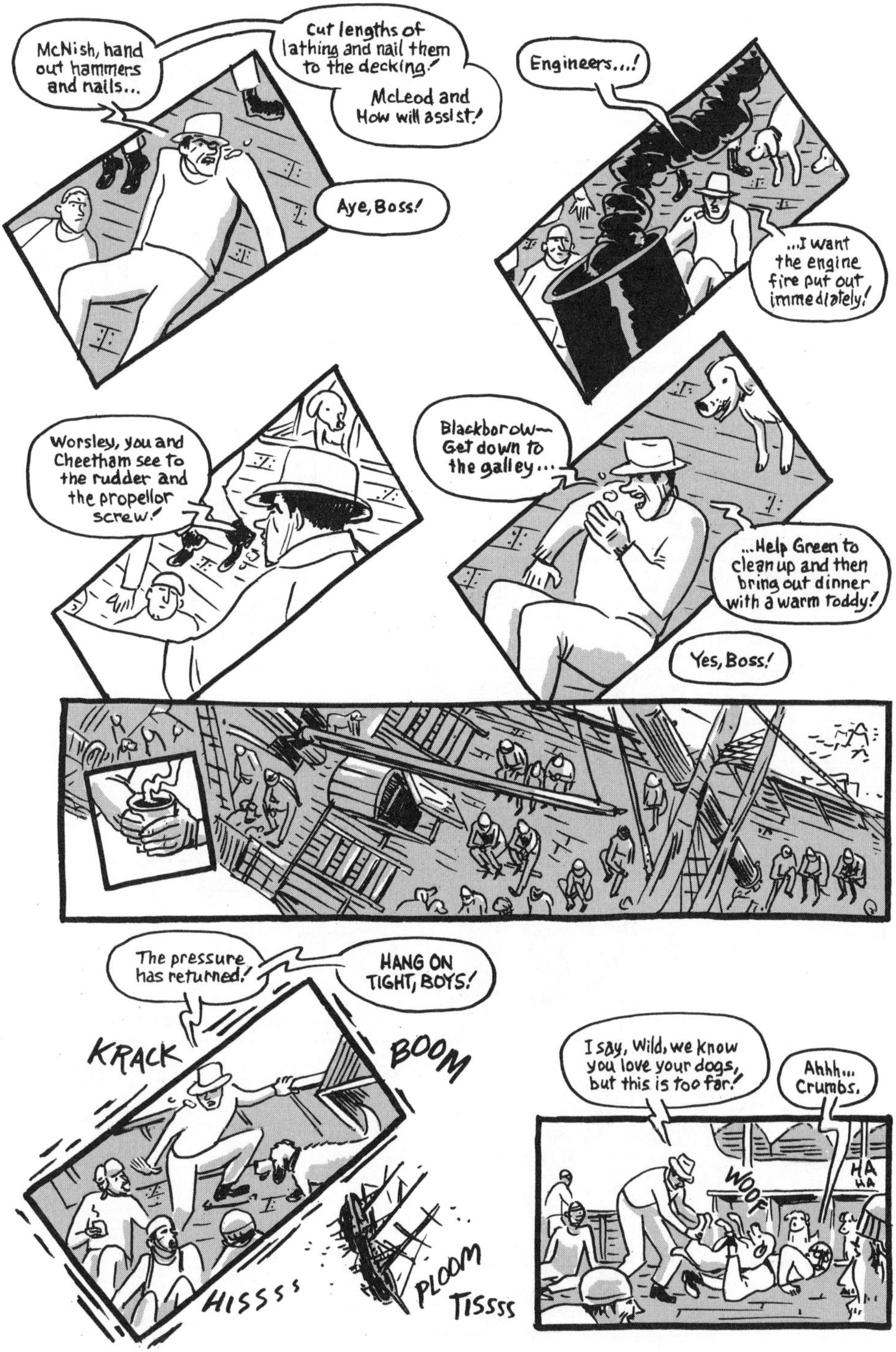
McNish, hand out hammers and nails...
Cut lengths of lathing and nail them to the decking!
McLeod and How will assist!
Aye, Boss!
Engineers...!
...I want the engine fire put out immediately!
Worsley, you and Cheetham see to the rudder and the propellor screw!
Blackborow— Get down to the galley...
...Help Green to clean up and then bring out dinner with a warm toddy!
Yes, Boss!
The pressure has returned!
HANG ON TIGHT, BOYS!
KRACK
BOOM
HISSSS
PLOOM
TISSSS
I say, Wild, we know you love your dogs, but this is too far!
Ahhh... Crumbs.
WOOF
HA HA

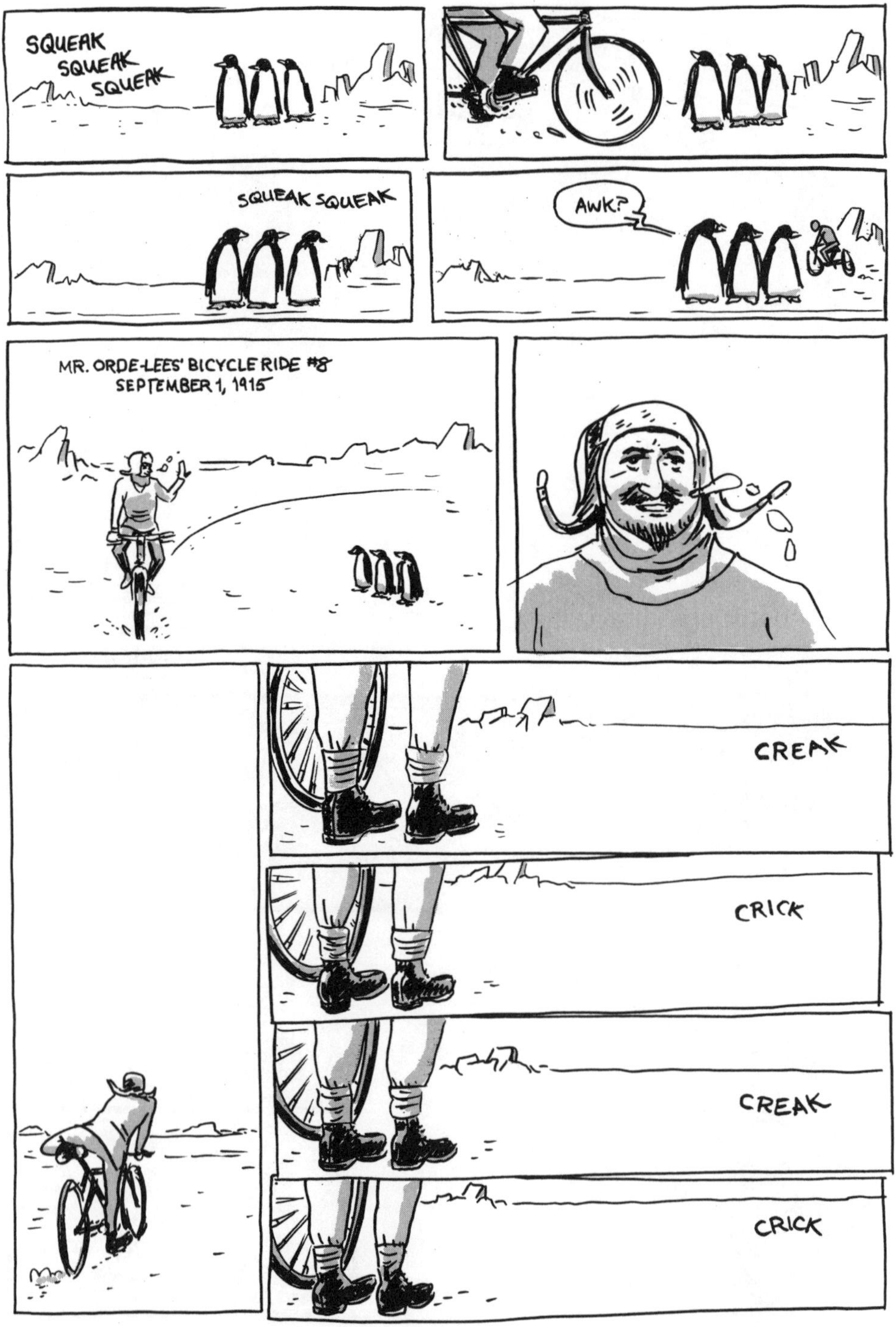
SQUEAK
SQUEAK
SQUEAK
SQUEAK SQUEAK
AWK?
MR. ORDE-LEES' BICYCLE RIDE #8
SEPTEMBER 1, 1915
CREAK
CRICK
CREAK
CRICK

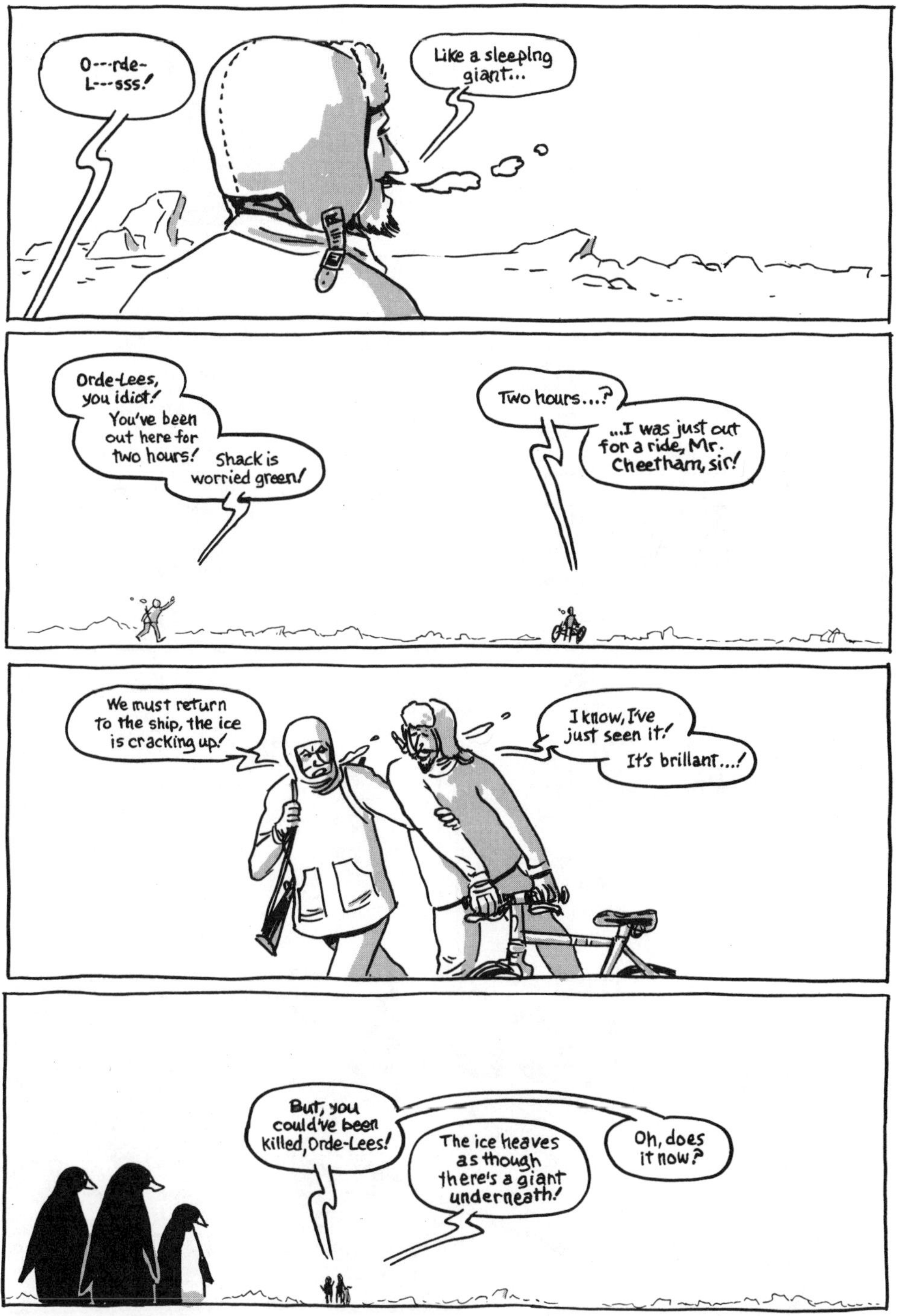
O---rde-
L---sss!
Like a sleeping giant...
Orde-Lees, you idiot! You've been out here for two hours!
Shack is worried green!
Two hours...?
...I was just out for a ride, Mr. Cheetham, sir!
We must return to the ship, the ice is cracking up!
I know, I've just seen it!
It's brillant...!
But, you could've been killed, Orde-Lees!
The ice heaves as though there's a giant underneath!
Oh, does it now?

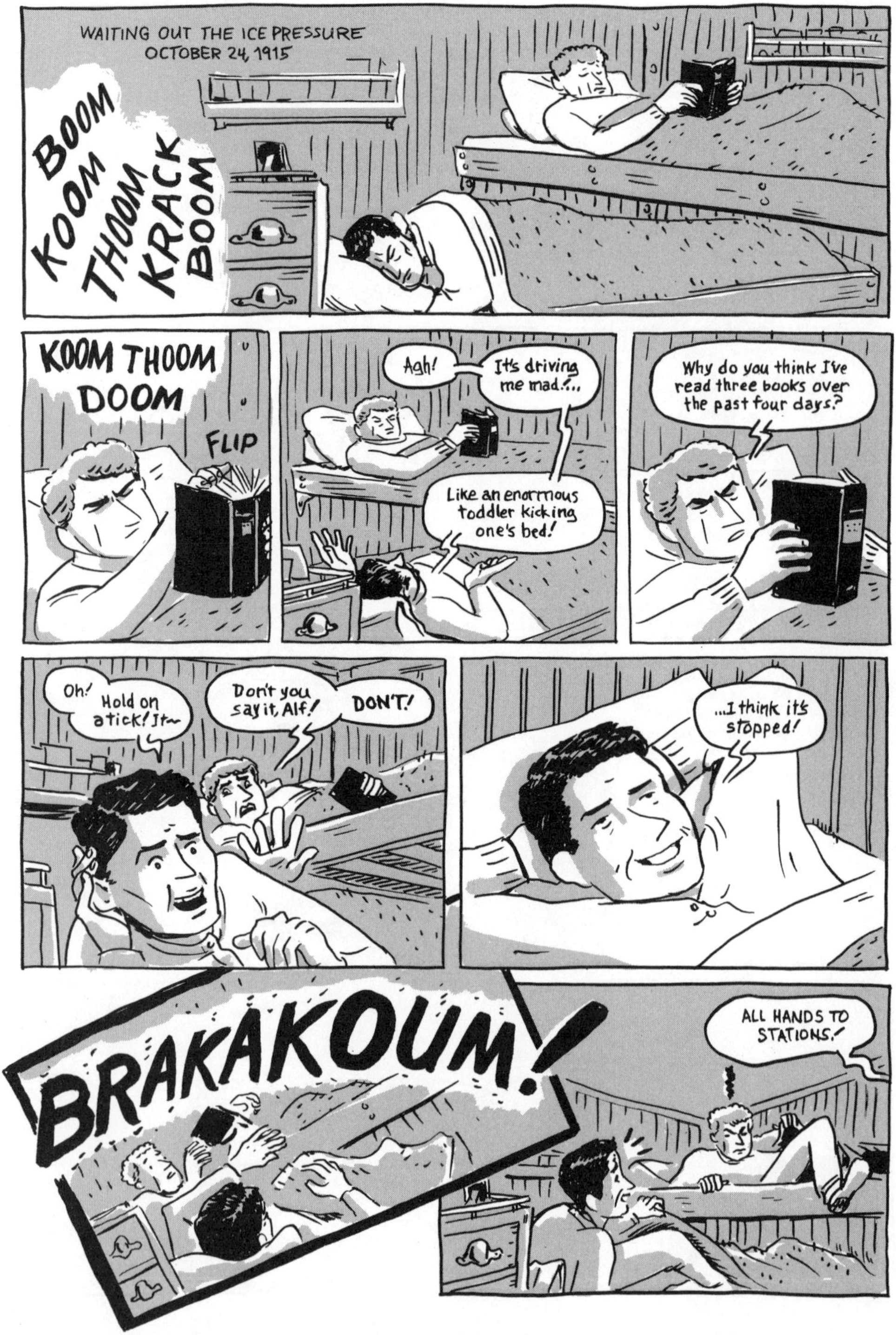
WAITING OUT THE ICE PRESSURE
OCTOBER 24, 1915
BOOM KOOM THOOM KRACK BOOM
KOOM THOOM DOOM
FLIP
Agh!
It's driving me mad!...
Like an enormous toddler kicking one's bed!
Why do you think I've read three books over the past four days?
Oh! Hold on a tick! It~
Don't you say it, Alf!
DON'T!
...I think it's stopped!
BRAKAKOUM!
ALL HANDS TO STATIONS!

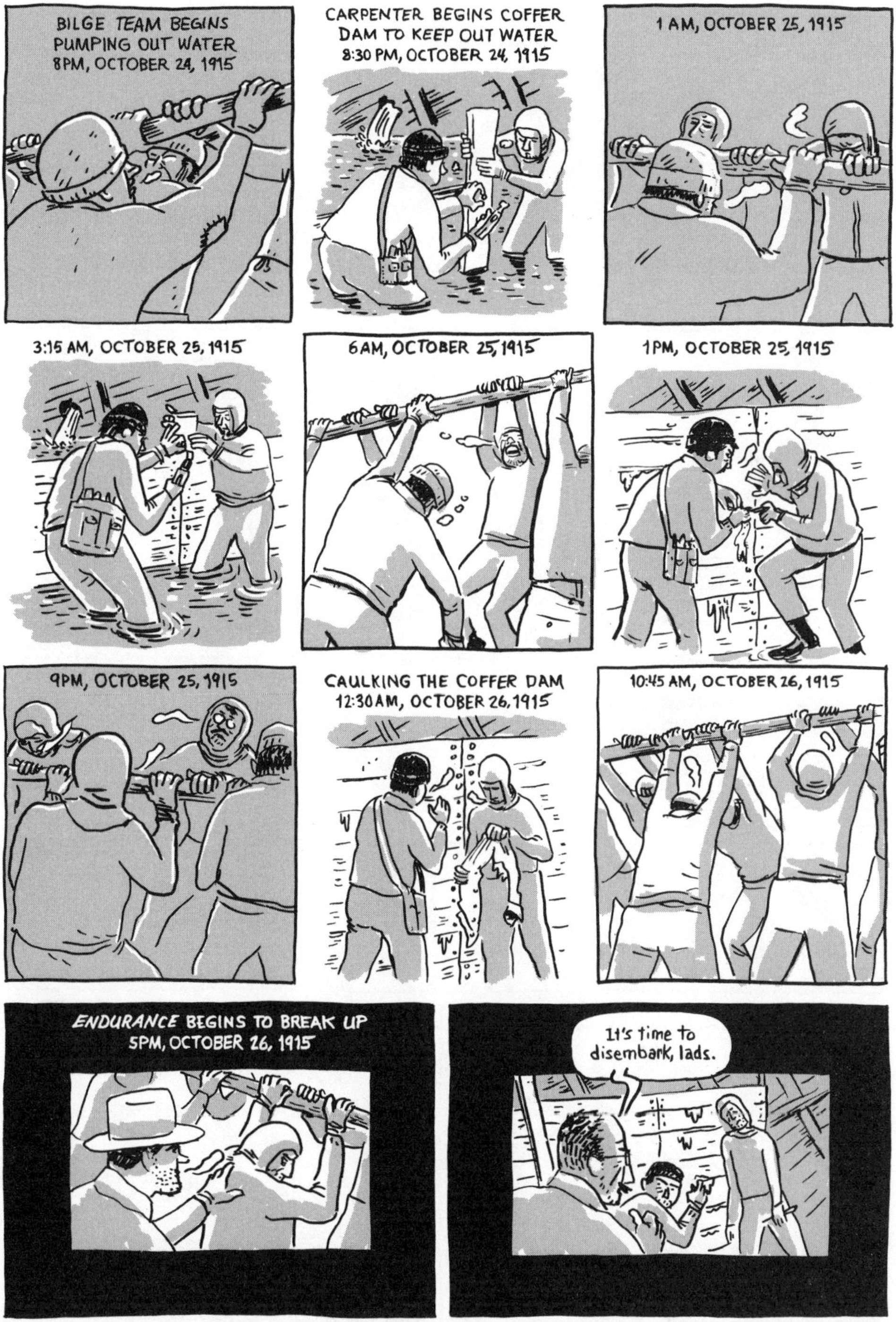
BILGE TEAM BEGINS PUMPING OUT WATER 8PM, OCTOBER 24, 1915
CARPENTER BEGINS COFFER DAM TO KEEP OUT WATER 8:30 PM, OCTOBER 24, 1915
1 AM, OCTOBER 25, 1915
3:15 AM, OCTOBER 25, 1915
6AM, OCTOBER 25, 1915
1PM, OCTOBER 25, 1915
9PM, OCTOBER 25, 1915
CAULKING THE COFFER DAM 12:30AM, OCTOBER 26, 1915
10:45 AM, OCTOBER 26, 1915
ENDURANCE BEGINS TO BREAK UP 5PM, OCTOBER 26, 1915
It's time to disembark, lads.

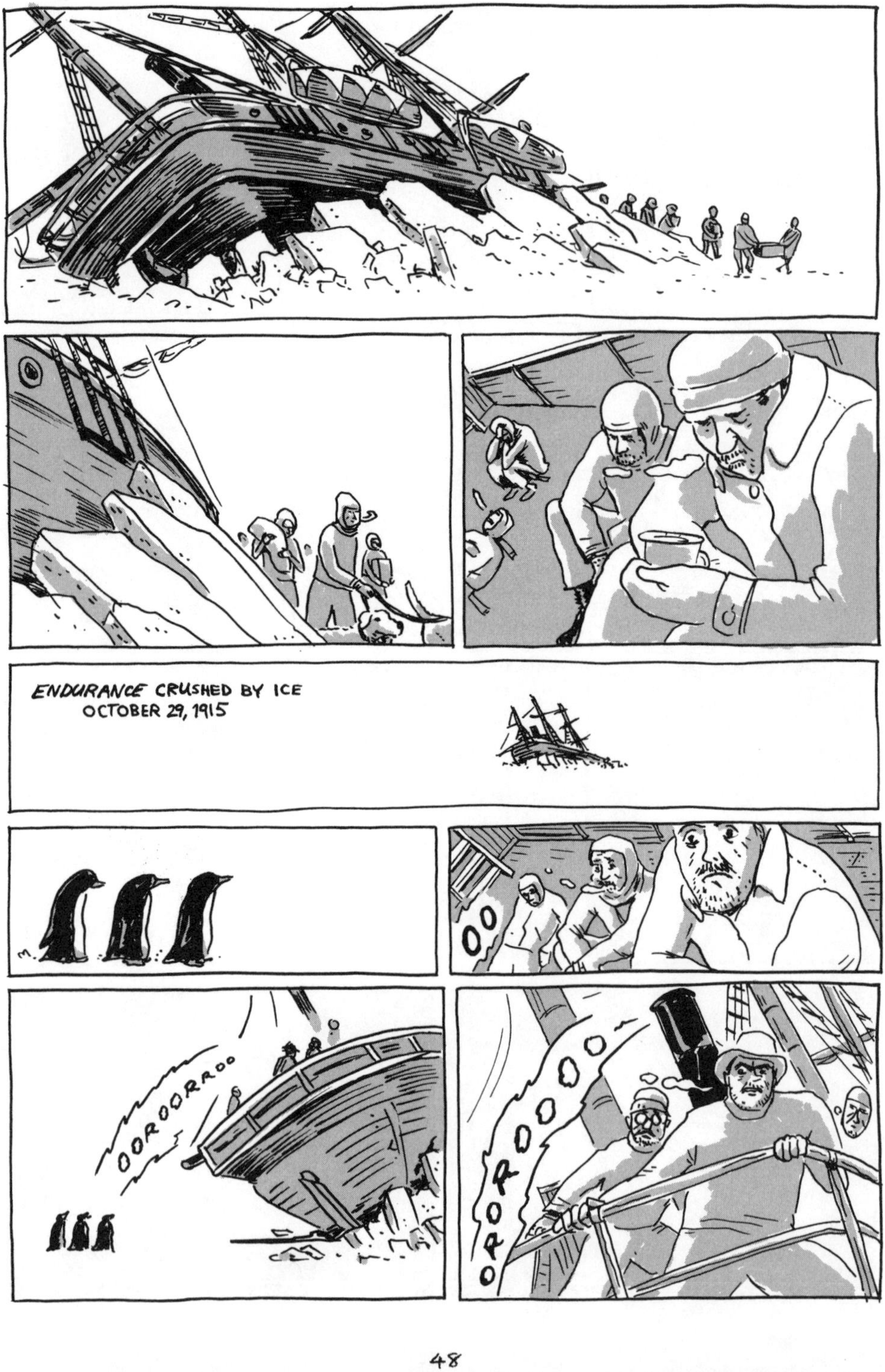
ENDURANCE CRUSHED BY ICE
OCTOBER 29, 1915
OO
OOROORROO

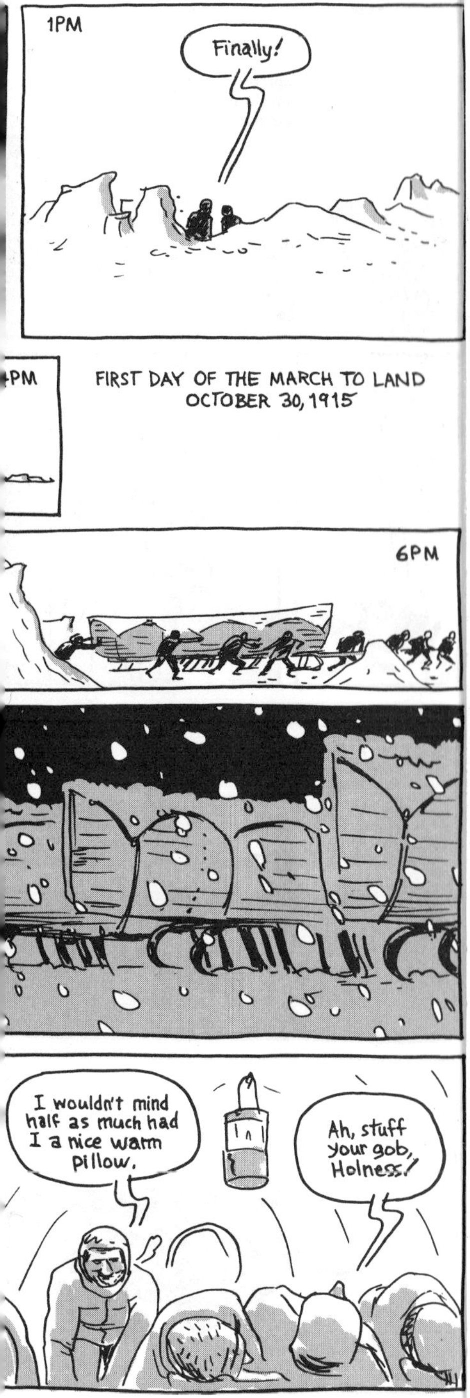
1PM
Finally!
FIRST DAY OF THE MARCH TO LAND
OCTOBER 30, 1915
6PM
I wouldn't mind half as much had I a nice warm pillow.
Ah, stuff your gob, Holness!

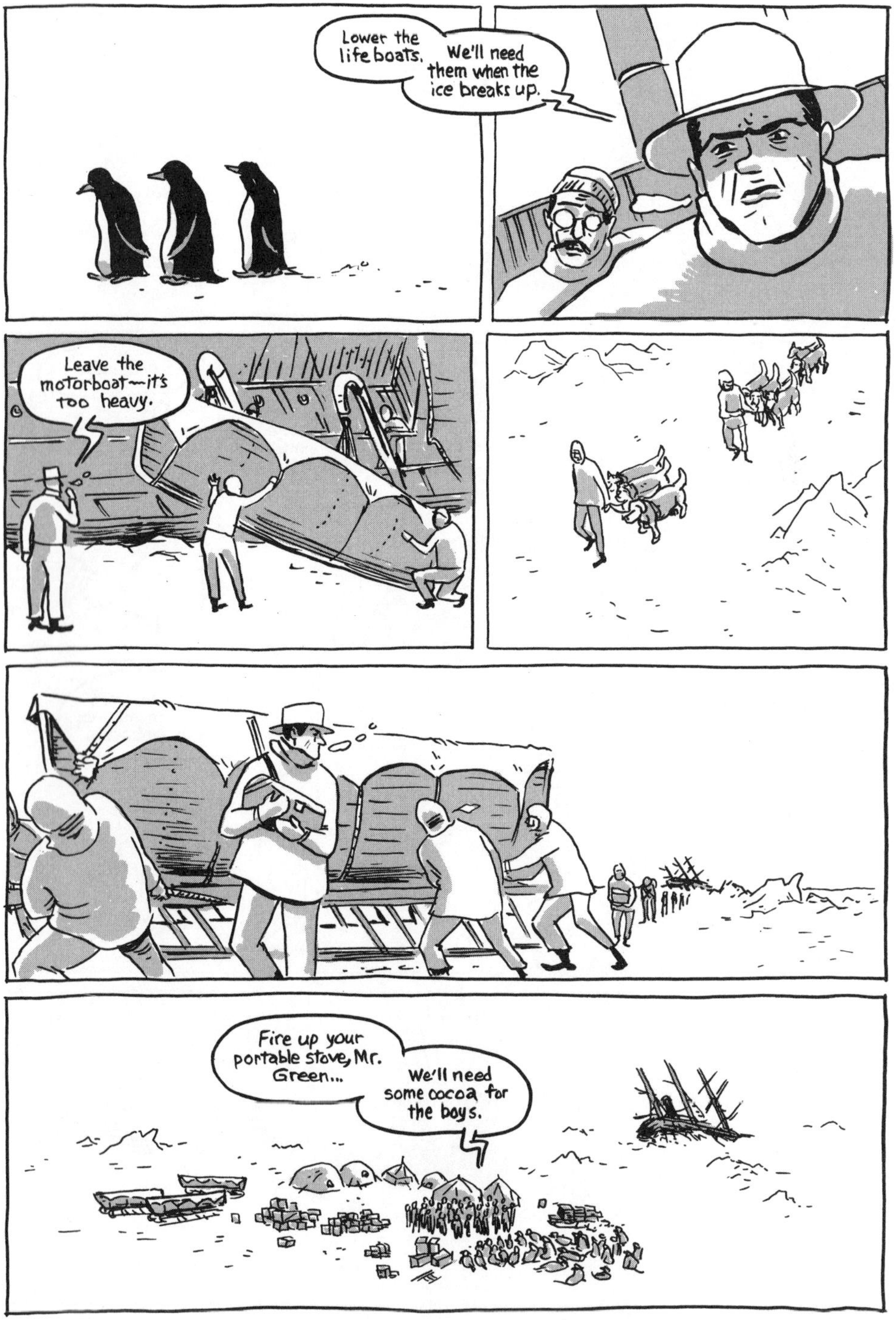
Lower the life boats.
We'll need them when the ice breaks up.
Leave the motorboat—it's too heavy.
Fire up your portable stove, Mr. Green...
We'll need some cocoa for the boys.

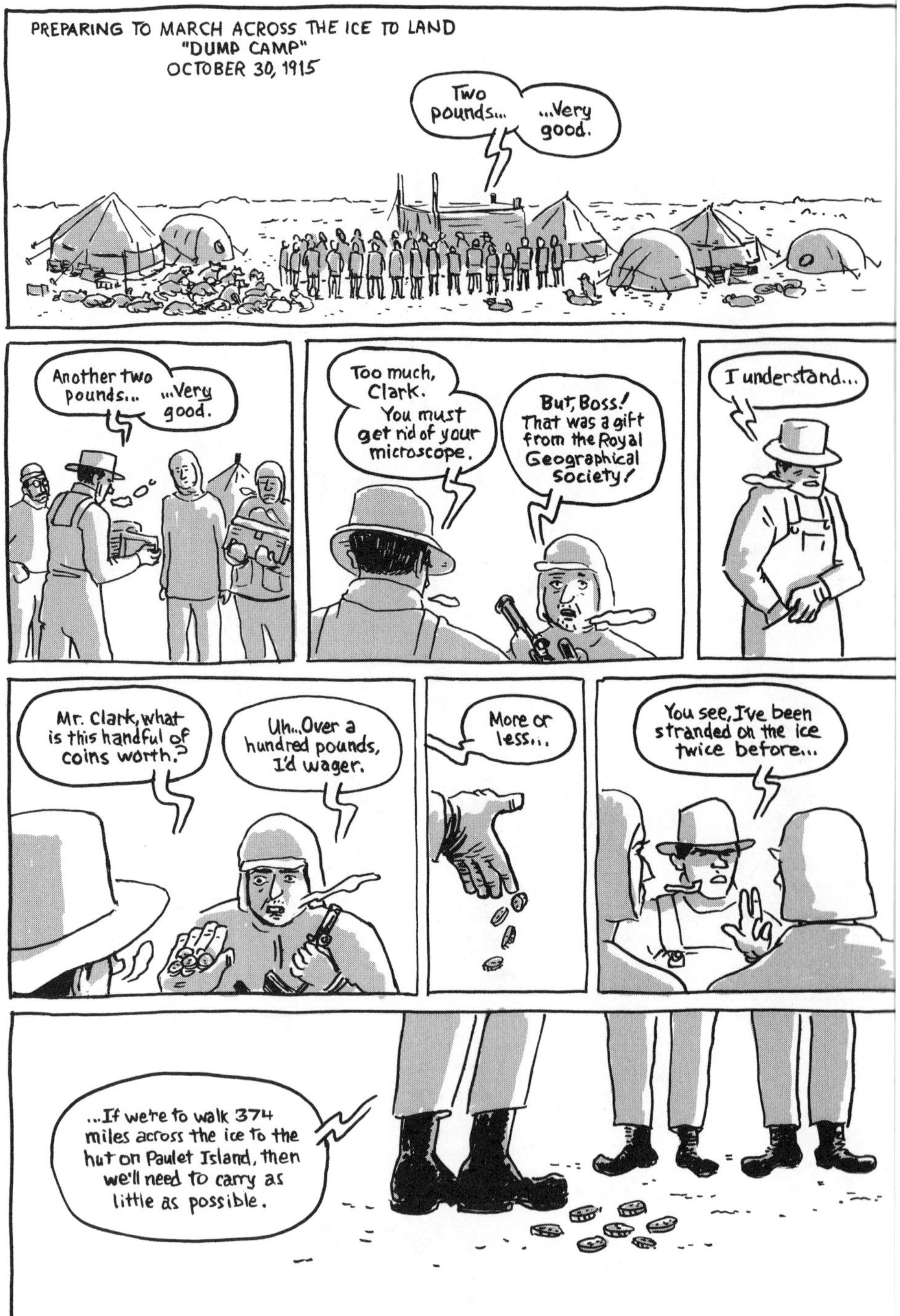
PREPARING TO MARCH ACROSS THE ICE TO LAND "DUMP CAMP" OCTOBER 30, 1915
Two pounds...
...Very good.
Another two pounds...
...Very good.
Too much, Clark. You must get rid of your microscope.
But, Boss! That was a gift from the Royal Geographical Society!
I understand...
Mr. Clark, what is this handful of coins worth?
Uh...Over a hundred pounds, I'd wager.
More or less...
You see, I've been stranded on the ice twice before...
...If we're to walk 374 miles across the ice to the hut on Paulet Island, then we'll need to carry as little as possible.

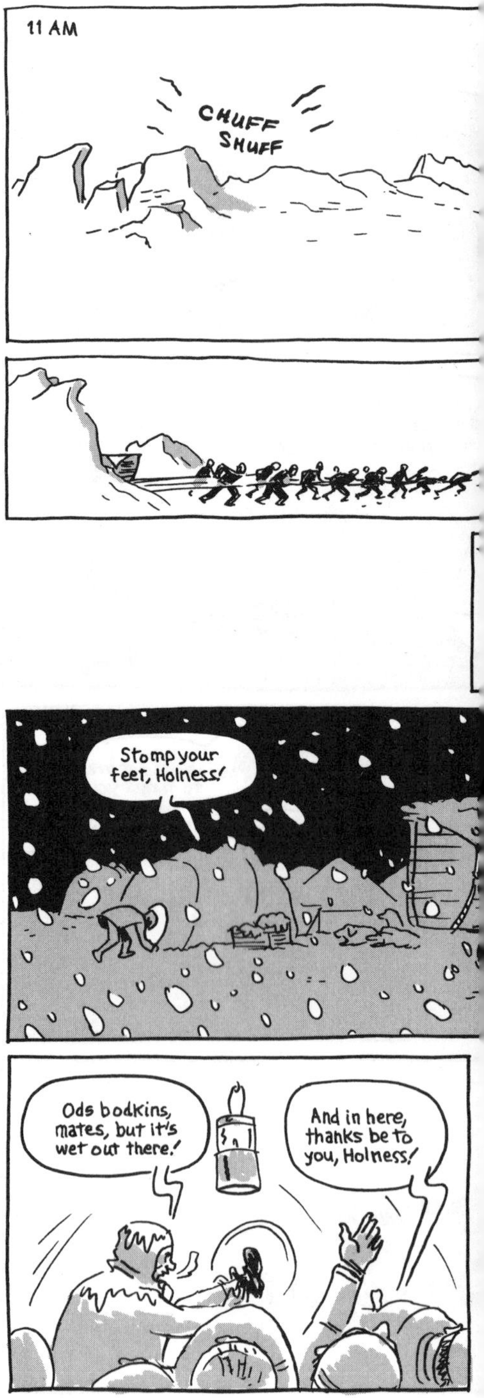
11 AM
CHUFF
SHUFF
Stomp your feet, Holness!
Ods bodkins, mates, but it's wet out there!
And in here, thanks be to you, Holness!

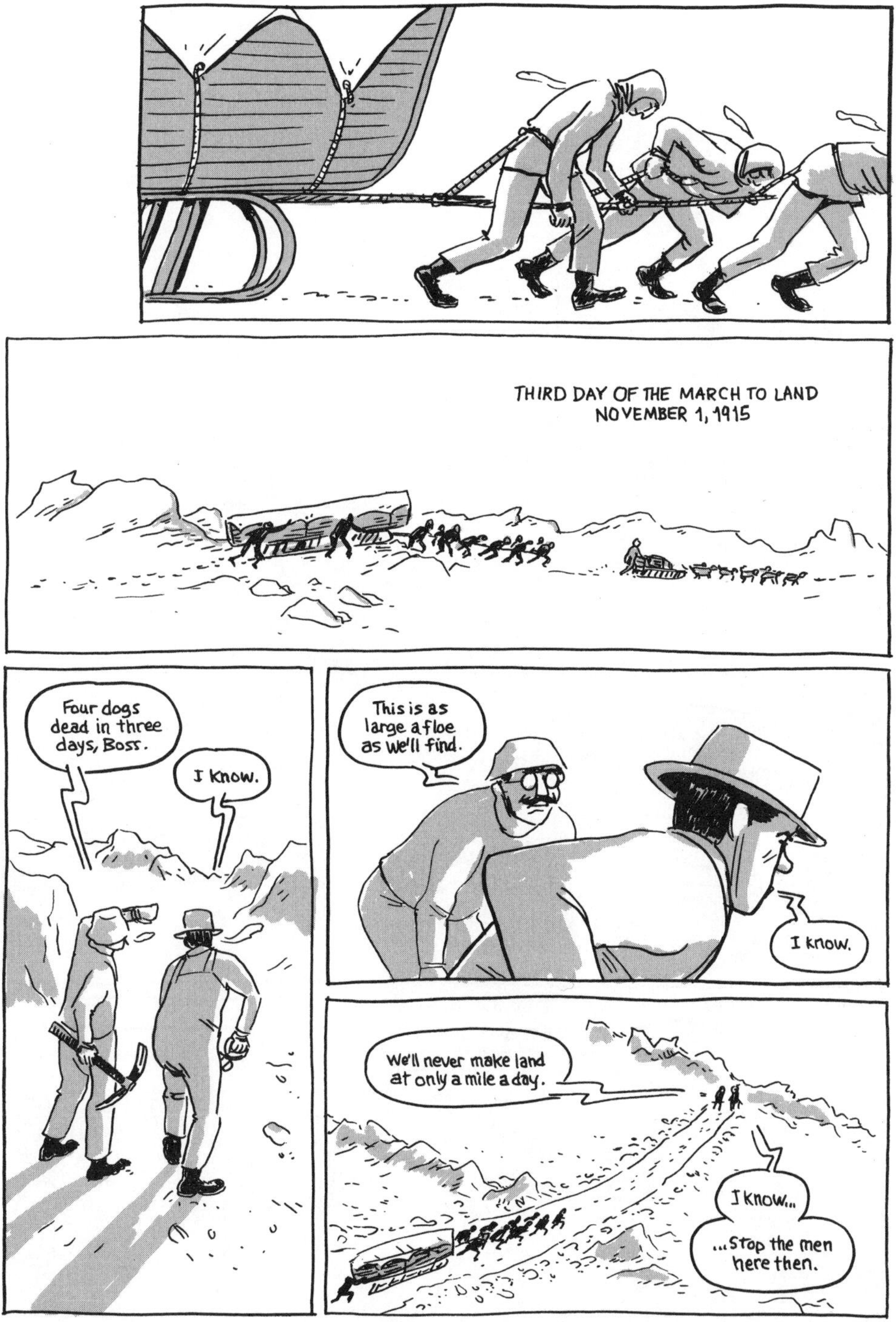
THIRD DAY OF THE MARCH TO LAND
NOVEMBER 1, 1915
Four dogs dead in three days, Boss.
I know.
This is as large a floe as we'll find.
I know.
We'll never make land at only a mile a day.
I know...
...Stop the men here then.

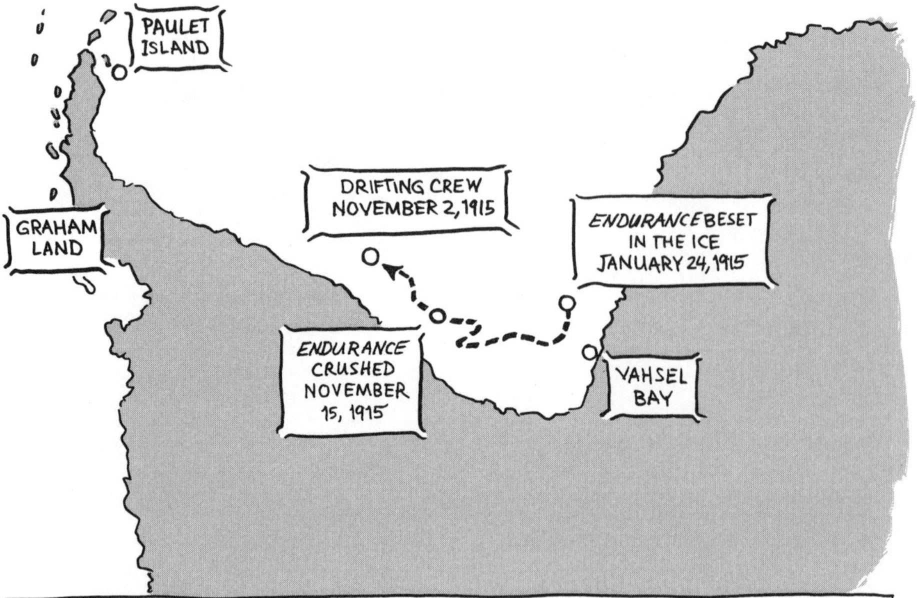
PAULET ISLAND
GRAHAM LAND
DRIFTING CREW NOVEMBER 2, 1915
ENDURANCE BESET IN THE ICE JANUARY 24, 1915
ENDURANCE CRUSHED NOVEMBER 15, 1915
VAHSEL BAY

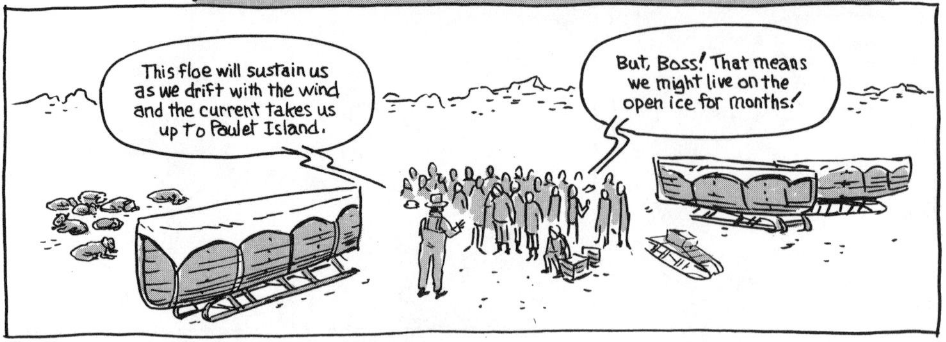
This floe will sustain us as we drift with the wind and the current takes us up to Paulet Island.
But, Boss! That means we might live on the open ice for months!

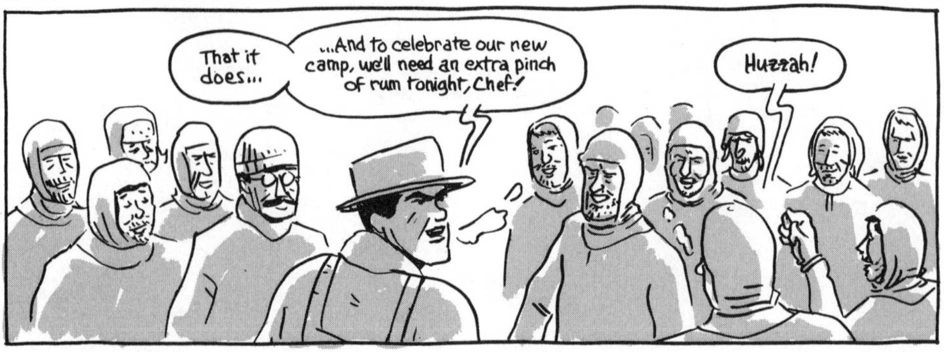
That it does...
...And to celebrate our new camp, we'll need an extra pinch of rum tonight, Chef!
Huzzah!

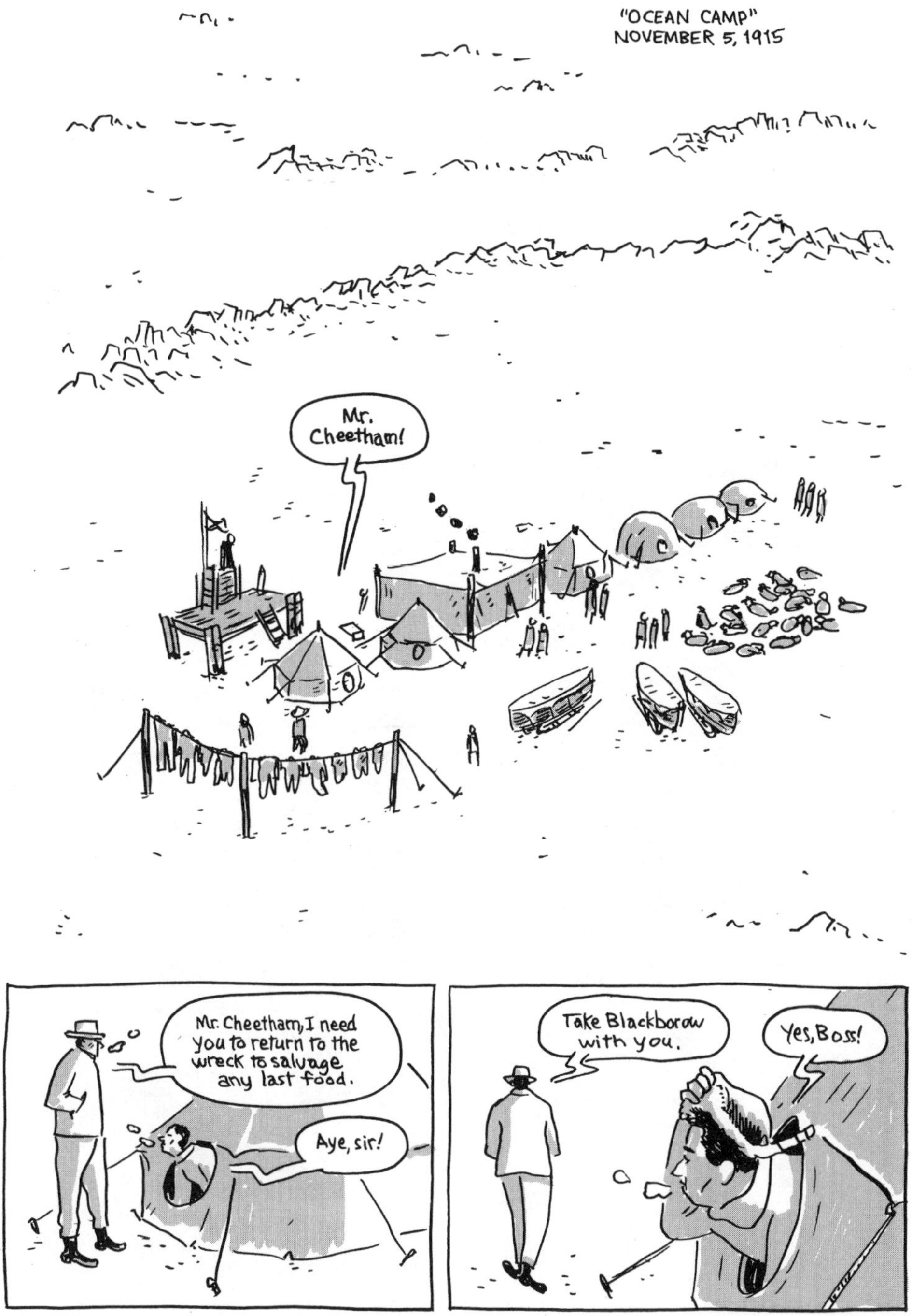
"OCEAN CAMP"
NOVEMBER 5, 1915
Mr. Cheetham!
Mr. Cheetham, I need you to return to the wreck to salvage any last food.
Aye, sir!
Take Blackborow with you.
Yes, Boss!

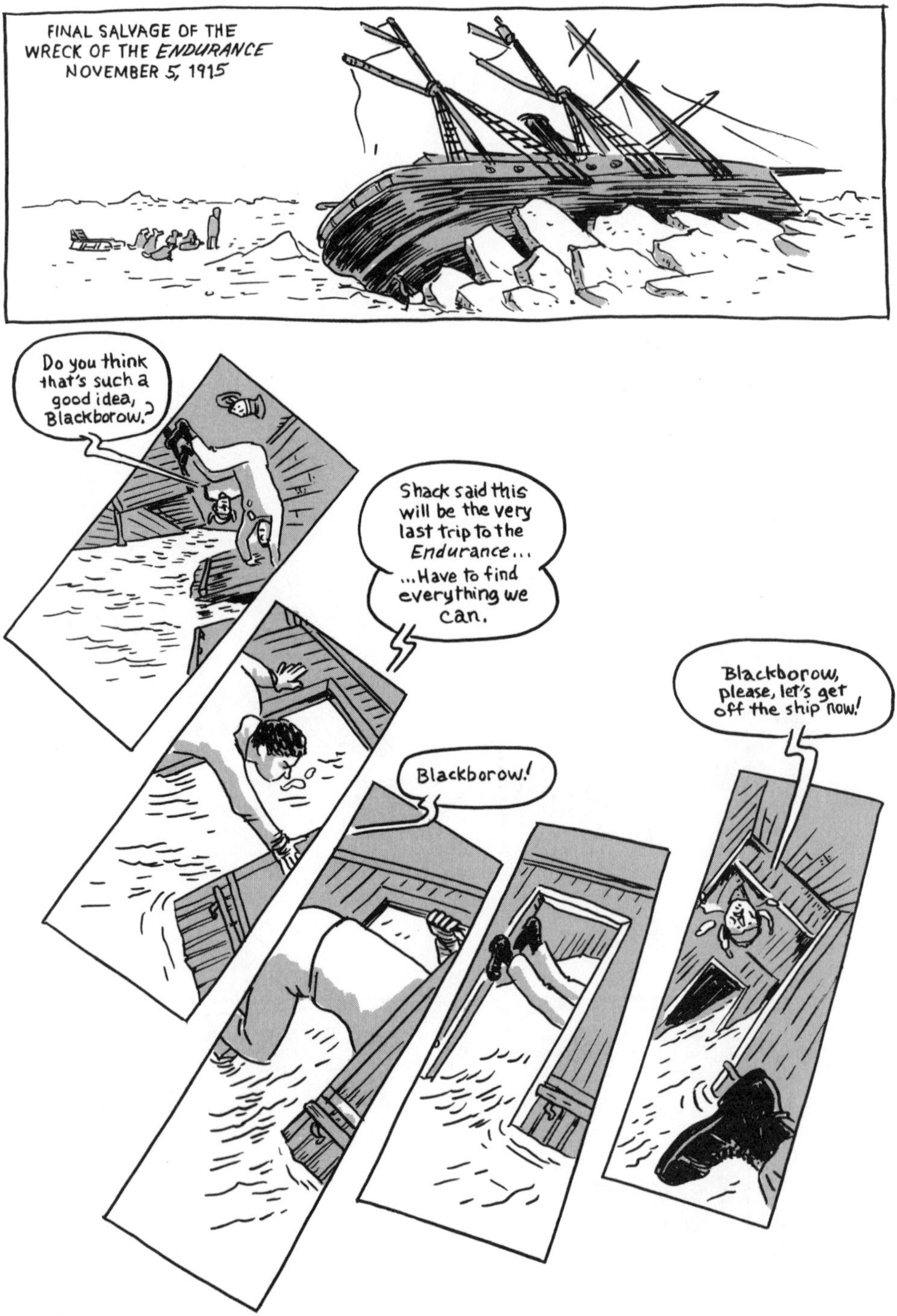
FINAL SALVAGE OF THE WRECK OF THE *ENDURANCE* NOVEMBER 5, 1915
Do you think that's such a good idea, Blackborow?
Shack said this will be the very last trip to the *Endurance*...
...Have to find everything we can.
Blackborow!
Blackborow, please, let's get off the ship now!

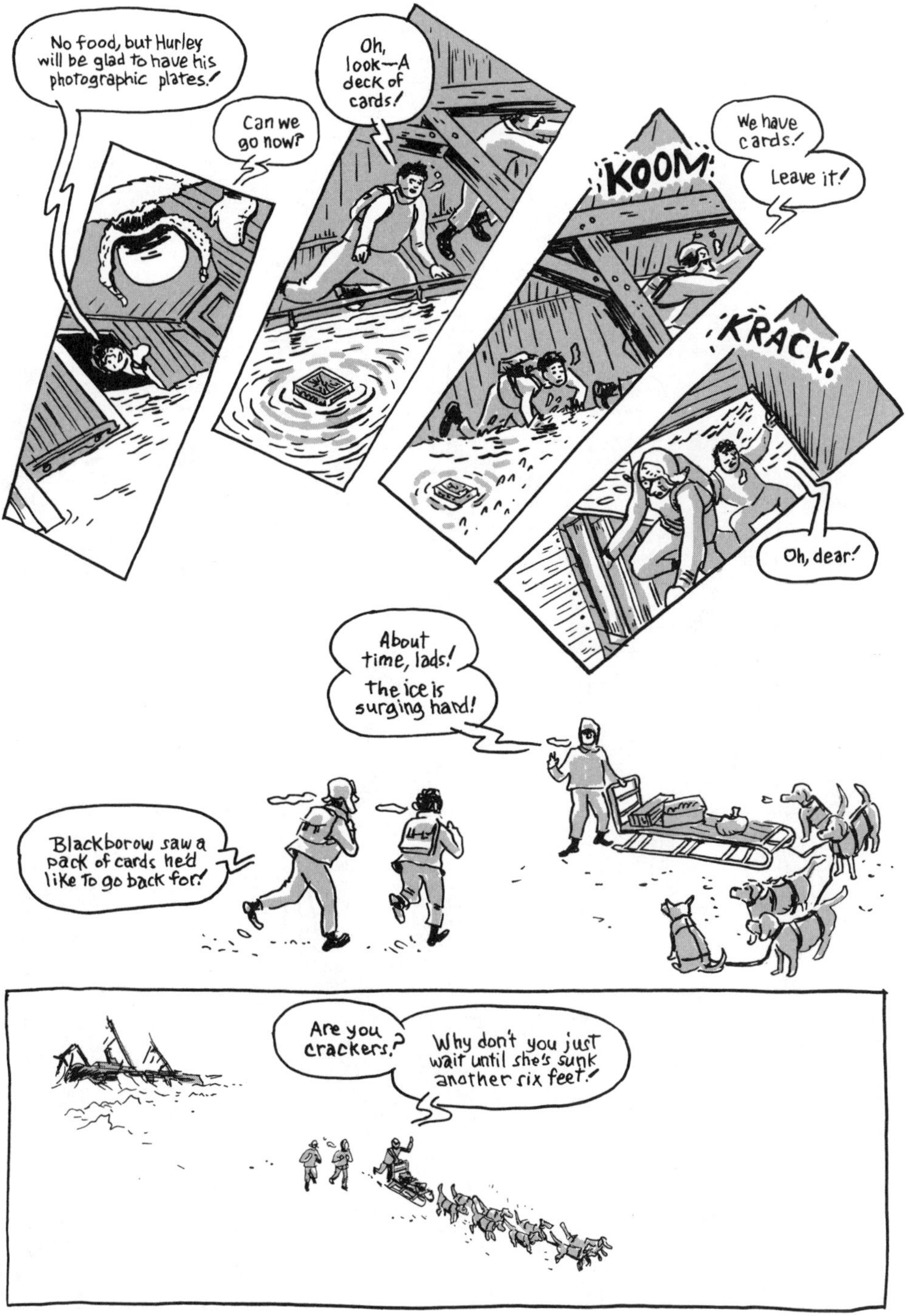

No food, but Hurley will be glad to have his photographic plates!
Can we go now?
Oh, look—A deck of cards!
KOOM
We have cards!
Leave it!
KRACK!
Oh, dear!
About time, lads!
The ice is surging hard!
Blackborow saw a pack of cards he'd like to go back for!
Are you crackers?
Why don't you just wait until she's sunk another six feet!

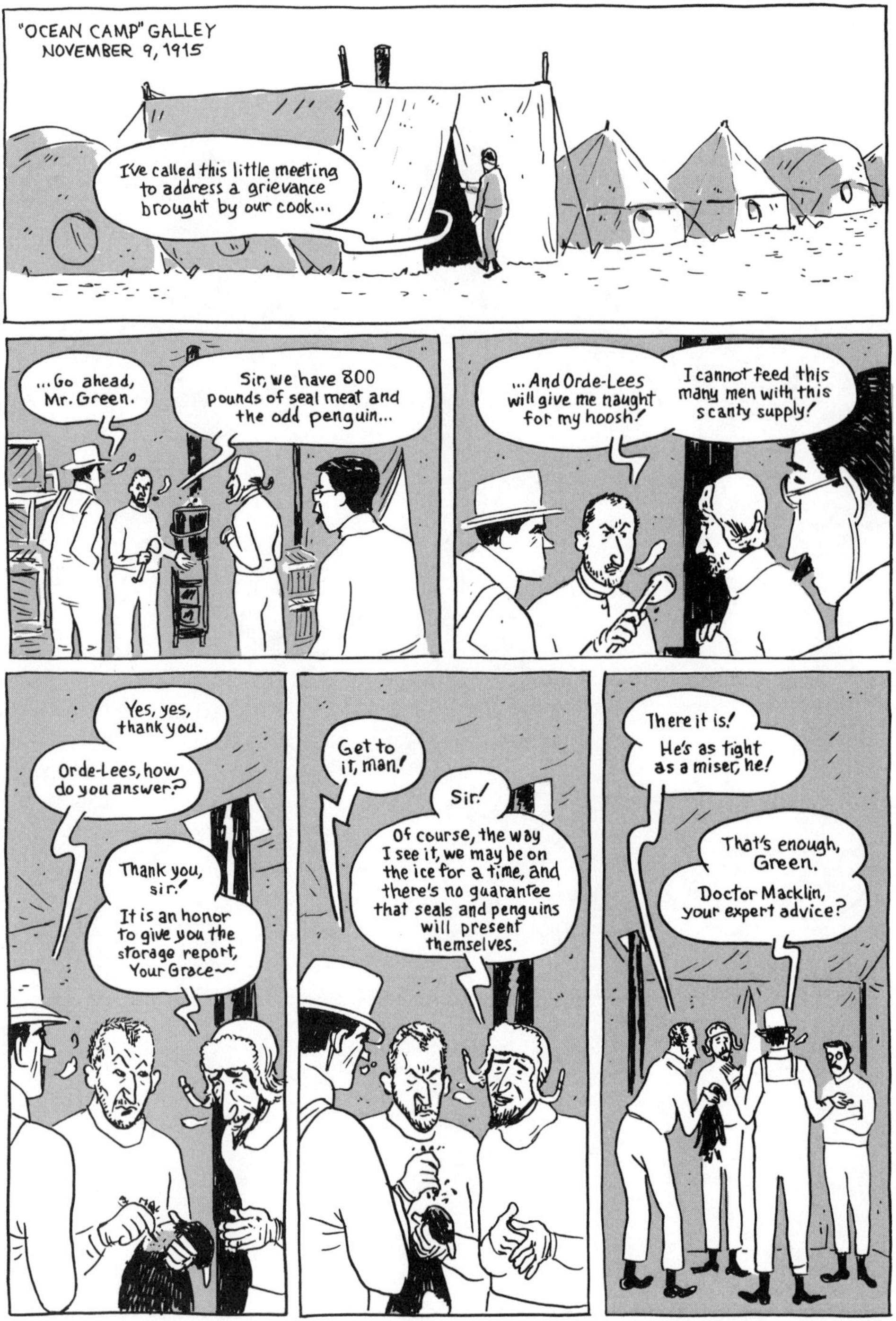
"OCEAN CAMP" GALLEY
NOVEMBER 9, 1915
I've called this little meeting to address a grievance brought by our cook...
...Go ahead, Mr. Green.
Sir, we have 800 pounds of seal meat and the odd penguin...
...And Orde-Lees will give me naught for my hoosh!
I cannot feed this many men with this scanty supply!
Yes, yes, thank you.
Orde-Lees, how do you answer?
Thank you, sir!
It is an honor to give you the storage report, Your Grace~
Get to it, man!
Sir!
Of course, the way I see it, we may be on the ice for a time, and there's no guarantee that seals and penguins will present themselves.
There it is!
He's as tight as a miser, he!
That's enough, Green.
Doctor Macklin, your expert advice?

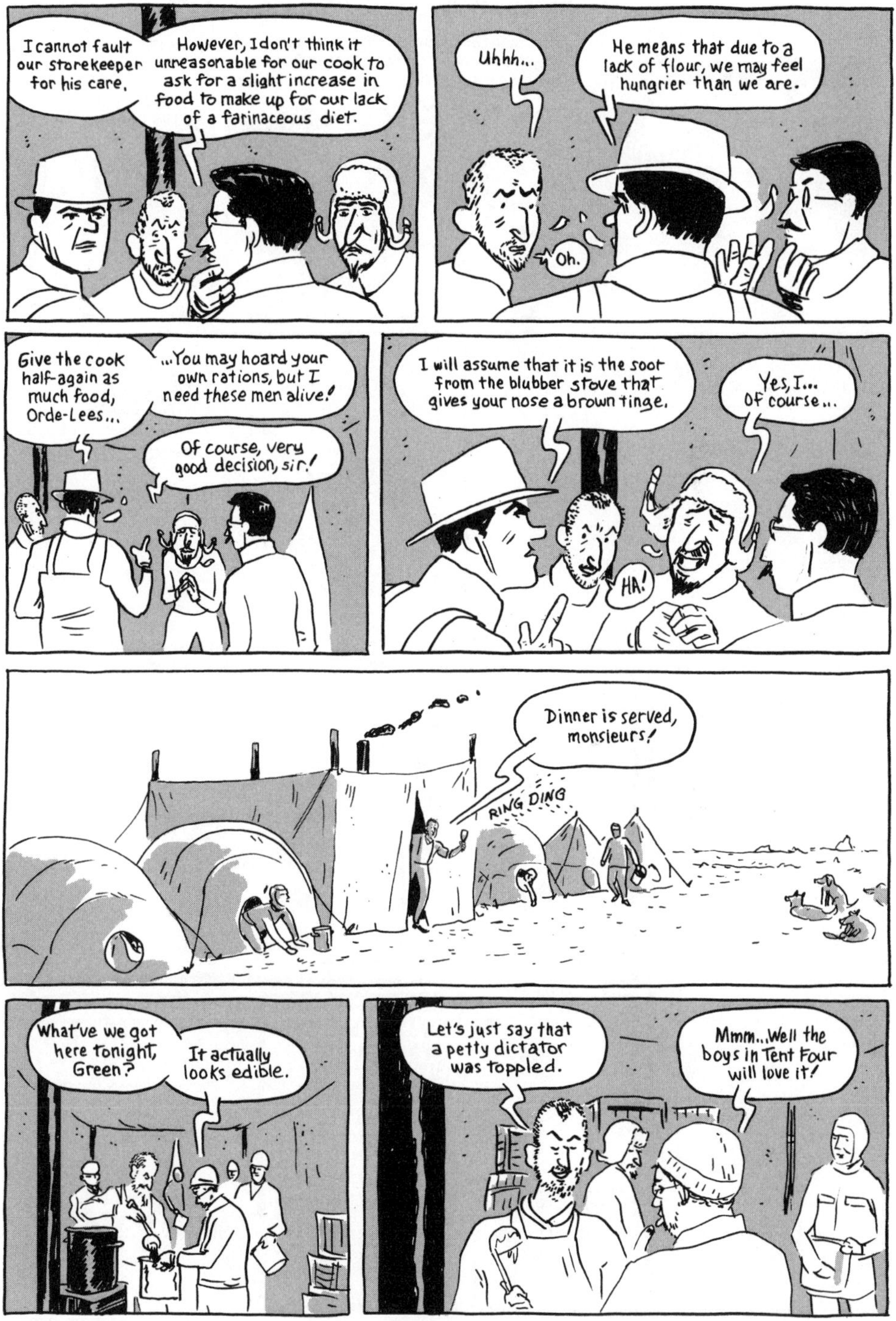

I cannot fault our storekeeper for his care.
However, I don't think it unreasonable for our cook to ask for a slight increase in food to make up for our lack of a farinaceous diet.
Uhhh...
He means that due to a lack of flour, we may feel hungrier than we are.
Oh.
Give the cook half-again as much food, Orde-Lees...
...You may hoard your own rations, but I need these men alive!
Of course, very good decision, sir!
I will assume that it is the soot from the blubber stove that gives your nose a brown tinge.
Yes, I... Of course...
HA!
Dinner is served, monsieurs!
RING DING
What've we got here tonight, Green?
It actually looks edible.
Let's just say that a petty dictator was toppled.
Mmm...Well the boys in Tent Four will love it!

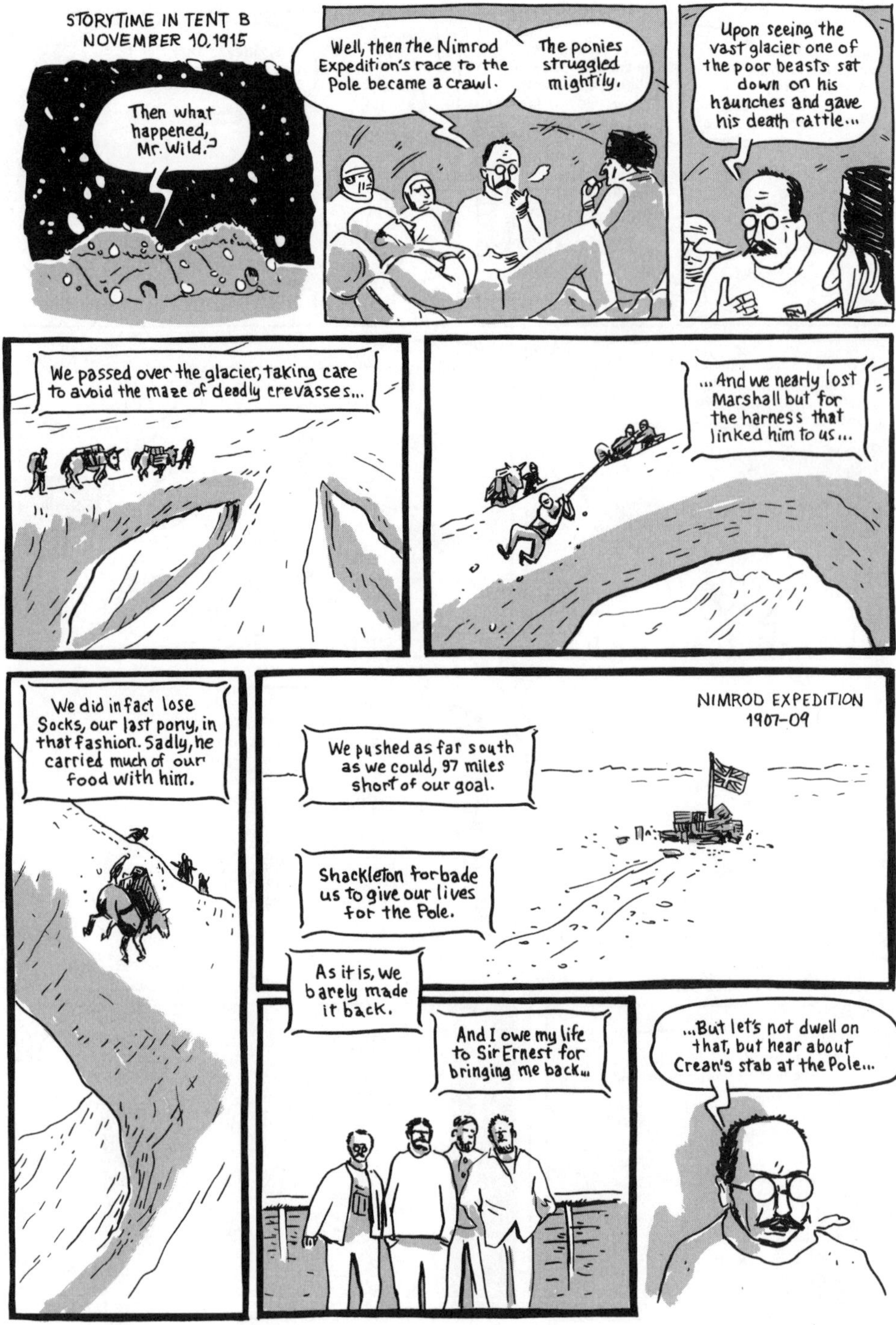
STORYTIME IN TENT B
NOVEMBER 10, 1915
Then what happened, Mr. Wild?
Well, then the Nimrod Expedition's race to the Pole became a crawl.
The ponies struggled mightily.
Upon seeing the vast glacier one of the poor beasts sat down on his haunches and gave his death rattle...
We passed over the glacier, taking care to avoid the maze of deadly crevasses...
...And we nearly lost Marshall but for the harness that linked him to us...
We did in fact lose Socks, our last pony, in that fashion. Sadly, he carried much of our food with him.
NIMROD EXPEDITION
1907-09
We pushed as far south as we could, 97 miles short of our goal.
Shackleton forbade us to give our lives for the Pole.
As it is, we barely made it back.
And I owe my life to Sir Ernest for bringing me back...
...But let's not dwell on that, but hear about Crean's stab at the Pole...

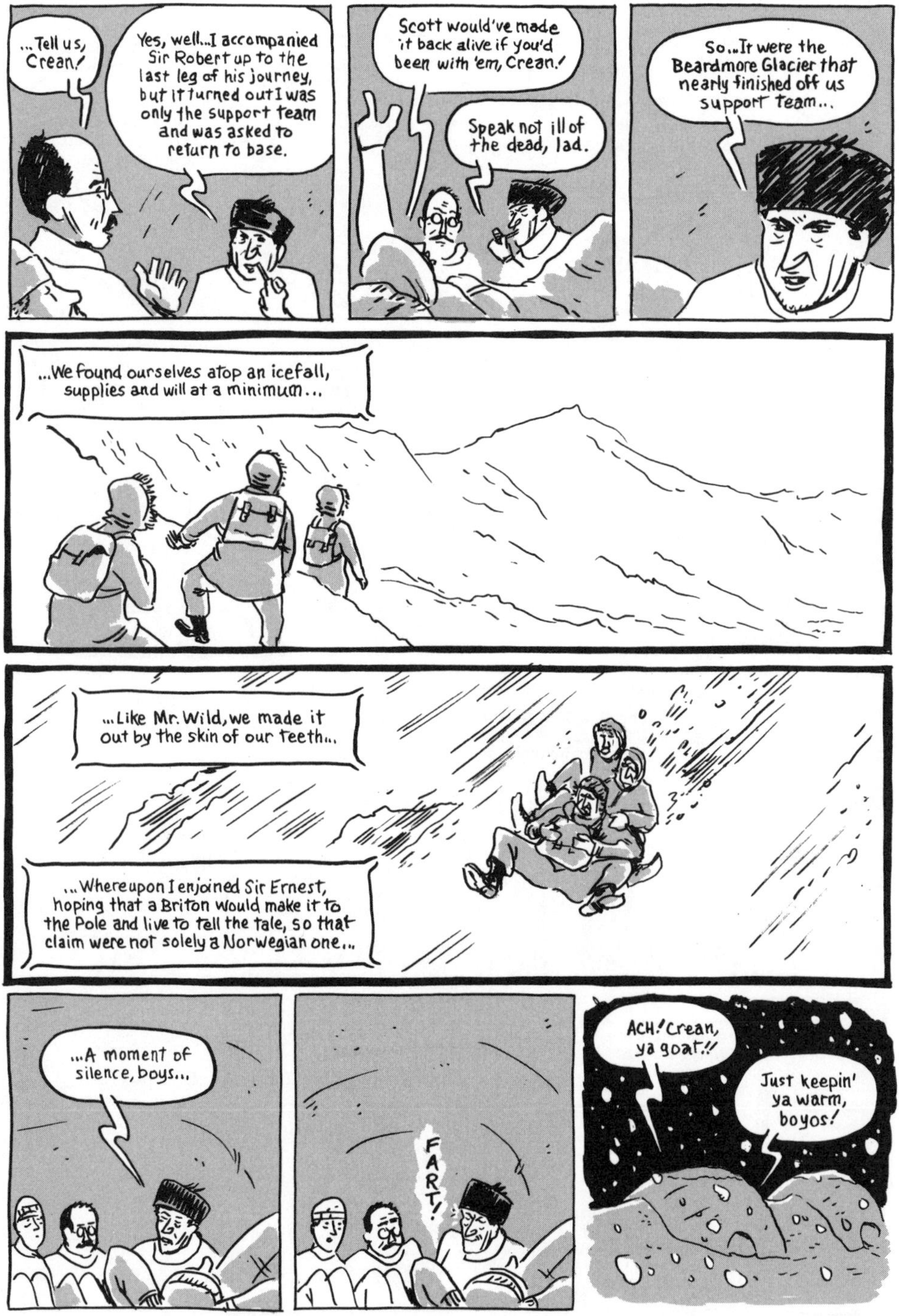
...Tell us, Crean!
Yes, well...I accompanied Sir Robert up to the last leg of his journey, but it turned out I was only the support team and was asked to return to base.
Scott would've made it back alive if you'd been with 'em, Crean!
Speak not ill of the dead, lad.
So...It were the Beardmore Glacier that nearly finished off us support team...
...We found ourselves atop an icefall, supplies and will at a minimum...
...Like Mr. Wild, we made it out by the skin of our teeth...
...Whereupon I enjoined Sir Ernest, hoping that a Briton would make it to the Pole and live to tell the tale, so that claim were not solely a Norwegian one...
...A moment of silence, boys...
FART!
ACH! Crean, ya goat!!
Just keepin' ya warm, boyos!

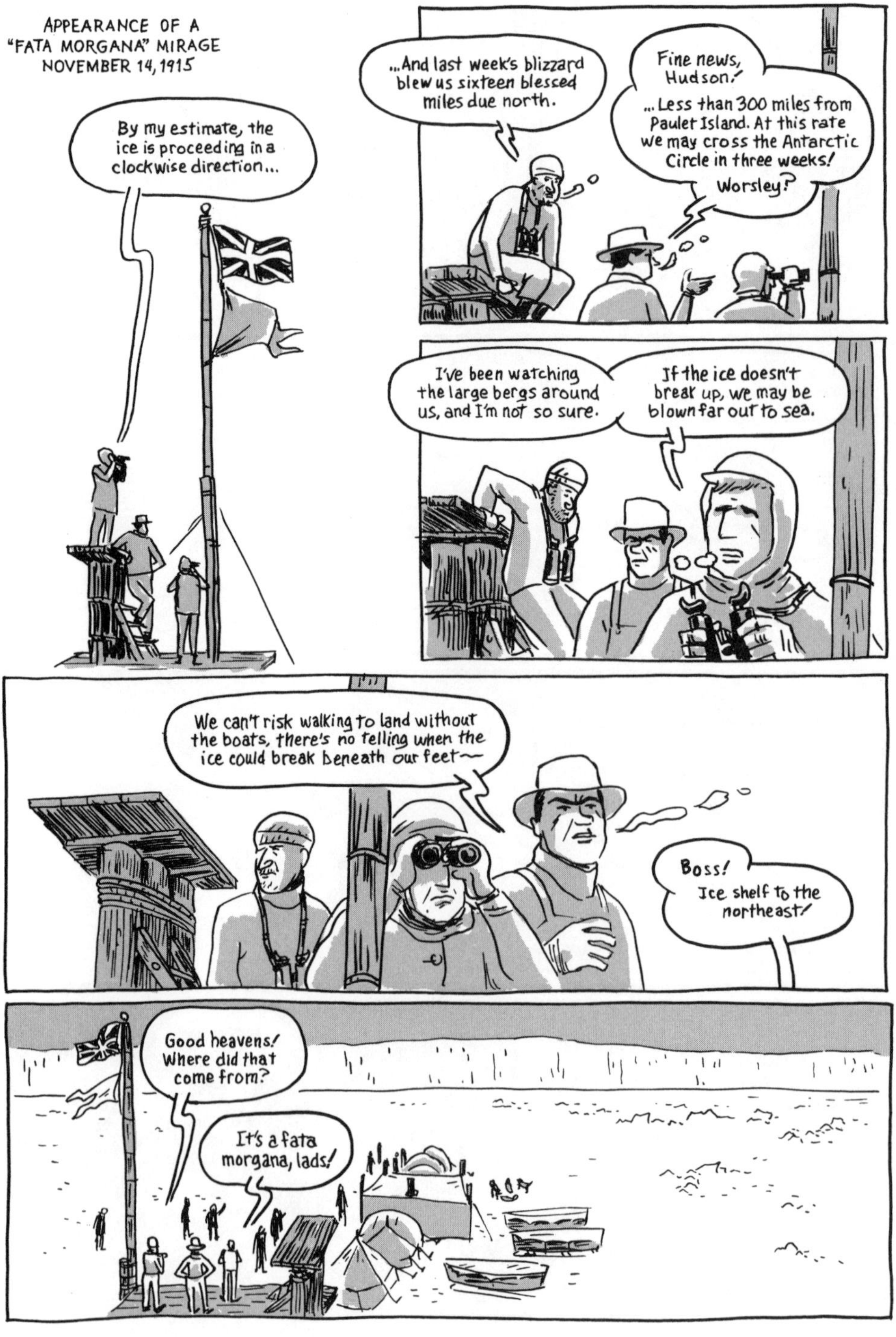

APPEARANCE OF A "FATA MORGANA" MIRAGE NOVEMBER 14, 1915
By my estimate, the ice is proceeding in a clockwise direction...
...And last week's blizzard blew us sixteen blessed miles due north.
Fine news, Hudson!
...Less than 300 miles from Paulet Island. At this rate we may cross the Antarctic Circle in three weeks!
Worsley?
I've been watching the large bergs around us, and I'm not so sure.
If the ice doesn't break up, we may be blown far out to sea.
We can't risk walking to land without the boats, there's no telling when the ice could break beneath our feet—
Boss!
Ice shelf to the northeast!
Good heavens! Where did that come from?
It's a fata morgana, lads!

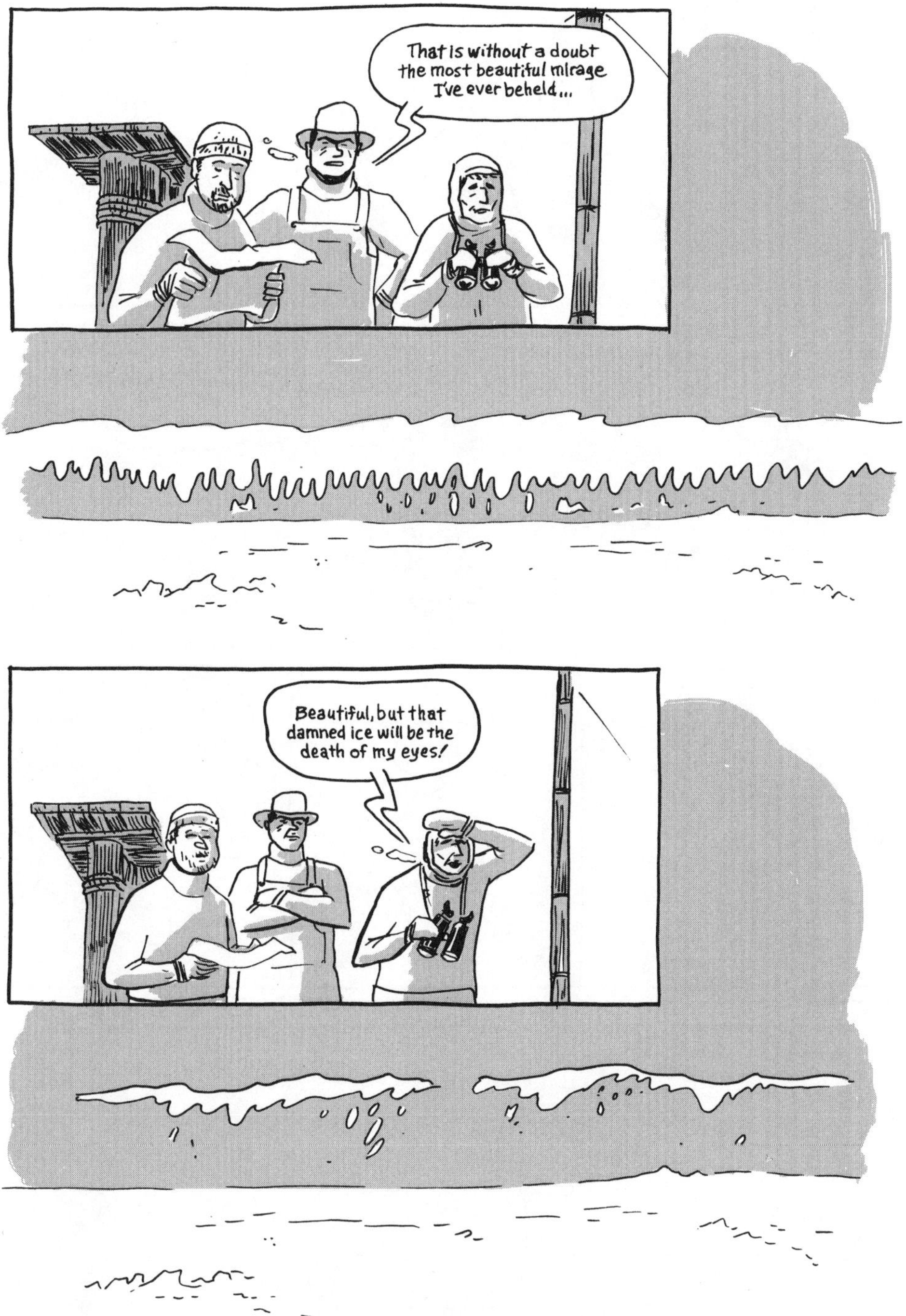
That is without a doubt the most beautiful mirage I've ever beheld...
Beautiful, but that damned ice will be the death of my eyes!

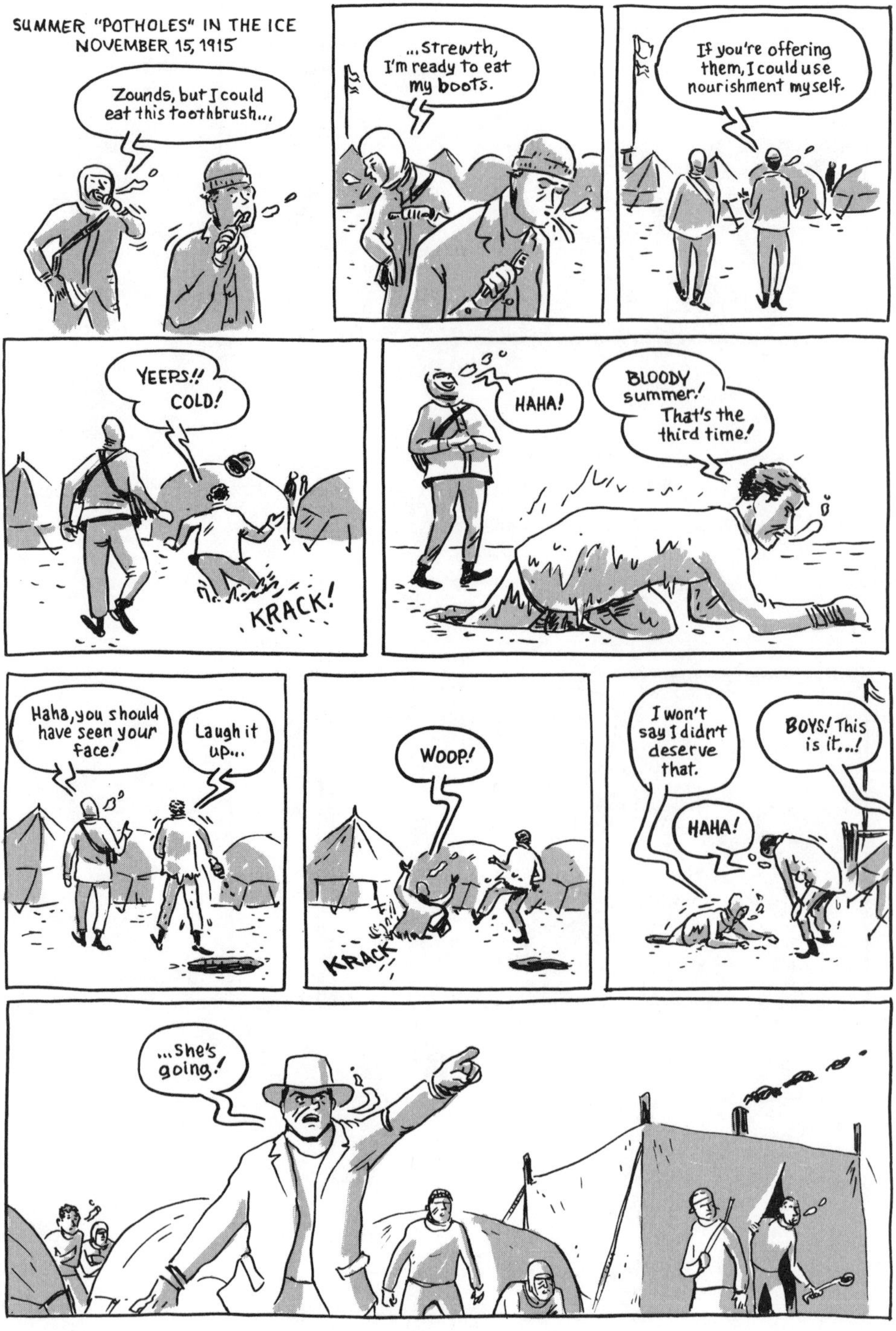
SUMMER "POTHOLES" IN THE ICE
NOVEMBER 15, 1915
Zounds, but I could eat this toothbrush...
...strewth, I'm ready to eat my boots.
If you're offering them, I could use nourishment myself.
YEEPS!! COLD!
KRACK!
HAHA!
BLOODY summer! That's the third time!
Haha, you should have seen your face!
Laugh it up...
WOOP!
KRACK
I won't say I didn't deserve that.
HAHA!
BOYS! This is it...!
...she's going!

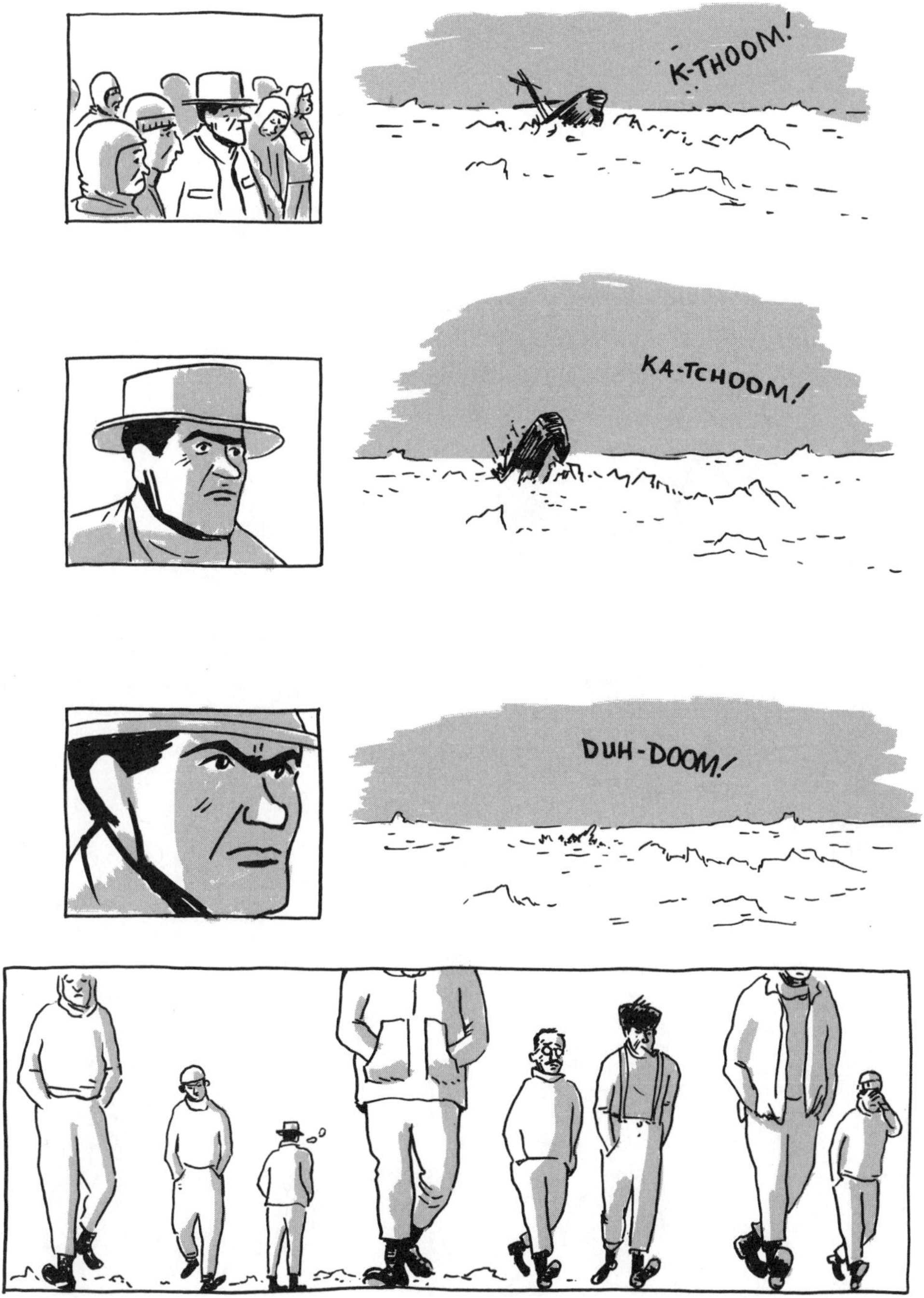
K-THOOM!
KA-TCHOOM!
DUH-DOOM!

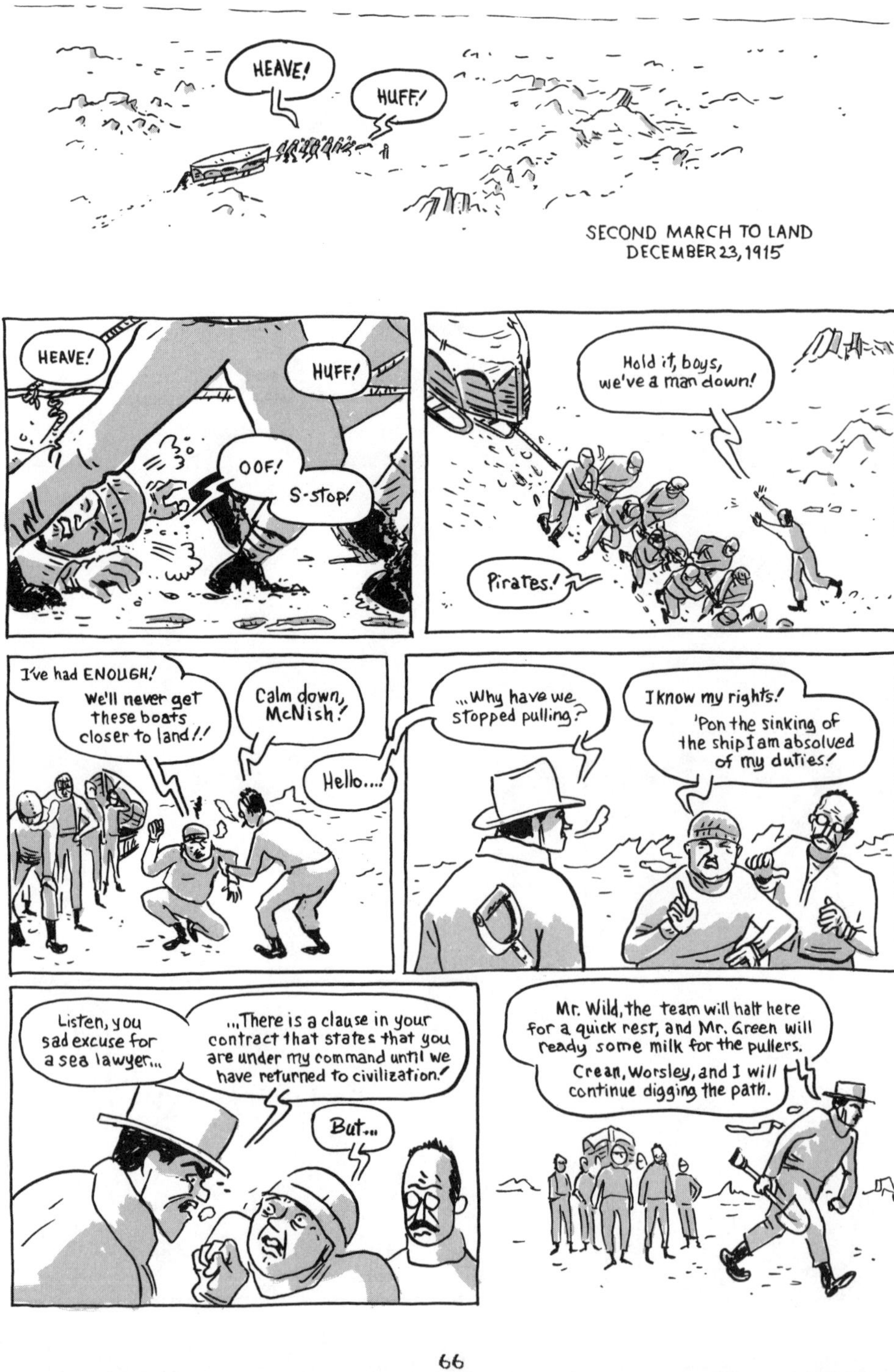
HEAVE!
HUFF!
SECOND MARCH TO LAND
DECEMBER 23, 1915
HEAVE!
HUFF!
OOF!
S-stop!
Hold it, boys, we've a man down!
Pirates!
I've had ENOUGH!
We'll never get these boats closer to land!!
Calm down, McNish!
Hello....
...Why have we stopped pulling?
I know my rights!
'Pon the sinking of the ship I am absolved of my duties!
Listen, you sad excuse for a sea lawyer...
...There is a clause in your contract that states that you are under my command until we have returned to civilization!
But...
Mr. Wild, the team will halt here for a quick rest, and Mr. Green will ready some milk for the pullers.
Crean, Worsley, and I will continue digging the path.

SCANNING FOR PASSAGE ACROSS THE ICE
DECEMBER 29, 1915

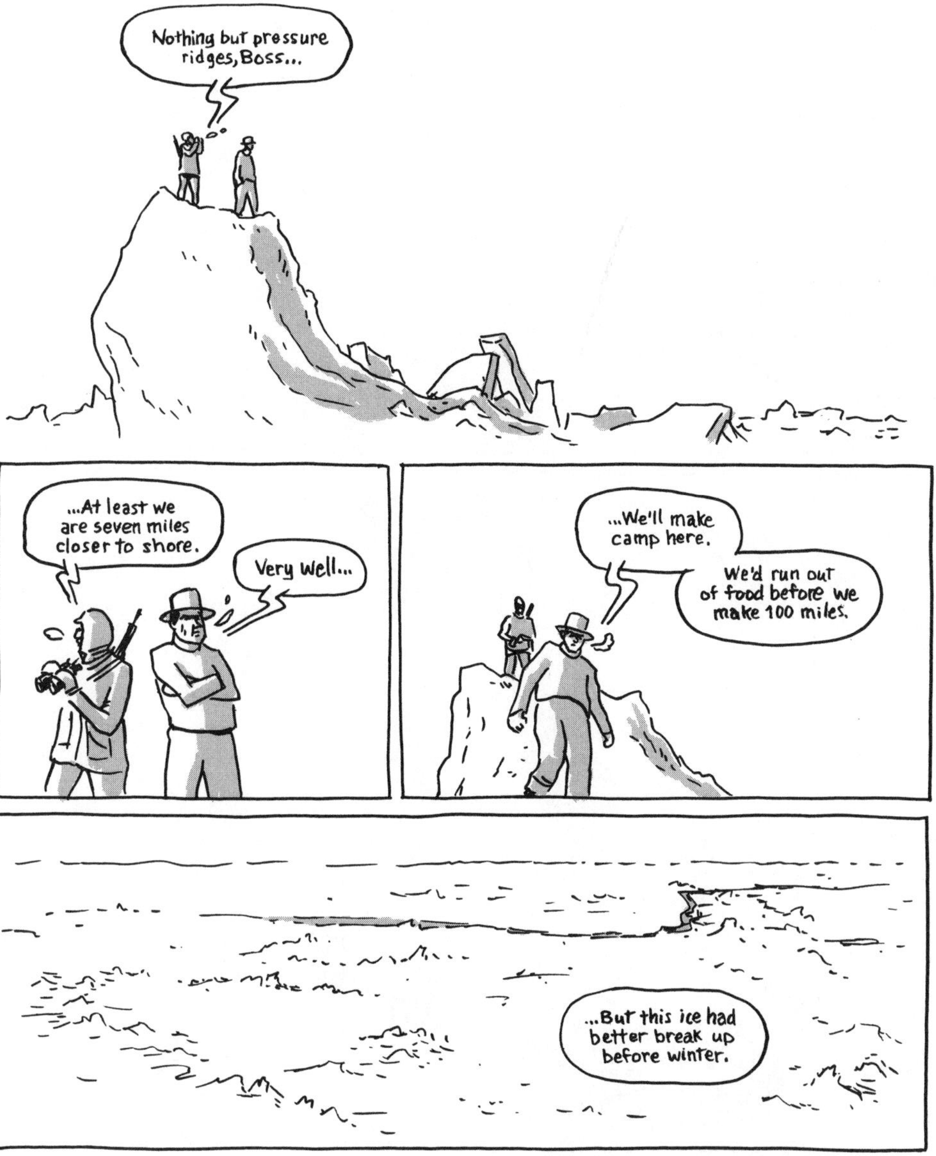
Nothing but pressure ridges, Boss...
...At least we are seven miles closer to shore.
Very well...
...We'll make camp here.
We'd run out of food before we make 100 miles.
...But this ice had better break up before winter.

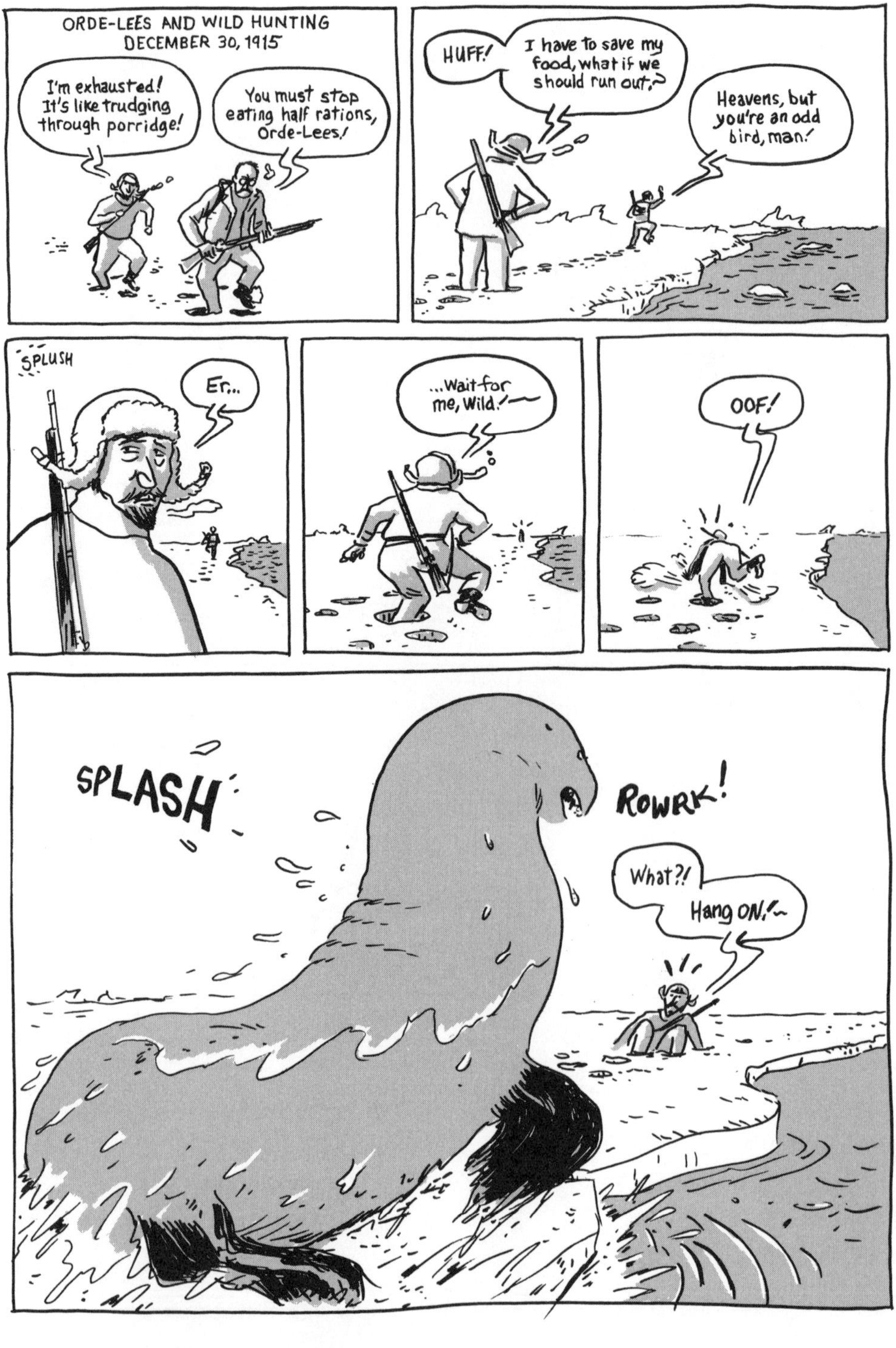
ORDE-LEES AND WILD HUNTING
DECEMBER 30, 1915
I'm exhausted! It's like trudging through porridge!
You must stop eating half rations, Orde-Lees!
HUFF!
I have to save my food, what if we should run out?
Heavens, but you're an odd bird, man!
SPLUSH
Er...
...Wait for me, Wild!
OOF!
SPLASH
ROWRK!
What?!
Hang ON!

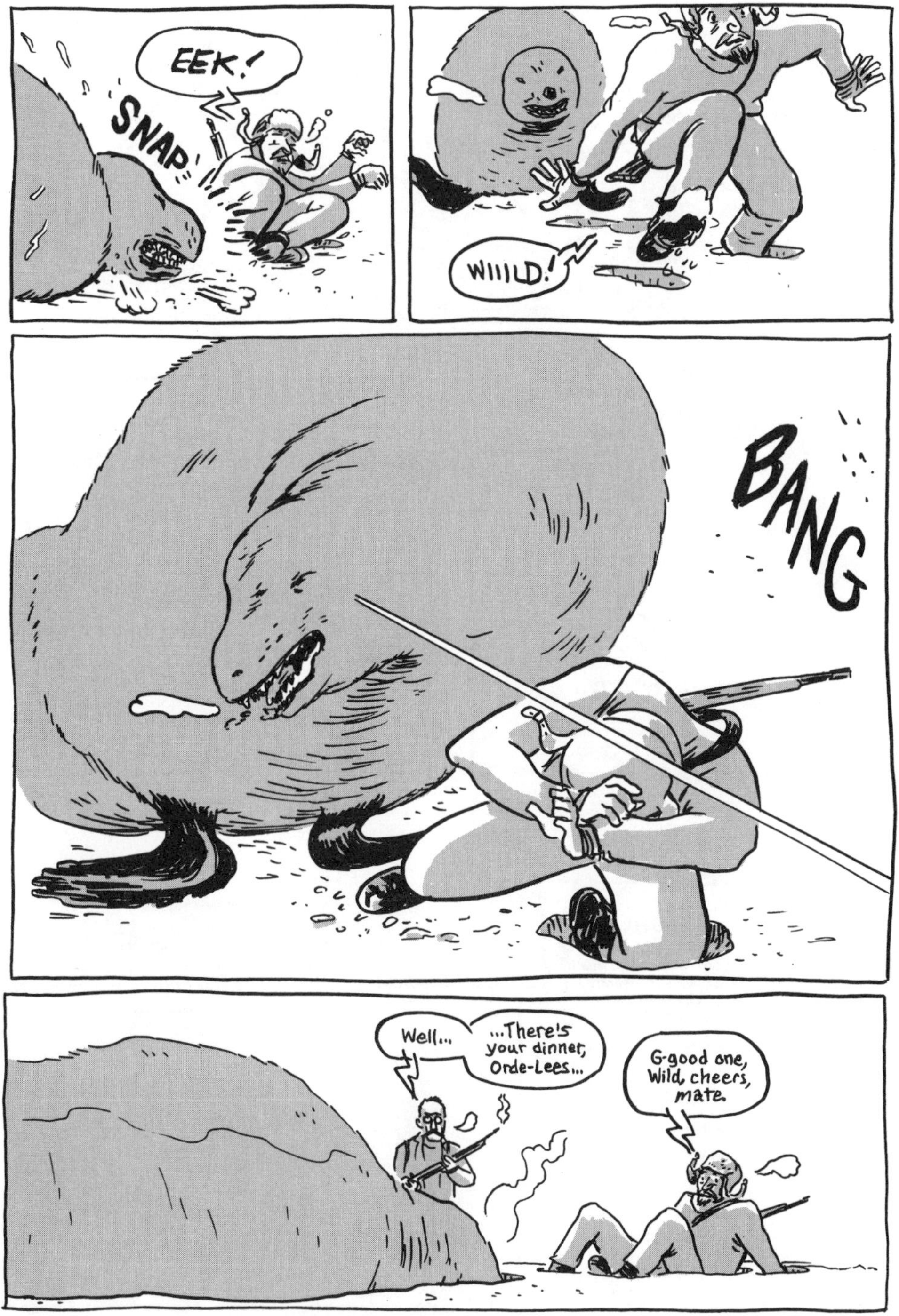
EEK!
SNAP
WIIILD!
BANG
Well...
...There's your dinner, Orde-Lees...
G-good one, Wild, cheers, mate.

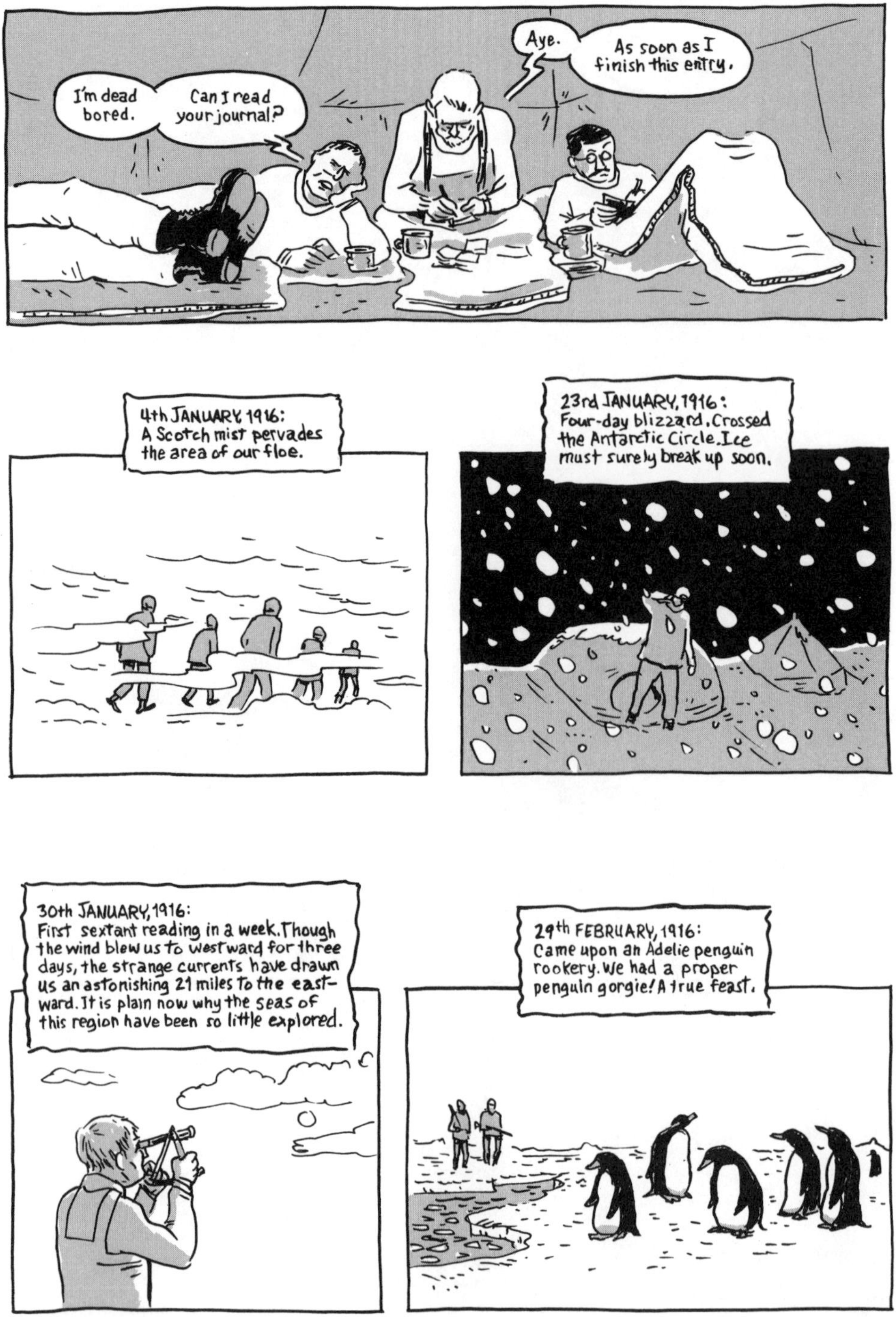
I'm dead bored.
Can I read your journal?
Aye.
As soon as I finish this entry.
4th JANUARY, 1916:
A Scotch mist pervades the area of our floe.
23rd JANUARY, 1916:
Four-day blizzard. Crossed the Antarctic Circle. Ice must surely break up soon.
30th JANUARY, 1916:
First sextant reading in a week. Though the wind blew us to westward for three days, the strange currents have drawn us an astonishing 21 miles to the east-ward. It is plain now why the seas of this region have been so little explored.
29th FEBRUARY, 1916:
Came upon an Adelie penguin rookery. We had a proper penguin gorgie! A true feast.

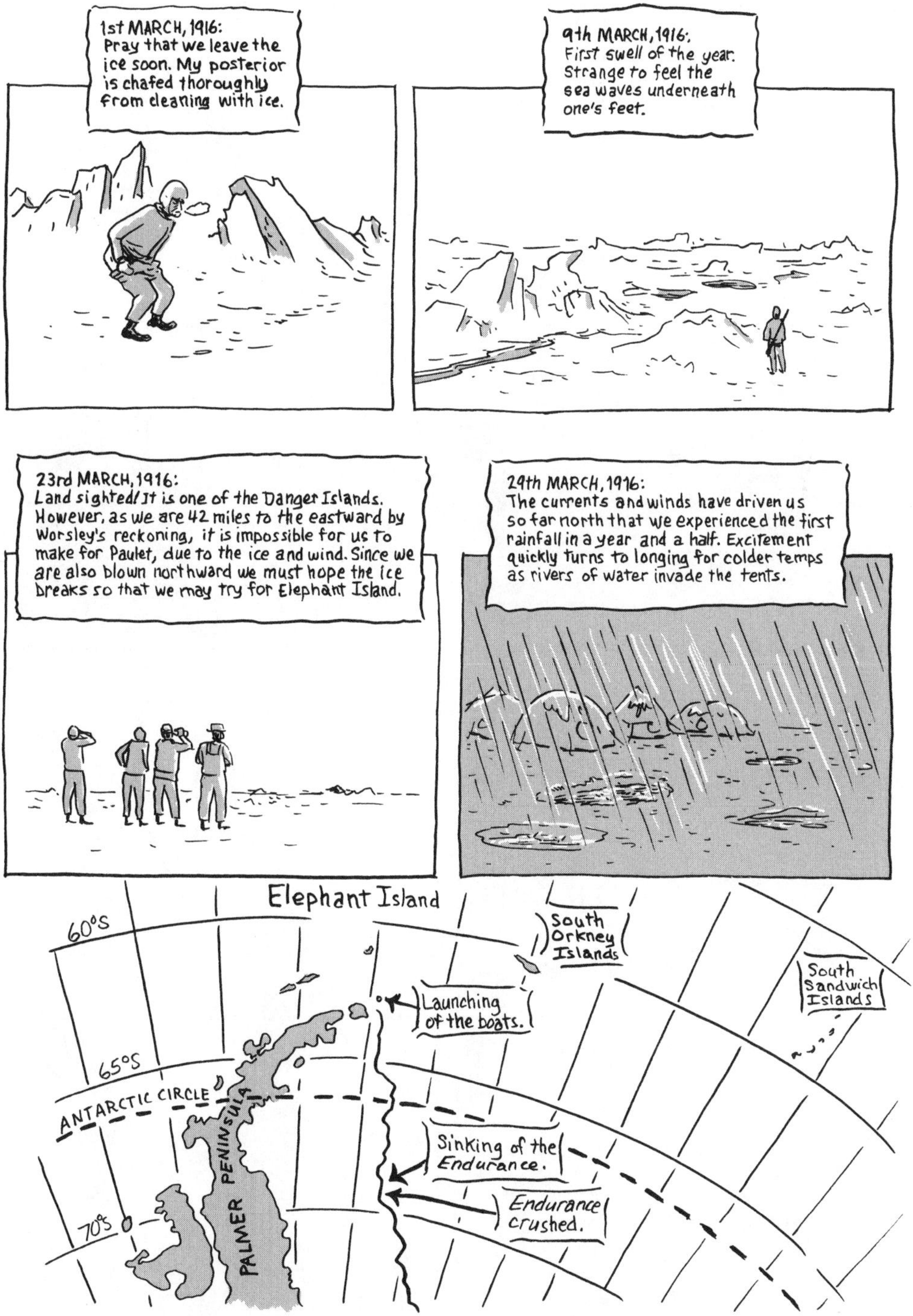
1st MARCH, 1916:
Pray that we leave the ice soon. My posterior is chafed thoroughly from cleaning with ice.
9th MARCH, 1916:
First swell of the year. Strange to feel the sea waves underneath one's feet.
23rd MARCH, 1916:
Land sighted! It is one of the Danger Islands. However, as we are 42 miles to the eastward by Worsley's reckoning, it is impossible for us to make for Paulet, due to the ice and wind. Since we are also blown northward we must hope the ice breaks so that we may try for Elephant Island.
24th MARCH, 1916:
The currents and winds have driven us so far north that we experienced the first rainfall in a year and a half. Excitement quickly turns to longing for colder temps as rivers of water invade the tents.
Elephant Island
60°S
South Orkney Islands
South Sandwich Islands
Launching of the boats.
65°S
ANTARCTIC CIRCLE
PALMER PENINSULA
Sinking of the *Endurance*.
Endurance crushed.
70°S

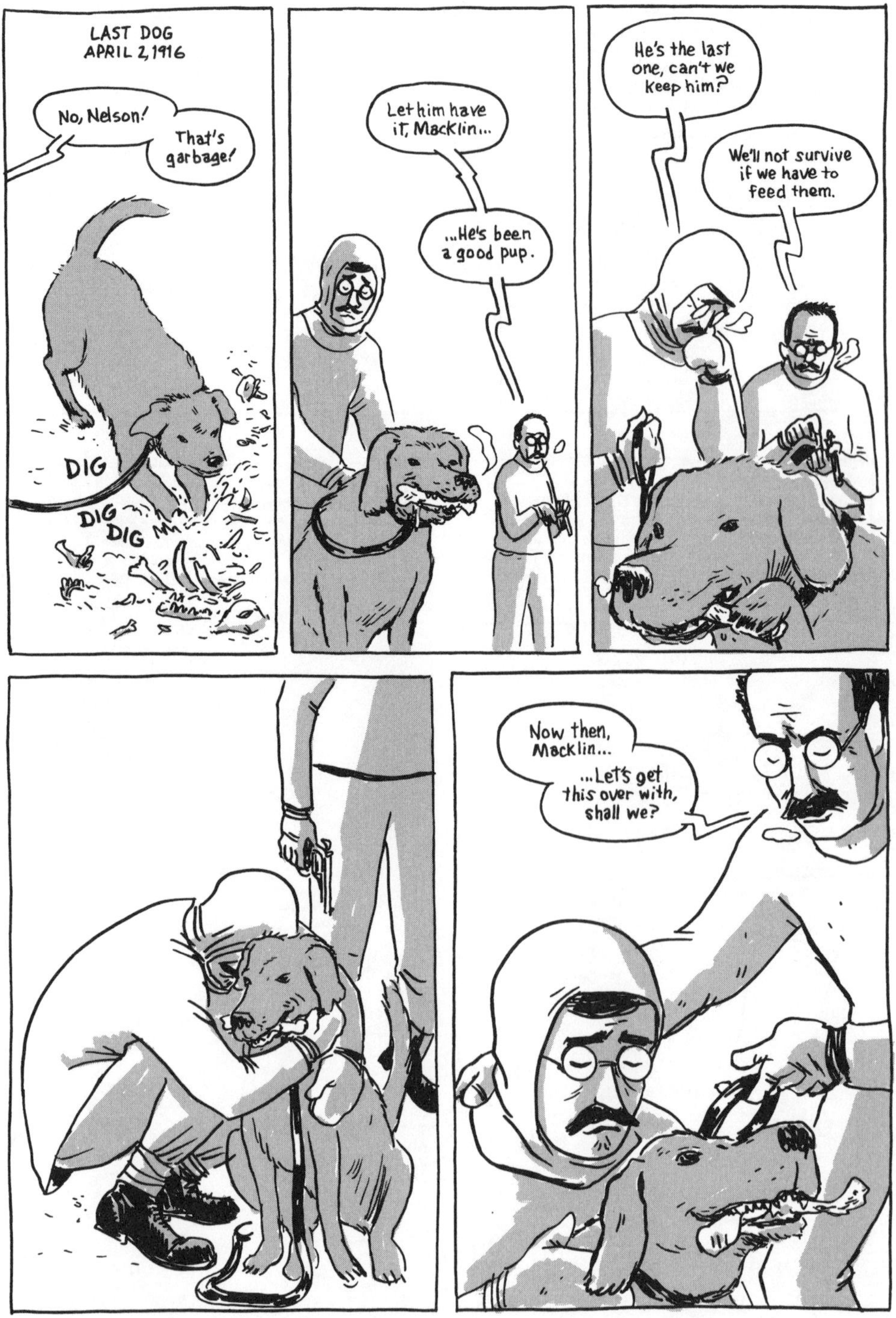
LAST DOG
APRIL 2, 1916
No, Nelson!
That's garbage!
DIG
DIG
DIG
Let him have it, Macklin...
...He's been a good pup.
He's the last one, can't we keep him?
We'll not survive if we have to feed them.
Now then, Macklin...
...Let's get this over with, shall we?

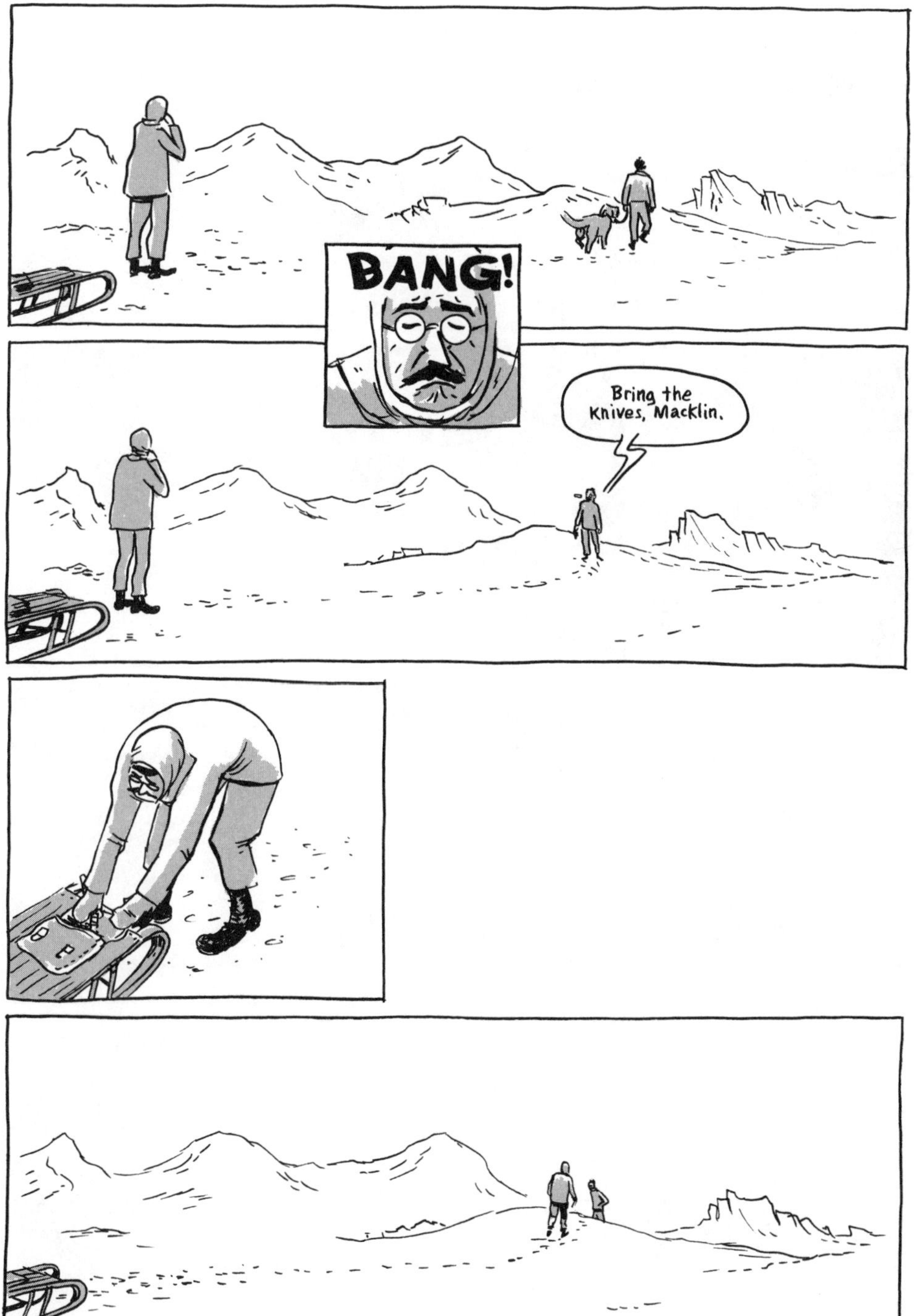
BANG!
Bring the knives, Macklin.

SHACKLETON CONSIDERS THE ICE
APRIL 5, 1916

CREAK

SLAM

CREAK
CREAK
CREAK

Crean... ...Crean, it's your watch.

Ice breaking up yet, Boss?

The swell has become more fierce, but I can make no sense of the currents.

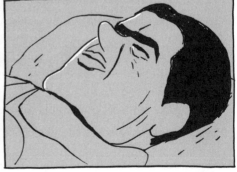

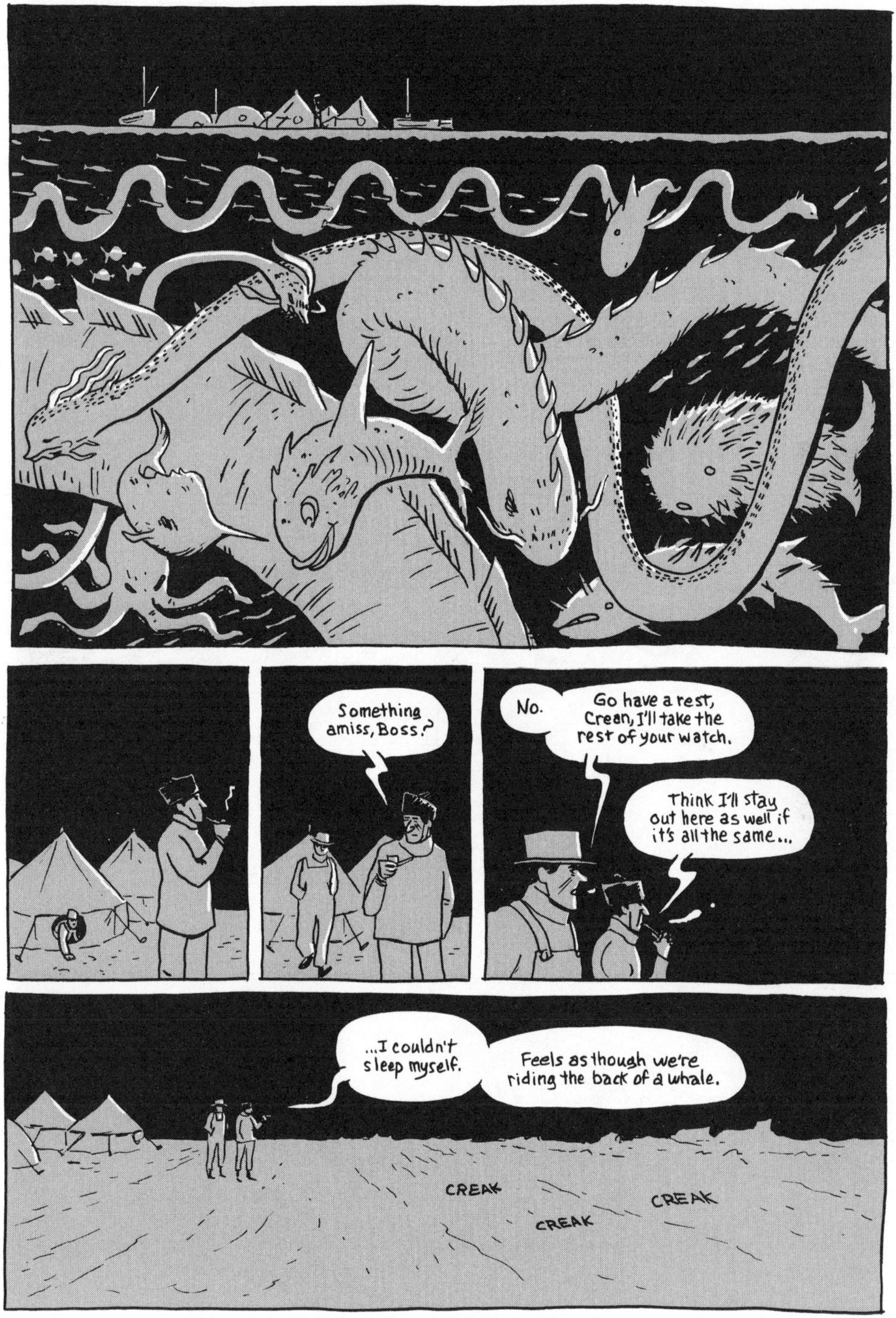

Something amiss, Boss?
No.
Go have a rest, Crean, I'll take the rest of your watch.
Think I'll stay out here as well if it's all the same...
...I couldn't sleep myself.
Feels as though we're riding the back of a whale.
CREAK
CREAK
CREAK

THE CRACKING FLOE
APRIL 8, 1916

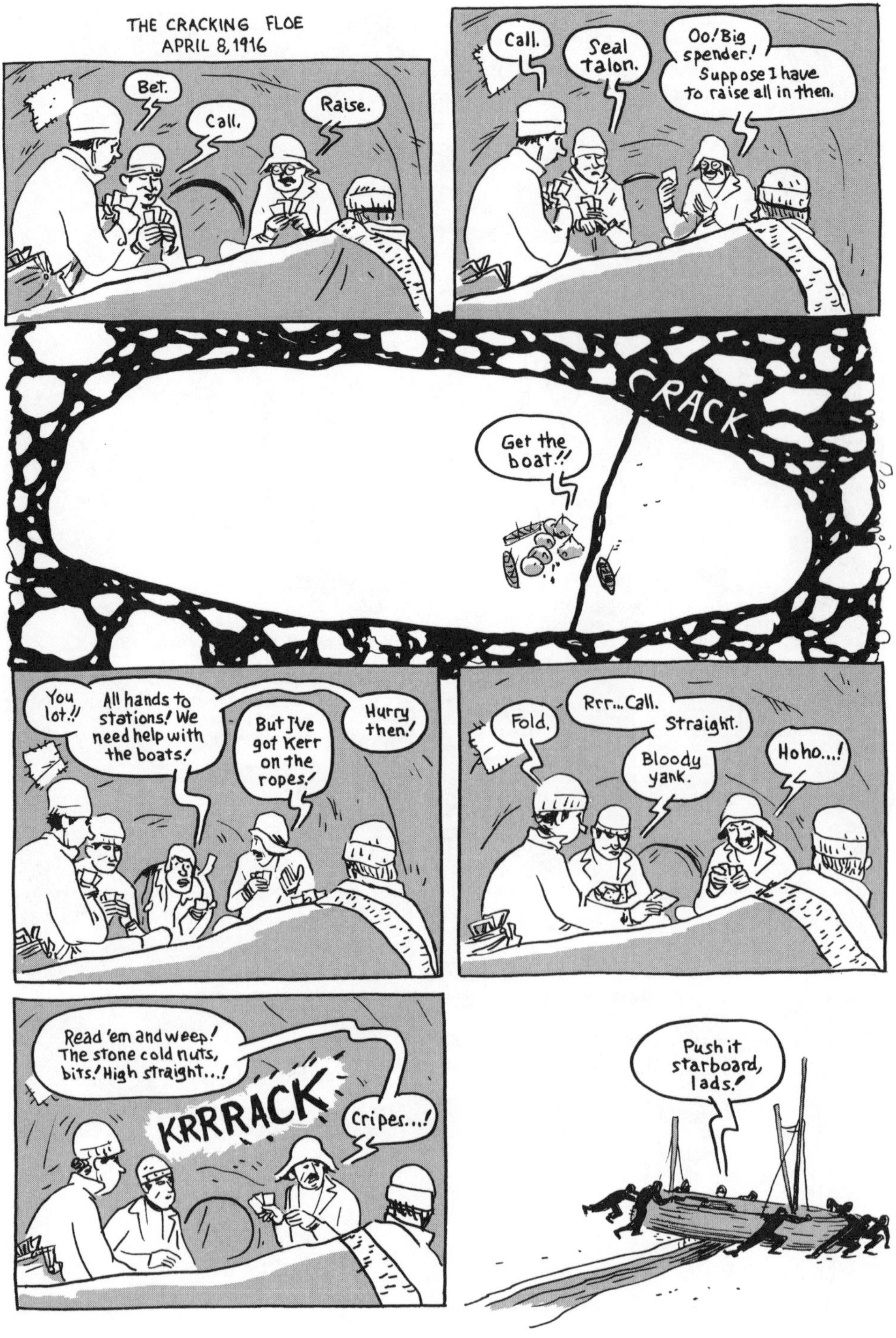
Bet.
Call.
Raise.
Call.
Seal talon.
Oo! Big spender! Suppose I have to raise all in then.
CRACK
Get the boat!!
You lot!!
All hands to stations! We need help with the boats!
But I've got Kerr on the ropes!
Hurry then!
Fold.
Rrr... Call.
Straight.
Bloody yank.
Hoho...!
Read 'em and weep! The stone cold nuts, bits! High straight...!
KRRRACK
Cripes...!
Push it starboard, lads!

WATCHING THE ICE, WAITING FOR THE WATER LEADS TO OPEN 11 AM, APRIL 9, 1916

SMASH

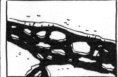

Launch the boats!

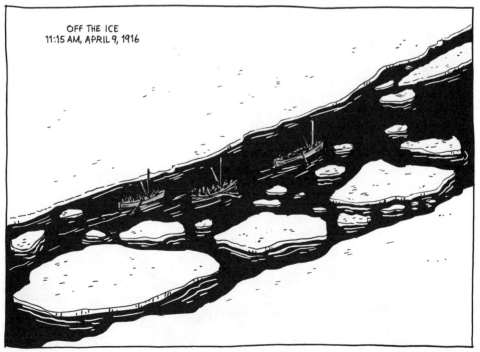

OFF THE ICE 11:15 AM, APRIL 9, 1916

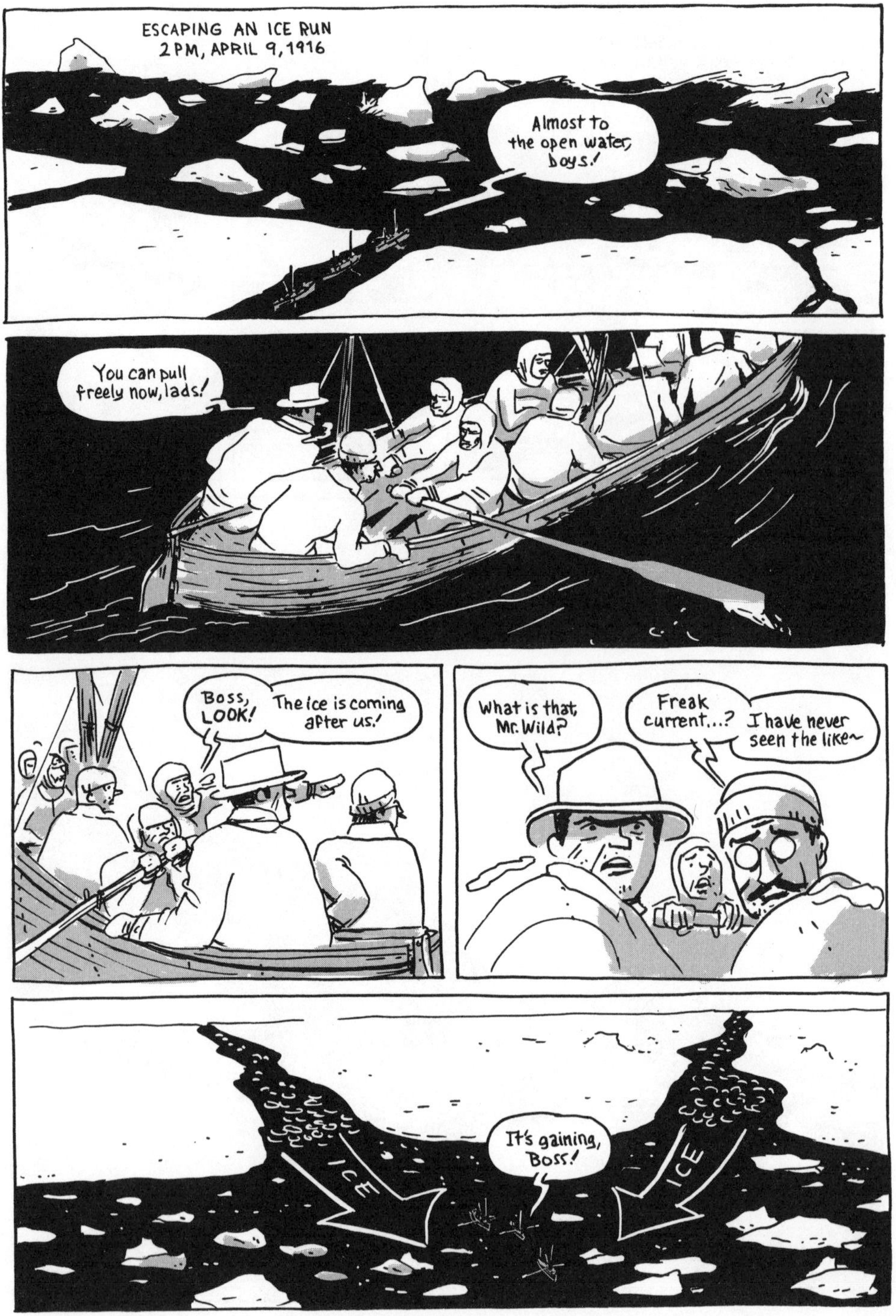
ESCAPING AN ICE RUN
2 PM, APRIL 9, 1916
Almost to the open water, boys!
You can pull freely now, lads!
Boss, LOOK!
The ice is coming after us!
What is that, Mr. Wild?
Freak current...?
I have never seen the like~
It's gaining, Boss!
ICE
ICE

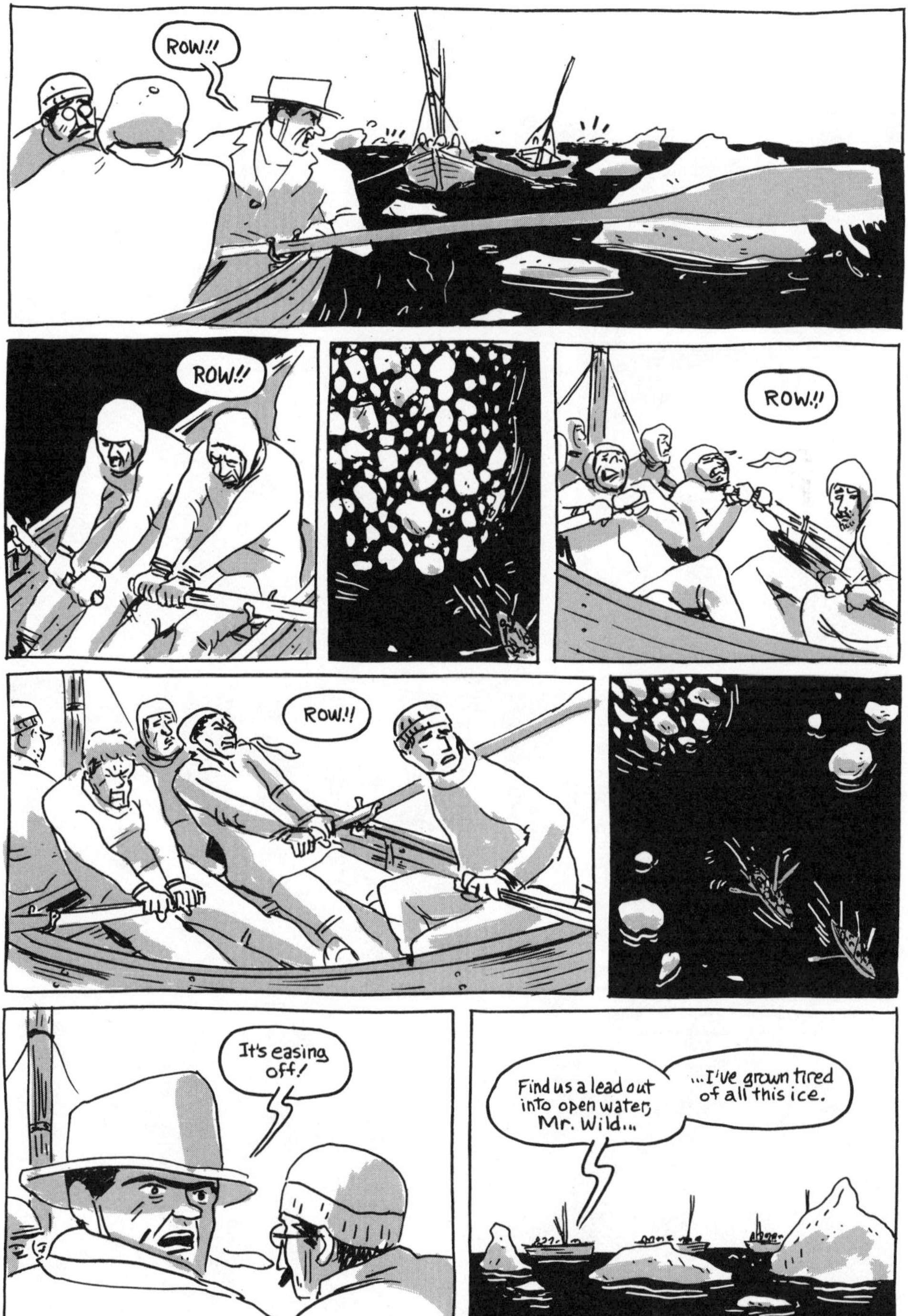
ROW!!
ROW!!
ROW!!
ROW!!
It's easing off!
Find us a lead out into open water, Mr. Wild...
...I've grown tired of all this ice.

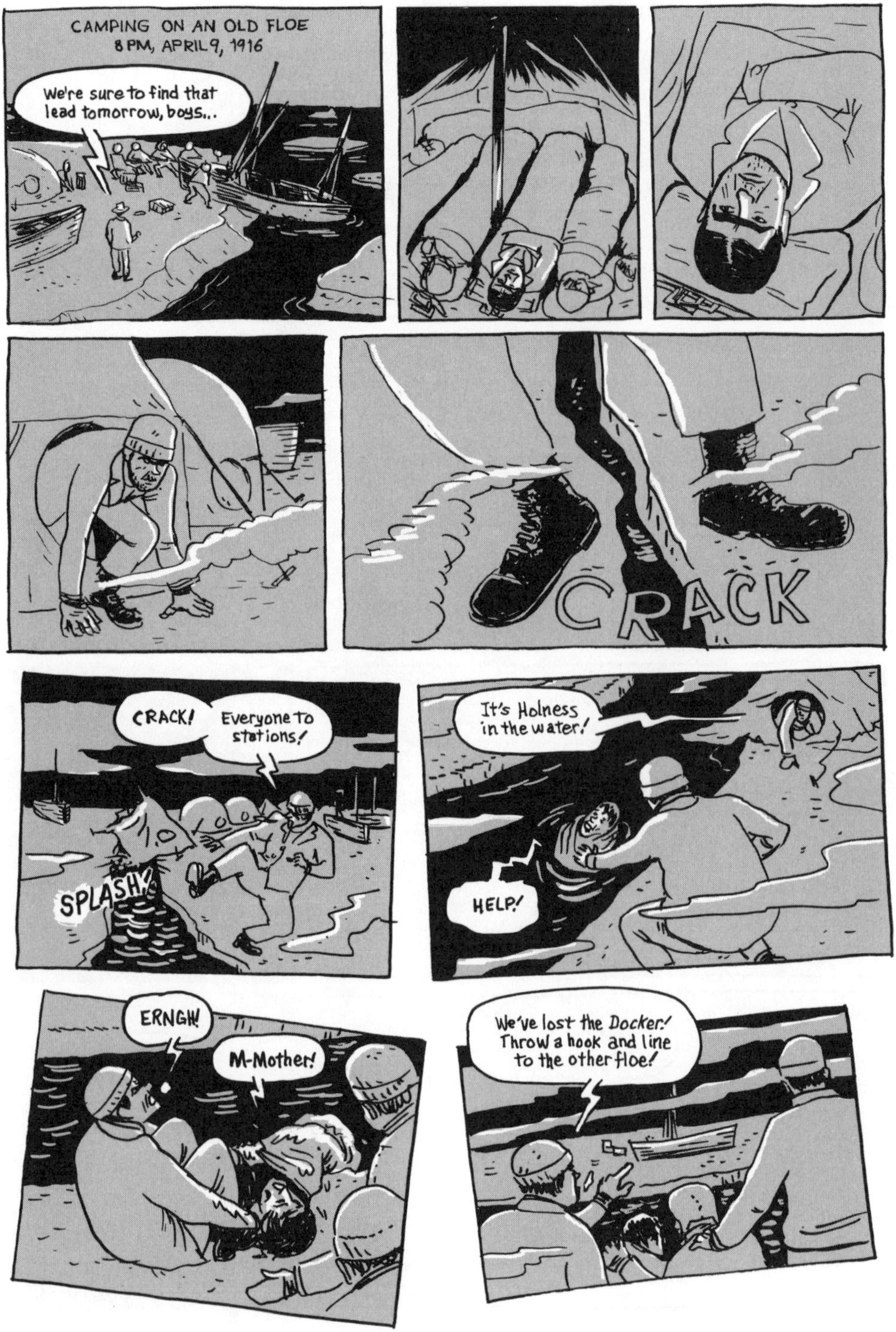

CAMPING ON AN OLD FLOE
8 PM, APRIL 9, 1916
We're sure to find that lead tomorrow, boys...
CRACK
CRACK!
Everyone to stations!
SPLASH!
It's Holness in the water!
HELP!
ERNGH!
M-Mother!
We've lost the *Docker!* Throw a hook and line to the other floe!

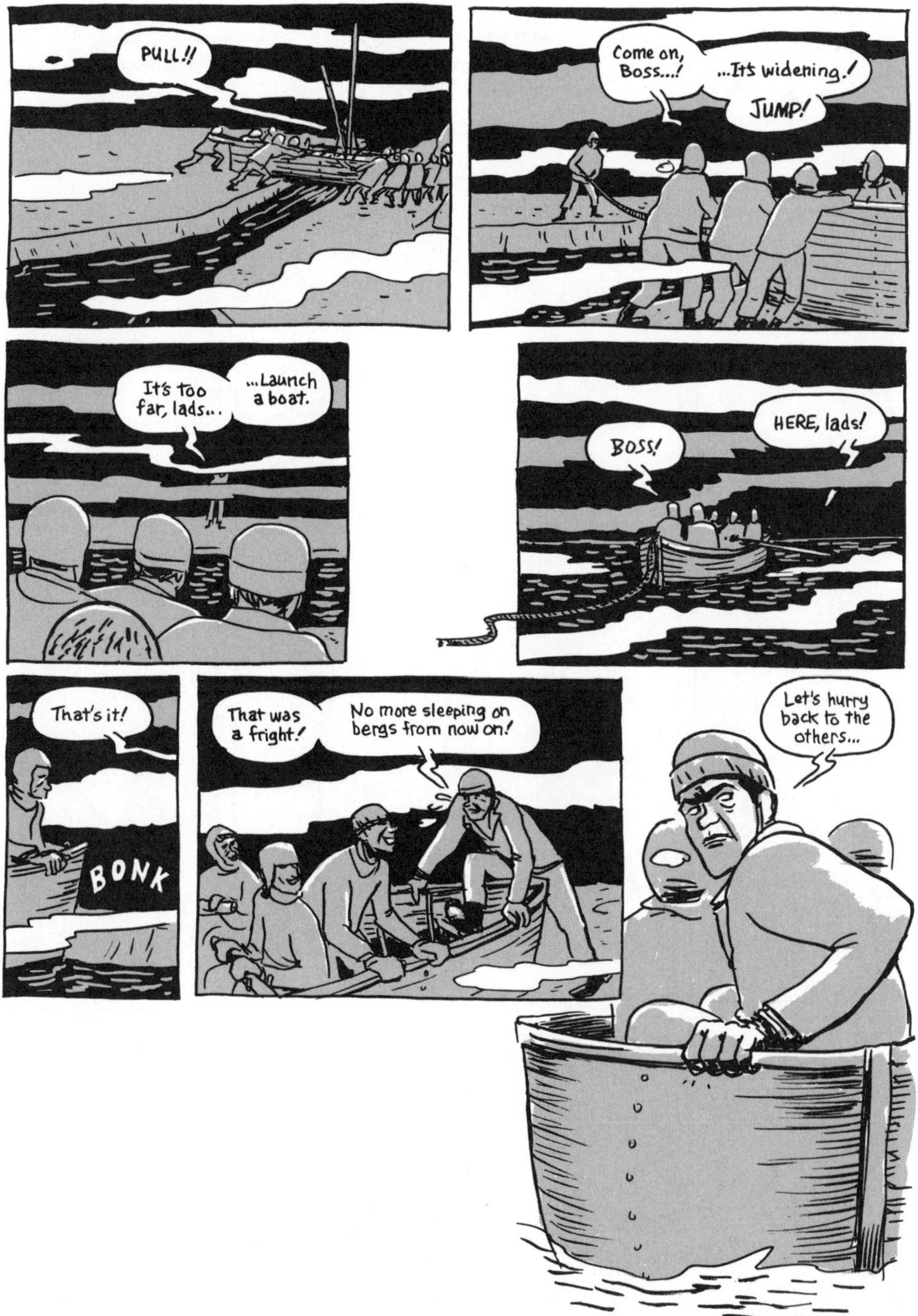
PULL!!
Come on, Boss...!
...It's widening!
JUMP!
It's too far, lads...
...Launch a boat.
BOSS!
HERE, lads!
That's it!
BONK
That was a fright!
No more sleeping on bergs from now on!
Let's hurry back to the others...

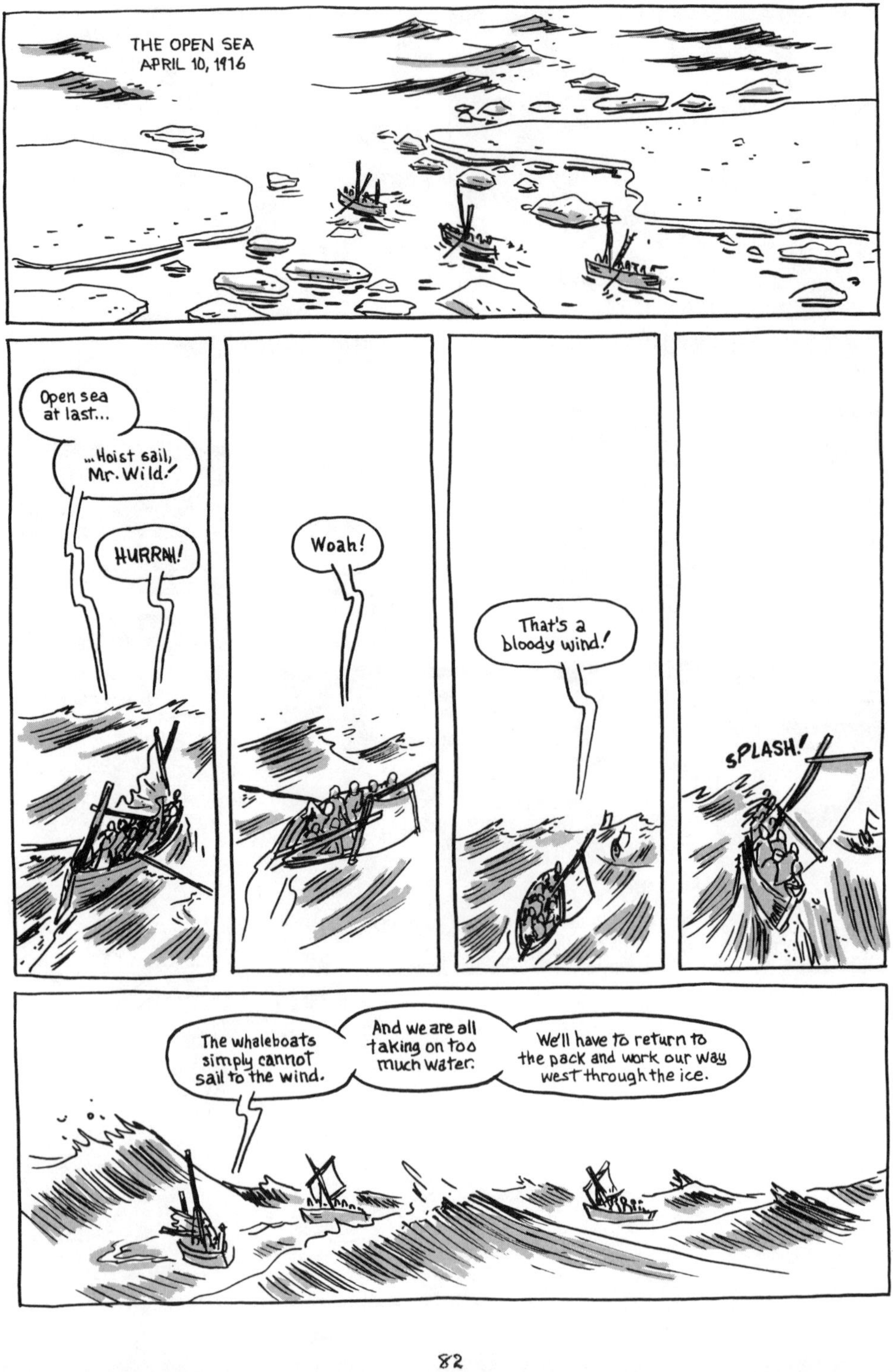
THE OPEN SEA
APRIL 10, 1916
Open sea at last...
...Hoist sail, Mr. Wild!
HURRAH!
Woah!
That's a bloody wind!
SPLASH!
The whaleboats simply cannot sail to the wind.
And we are all taking on too much water.
We'll have to return to the pack and work our way west through the ice.

RETURN TO THE FLOE
6 PM, APRIL 10, 1916

Boss, no disrespect, but I can't see an alternative to pulling up on the floe berg.

I understand, Worsley, but I've seen bergs ten times this one's size break and upend in seconds. It could cast us all into the water.

Begging your pardon, Boss, but if my men don't sleep they won't be able to ROW across the water.

URK!

Of course... ...Very well...

...But one crack and we return to the boats.

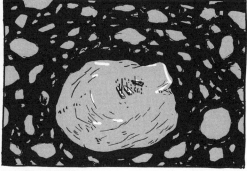

DAWN, APRIL 10, 1916

Worsley...

...Look.

RETURN TO THE OPEN SEA
DAWN, APRIL 11, 1916

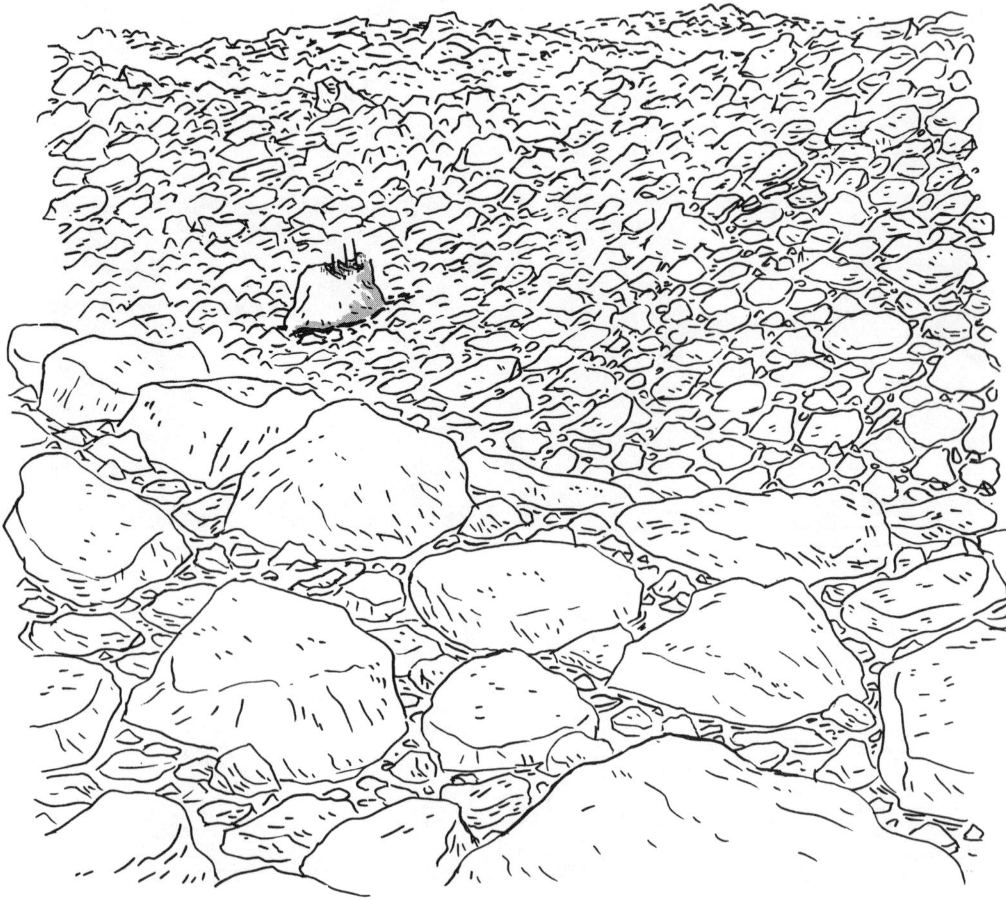

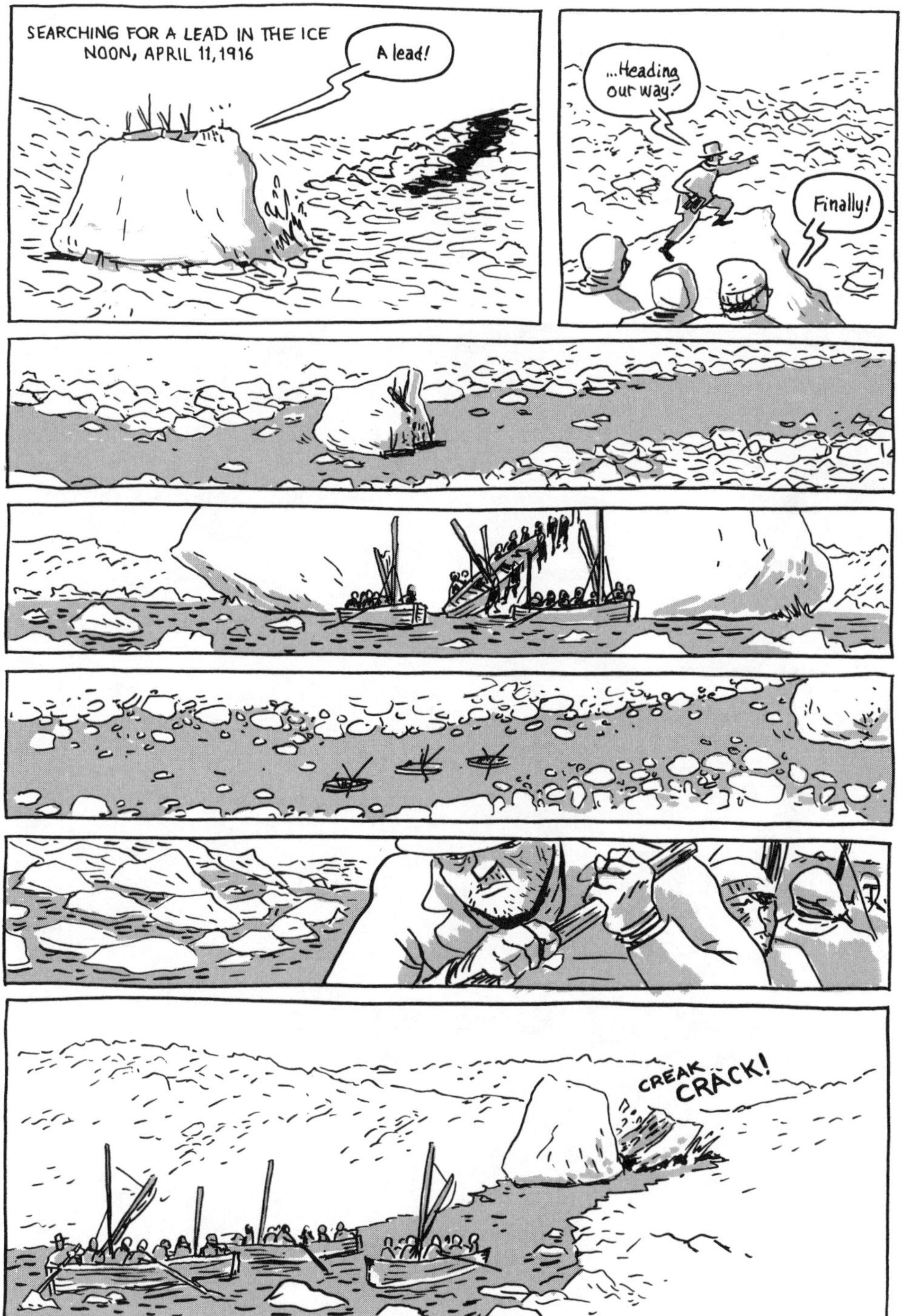
SEARCHING FOR A LEAD IN THE ICE
NOON, APRIL 11, 1916
A lead!
...Heading our way!
Finally!
CREAK
CRACK!

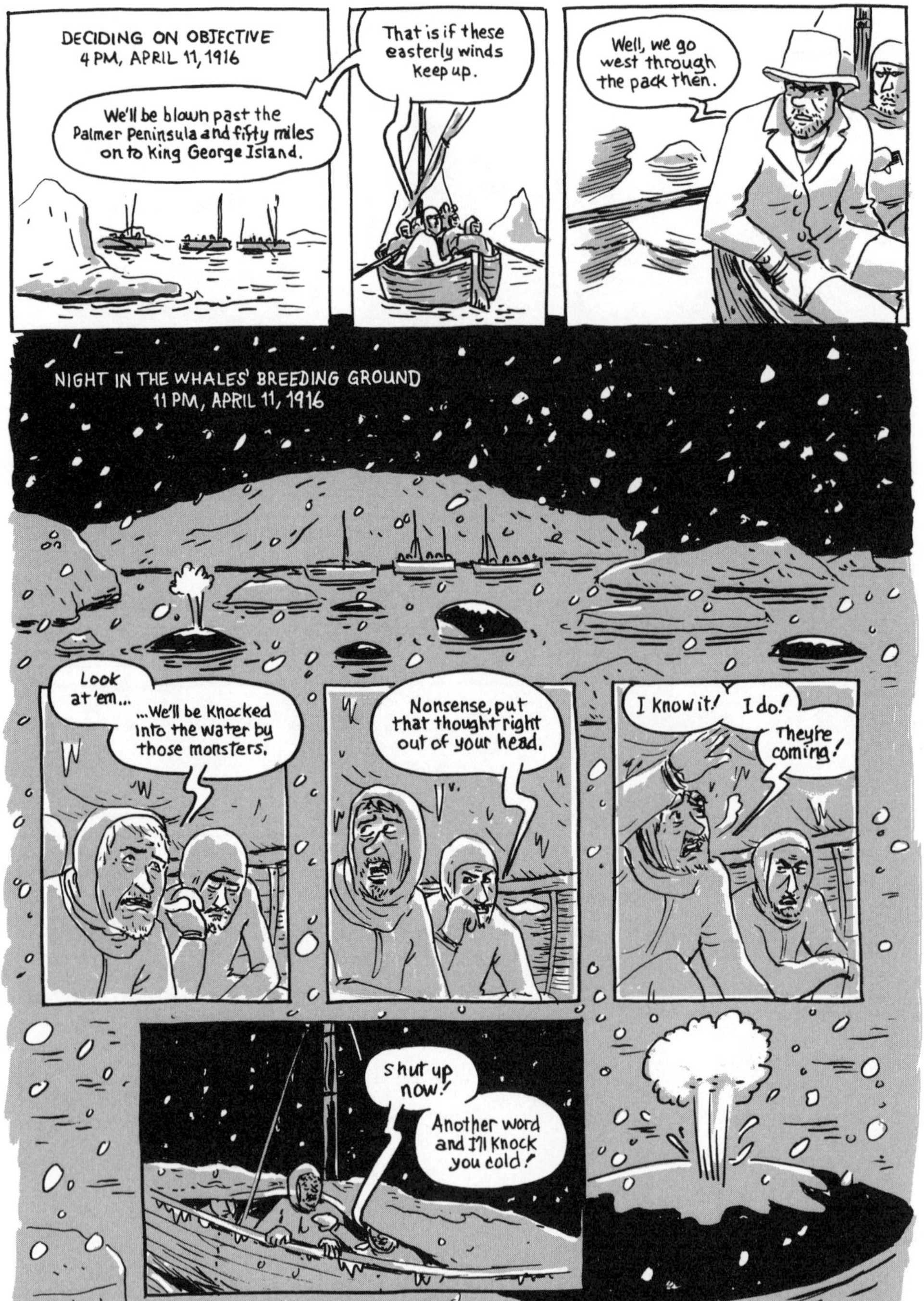
DECIDING ON OBJECTIVE
4 PM, APRIL 11, 1916
We'll be blown past the Palmer Peninsula and fifty miles on to King George Island.
That is if these easterly winds keep up.
Well, we go west through the pack then.
NIGHT IN THE WHALES' BREEDING GROUND
11 PM, APRIL 11, 1916
Look at 'em...
...We'll be knocked into the water by those monsters.
Nonsense, put that thought right out of your head.
I know it!
I do!
They're coming!
shut up now!
Another word and I'll knock you cold!

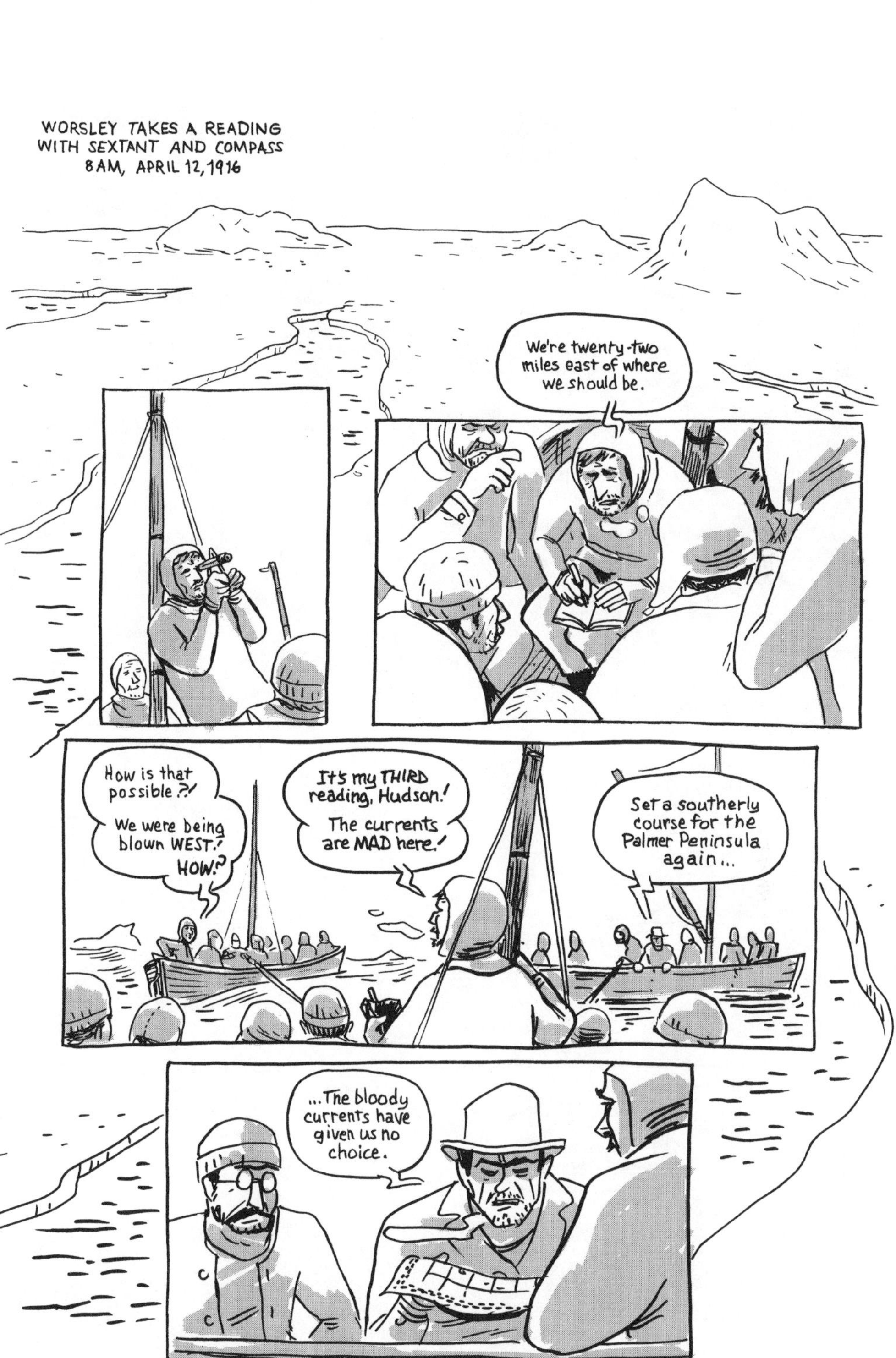
WORSLEY TAKES A READING WITH SEXTANT AND COMPASS 8AM, APRIL 12, 1916
We're twenty-two miles east of where we should be.
How is that possible?! We were being blown WEST! HOW?
It's my THIRD reading, Hudson! The currents are MAD here!
Set a southerly course for the Palmer Peninsula again...
...The bloody currents have given us no choice.

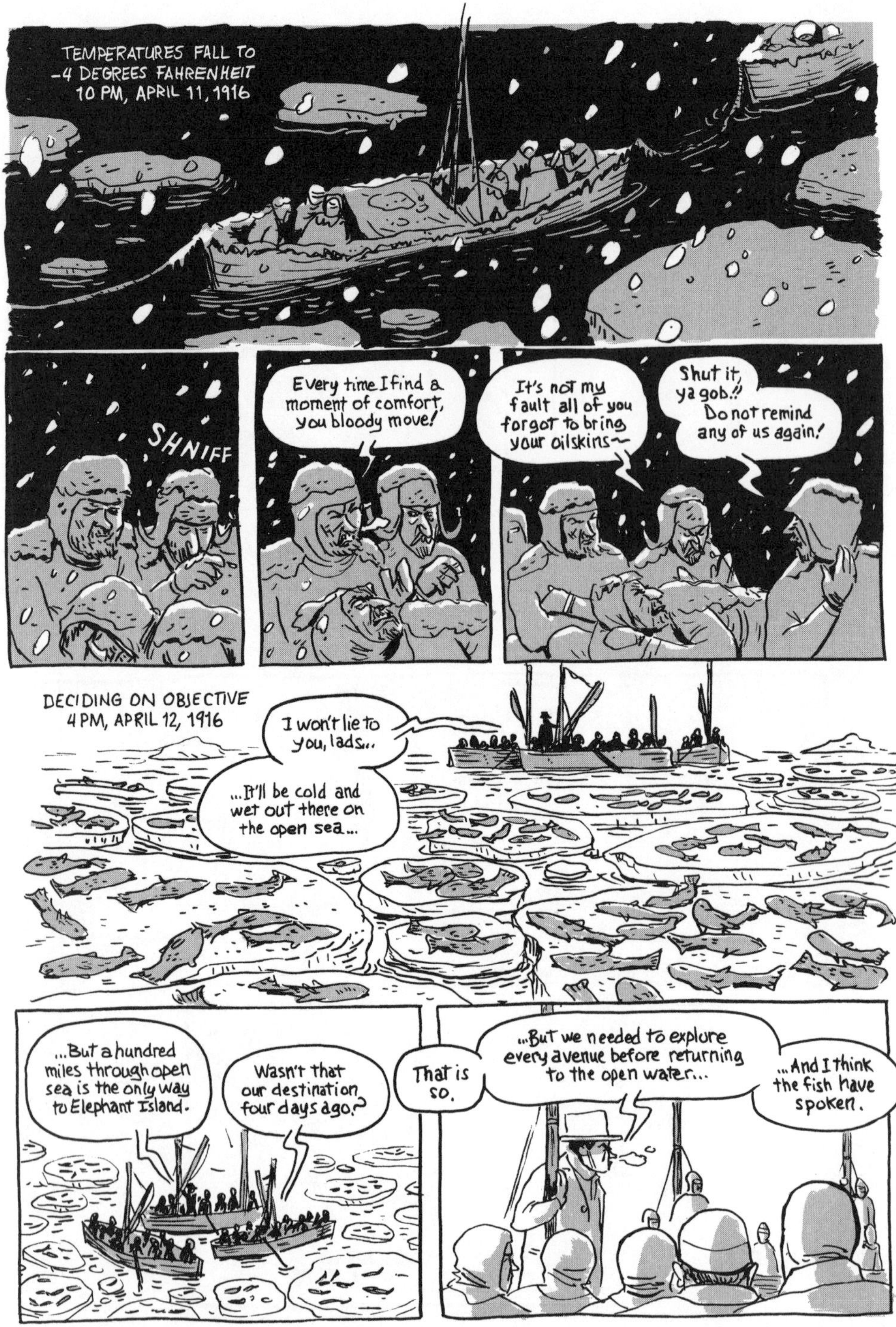
TEMPERATURES FALL TO -4 DEGREES FAHRENHEIT 10 PM, APRIL 11, 1916
SHNIFF
Every time I find a moment of comfort, you bloody move!
It's not my fault all of you forgot to bring your oilskins~
Shut it, ya gob!! Do not remind any of us again!
DECIDING ON OBJECTIVE 4 PM, APRIL 12, 1916
I won't lie to you, lads...
...It'll be cold and wet out there on the open sea...
...But a hundred miles through open sea is the only way to Elephant Island.
Wasn't that our destination four days ago?
That is so.
...But we needed to explore every avenue before returning to the open water...
...And I think the fish have spoken.

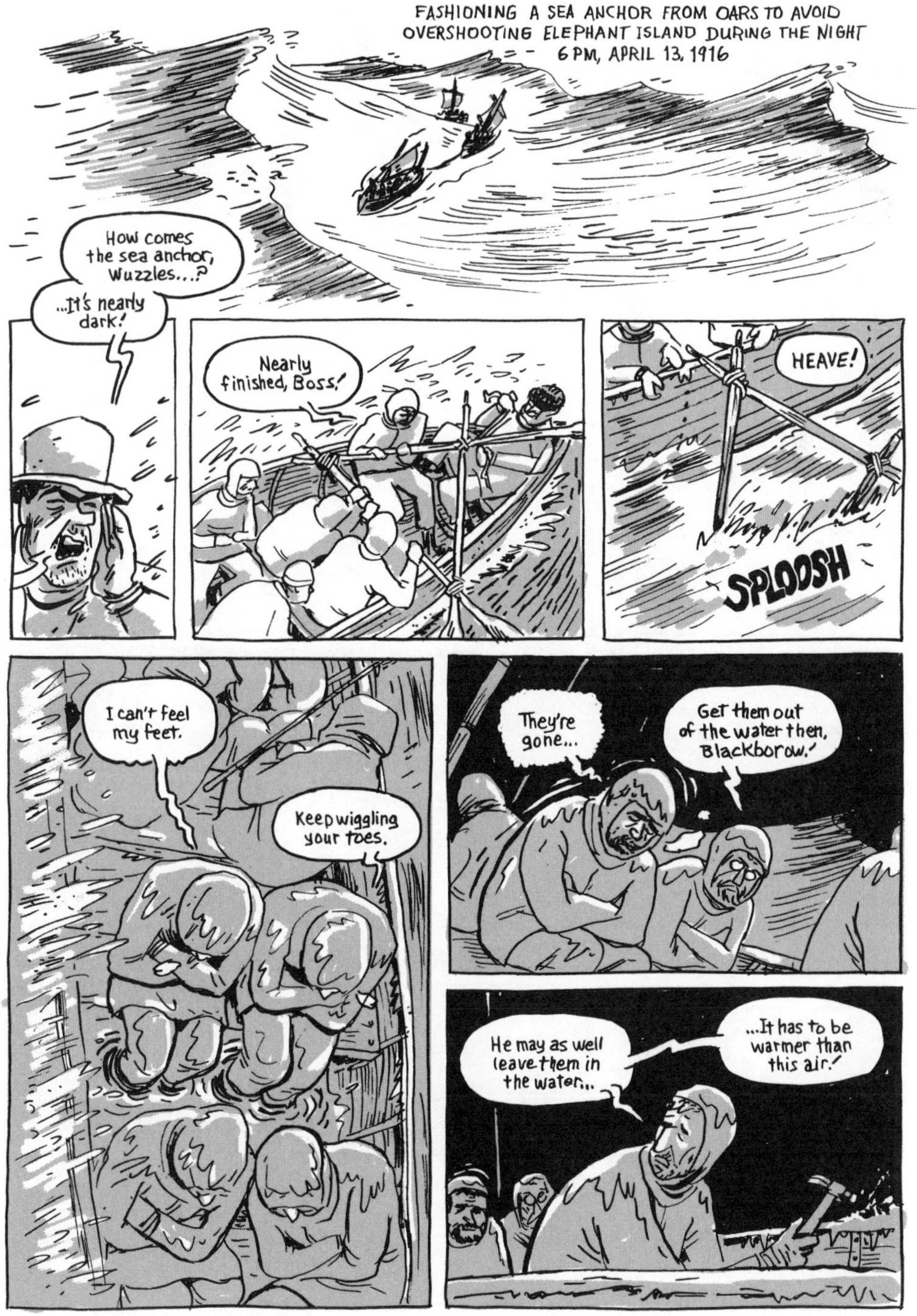

FASHIONING A SEA ANCHOR FROM OARS TO AVOID OVERSHOOTING ELEPHANT ISLAND DURING THE NIGHT
6 PM, APRIL 13, 1916
How comes the sea anchor, Wuzzles...?
...It's nearly dark!
Nearly finished, Boss!
HEAVE!
SPLOOSH
I can't feel my feet.
Keep wiggling your toes.
They're gone...
Get them out of the water then, Blackborow!
He may as well leave them in the water...
...It has to be warmer than this air!

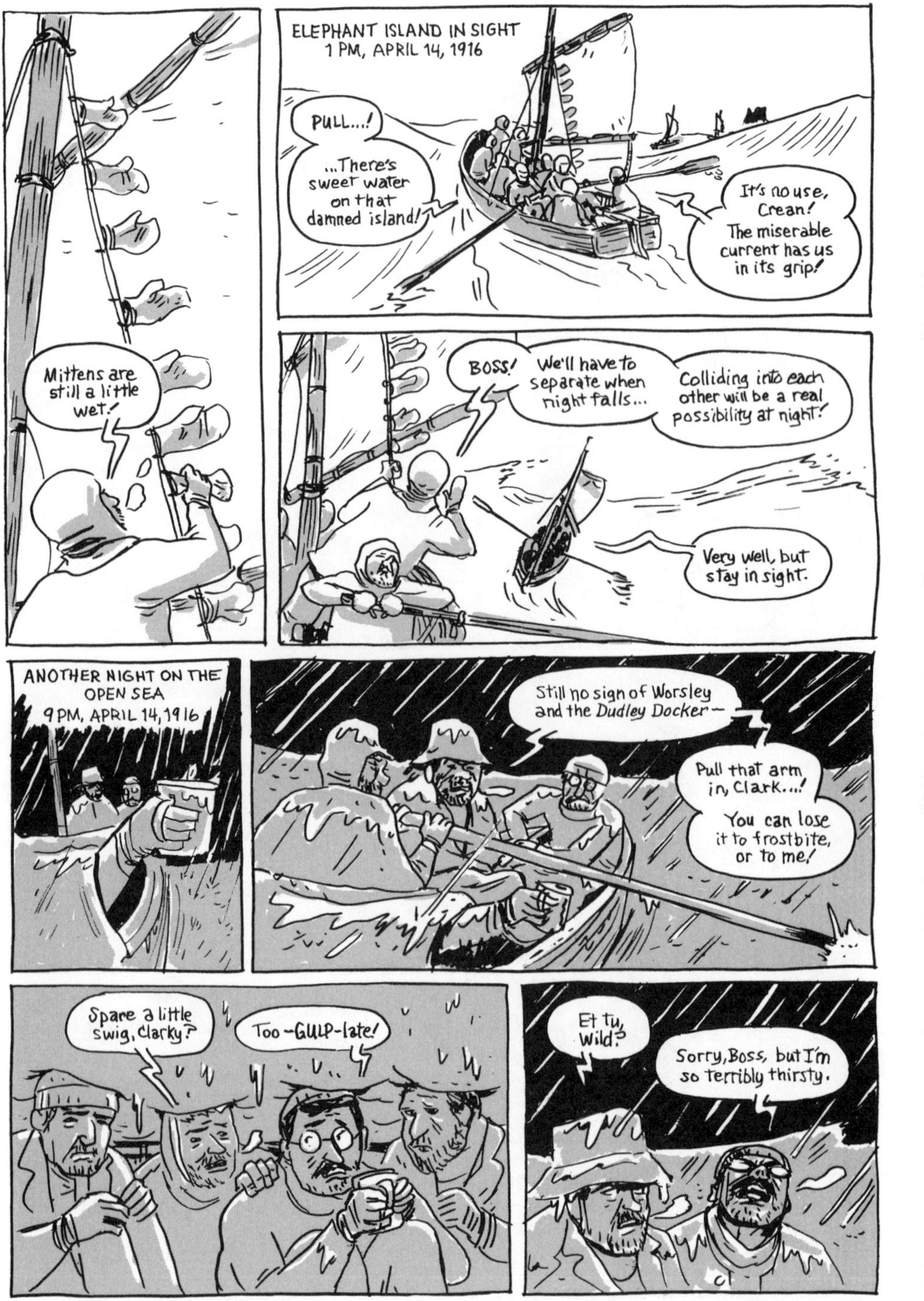
Mittens are still a little wet!
ELEPHANT ISLAND IN SIGHT 1 PM, APRIL 14, 1916
PULL...!
...There's sweet water on that damned island!
It's no use, Crean! The miserable current has us in its grip!
BOSS!
We'll have to separate when night falls...
Colliding into each other will be a real possibility at night!
Very well, but stay in sight.
ANOTHER NIGHT ON THE OPEN SEA 9 PM, APRIL 14, 1916
Still no sign of Worsley and the Dudley Docker—
Pull that arm in, Clark...!
You can lose it to frostbite, or to me!
Spare a little swig, Clarky?
Too—GULP—late!
Et tu, Wild?
Sorry, Boss, but I'm so terribly thirsty.

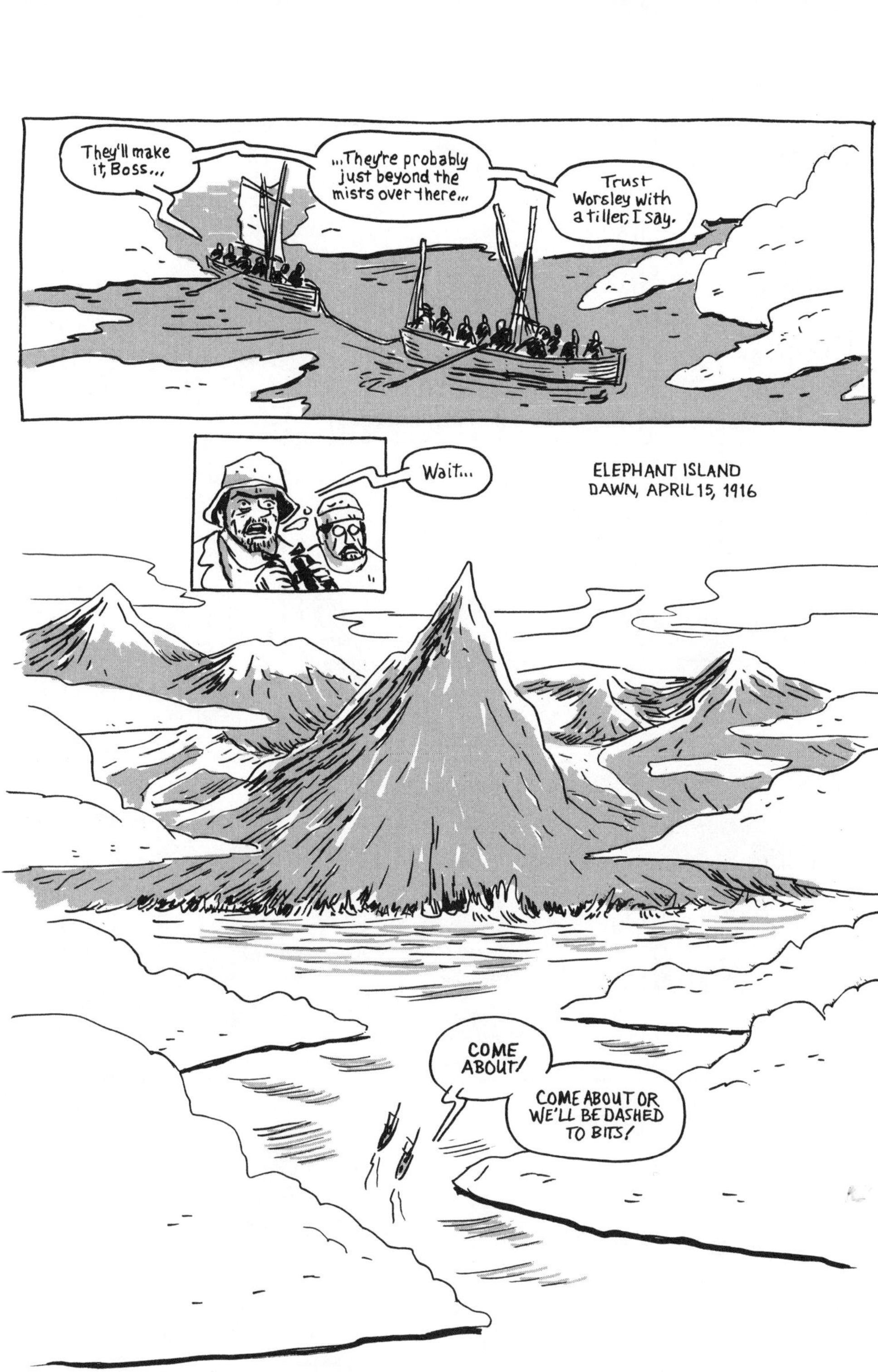
They'll make it, Boss...
...They're probably just beyond the mists over there...
Trust Worsley with a tiller, I say.
Wait...
ELEPHANT ISLAND
DAWN, APRIL 15, 1916
COME ABOUT!
COME ABOUT OR WE'LL BE DASHED TO BITS!

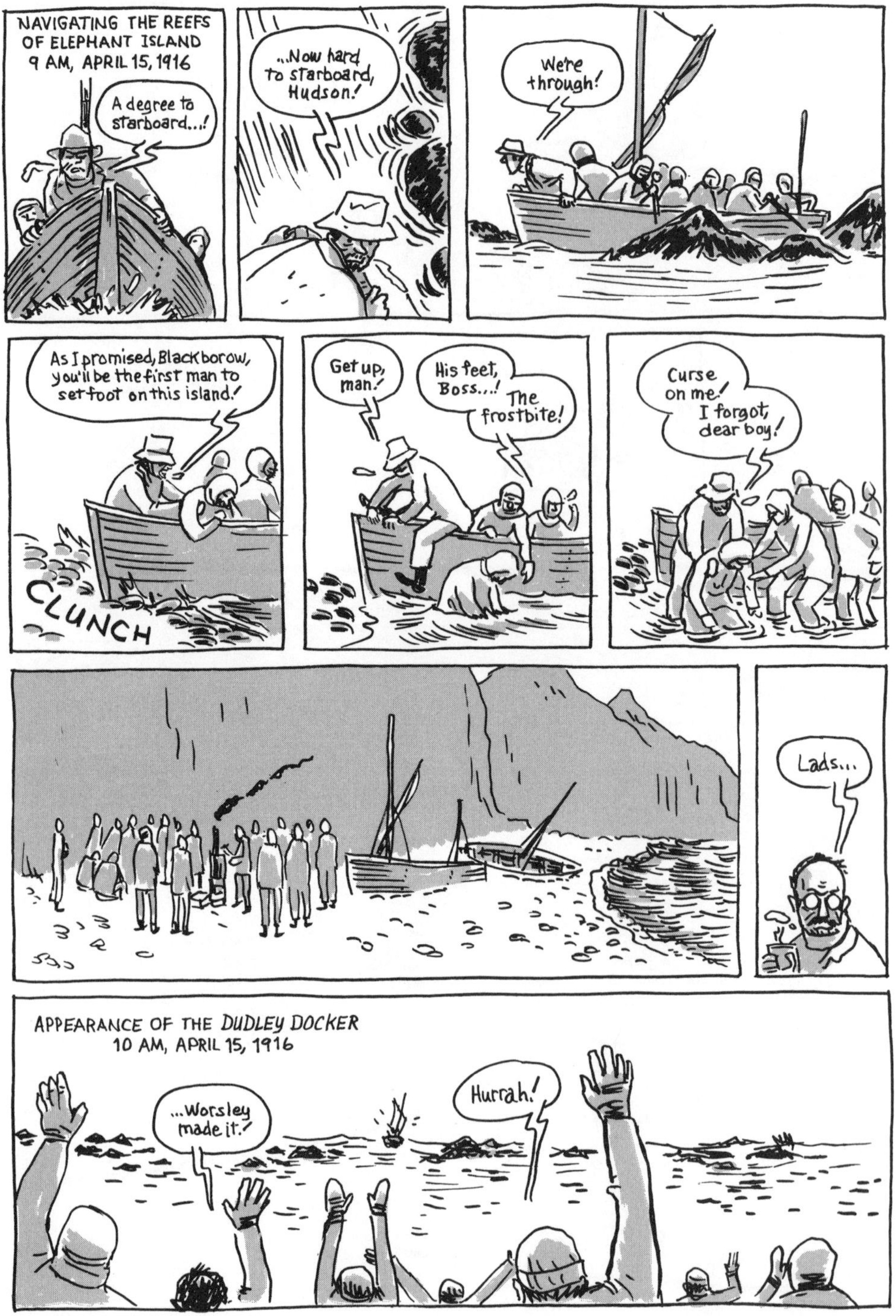
NAVIGATING THE REEFS OF ELEPHANT ISLAND 9 AM, APRIL 15, 1916
A degree to starboard...!
...Now hard to starboard, Hudson!
We're through!
As I promised, Blackborow, you'll be the first man to set foot on this island!
CLUNCH
Get up, man!
His feet, Boss...!
The frostbite!
Curse on me!
I forgot, dear boy!
Lads...
APPEARANCE OF THE DUDLEY DOCKER 10 AM, APRIL 15, 1916
...Worsley made it!
Hurrah!

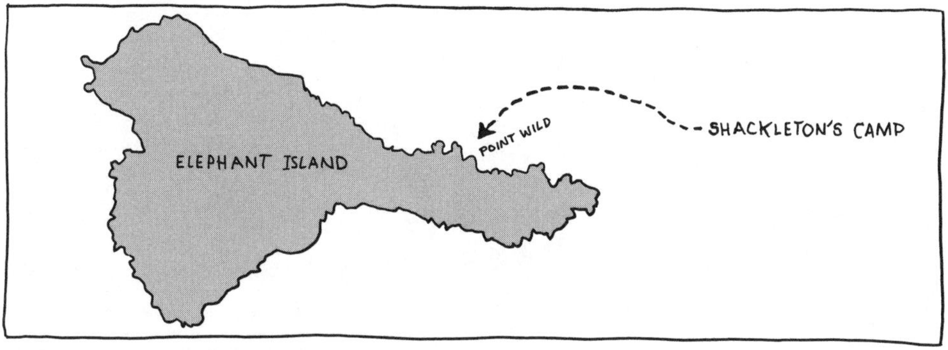
ELEPHANT ISLAND
POINT WILD
SHACKLETON'S CAMP

KERR AND GREENSTREET RETURN TO ELEPHANT ISLAND CAMP AFTER HUNTING FOR DINNER
DAWN, APRIL 22, 1916

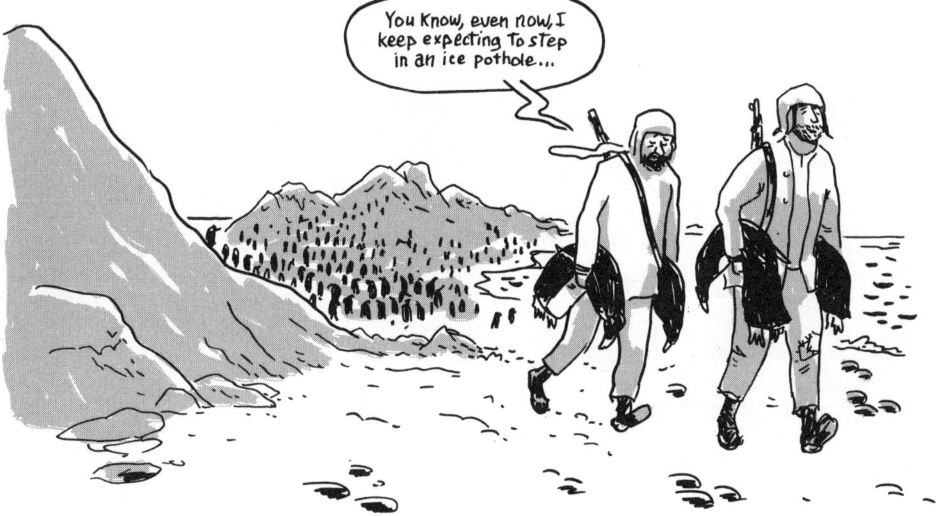
You know, even now, I keep expecting to step in an ice pothole...

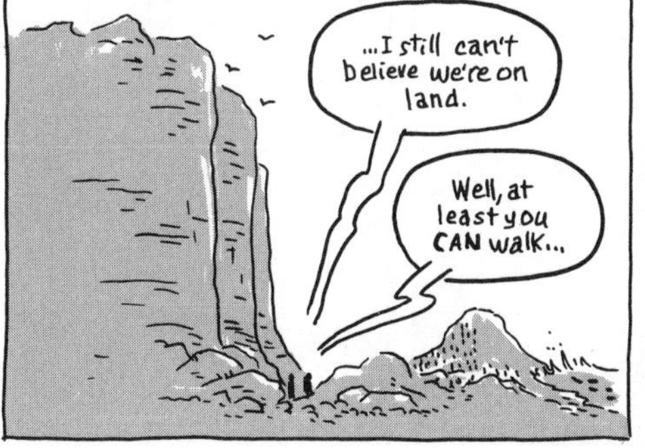
...I still can't believe we're on land.
Well, at least you CAN walk...

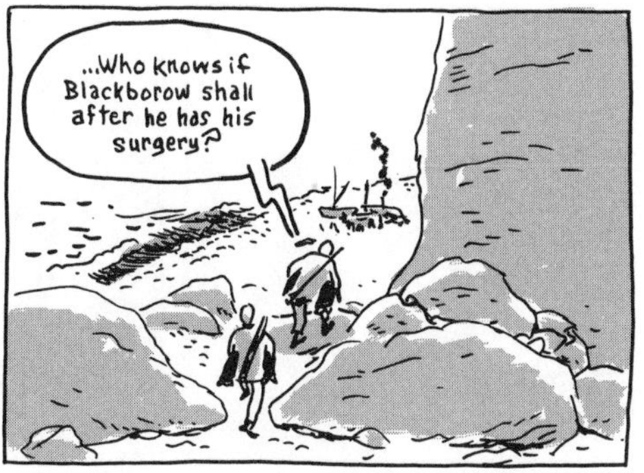
...Who knows if Blackborow shall after he has his surgery?

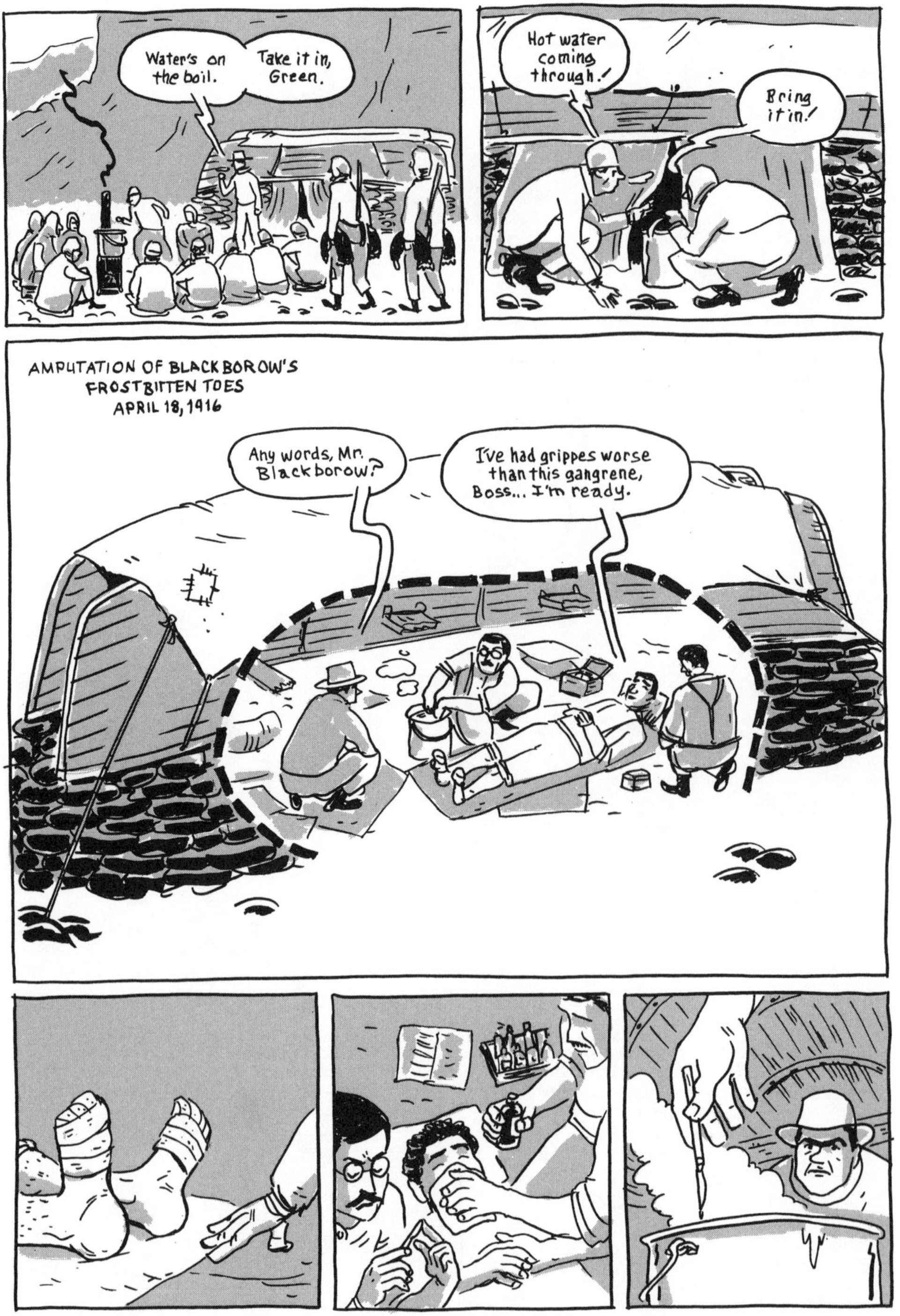

Water's on the boil.
Take it in, Green.
Hot water coming through!
Bring it in!
AMPUTATION OF BLACKBOROW'S FROSTBITTEN TOES APRIL 18, 1916
Any words, Mr. Blackborow?
I've had grippes worse than this gangrene, Boss... I'm ready.

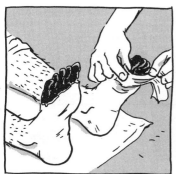

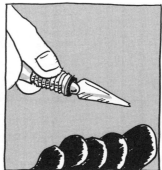

Strange to have the doctors fussing over someone other than you, Rickinson?

'Tis. I'm well tired of that bloody freezing stethoscope shoved down me shirt at all hours.

Your mild heart attack, frostbitten toes—I'd say we've had it easy for a crew that spent a year on the ice.

He'll live!

They couldn't kill me, lads!

HURRAH!

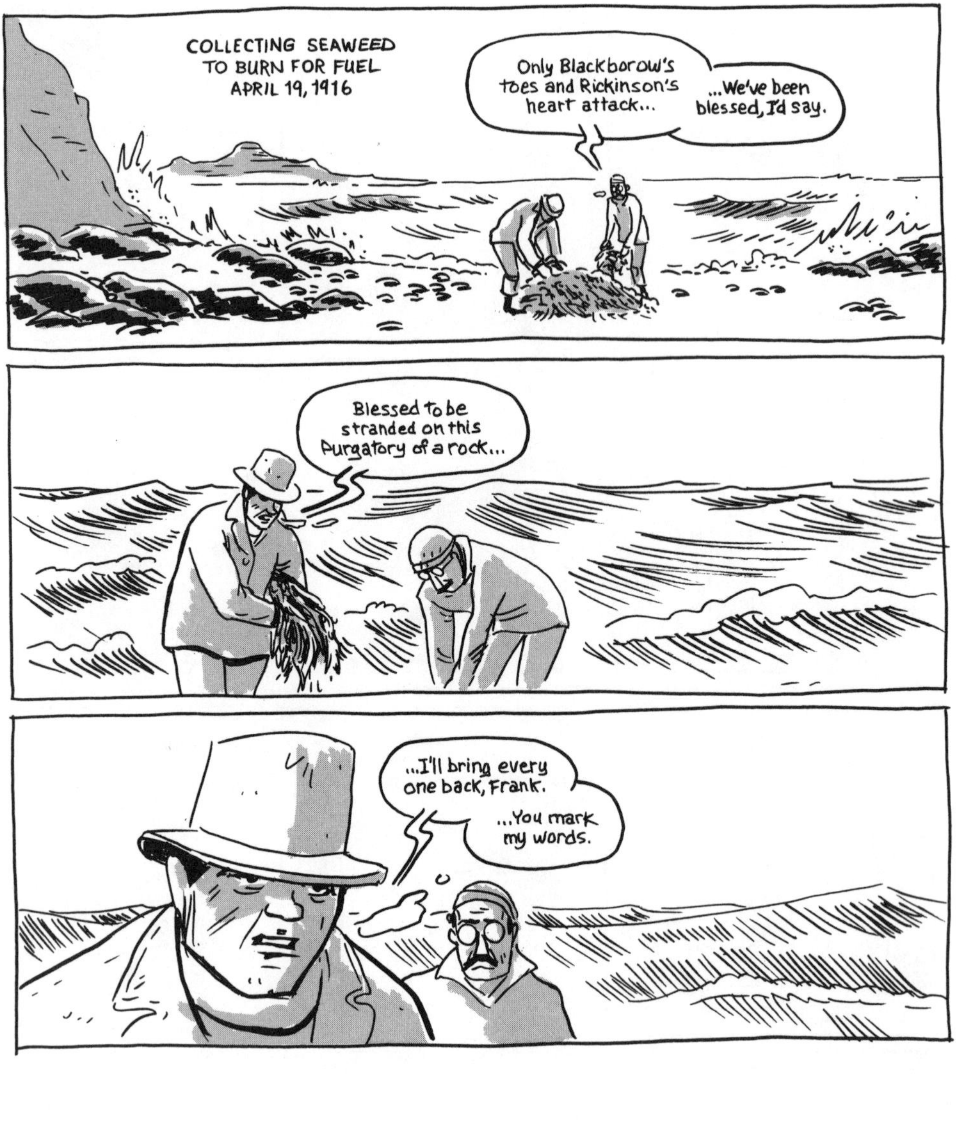
COLLECTING SEAWEED TO BURN FOR FUEL APRIL 19, 1916
Only Blackborow's toes and Rickinson's heart attack...
...We've been blessed, I'd say.
Blessed to be stranded on this Purgatory of a rock...
...I'll bring every one back, Frank.
...You mark my words.

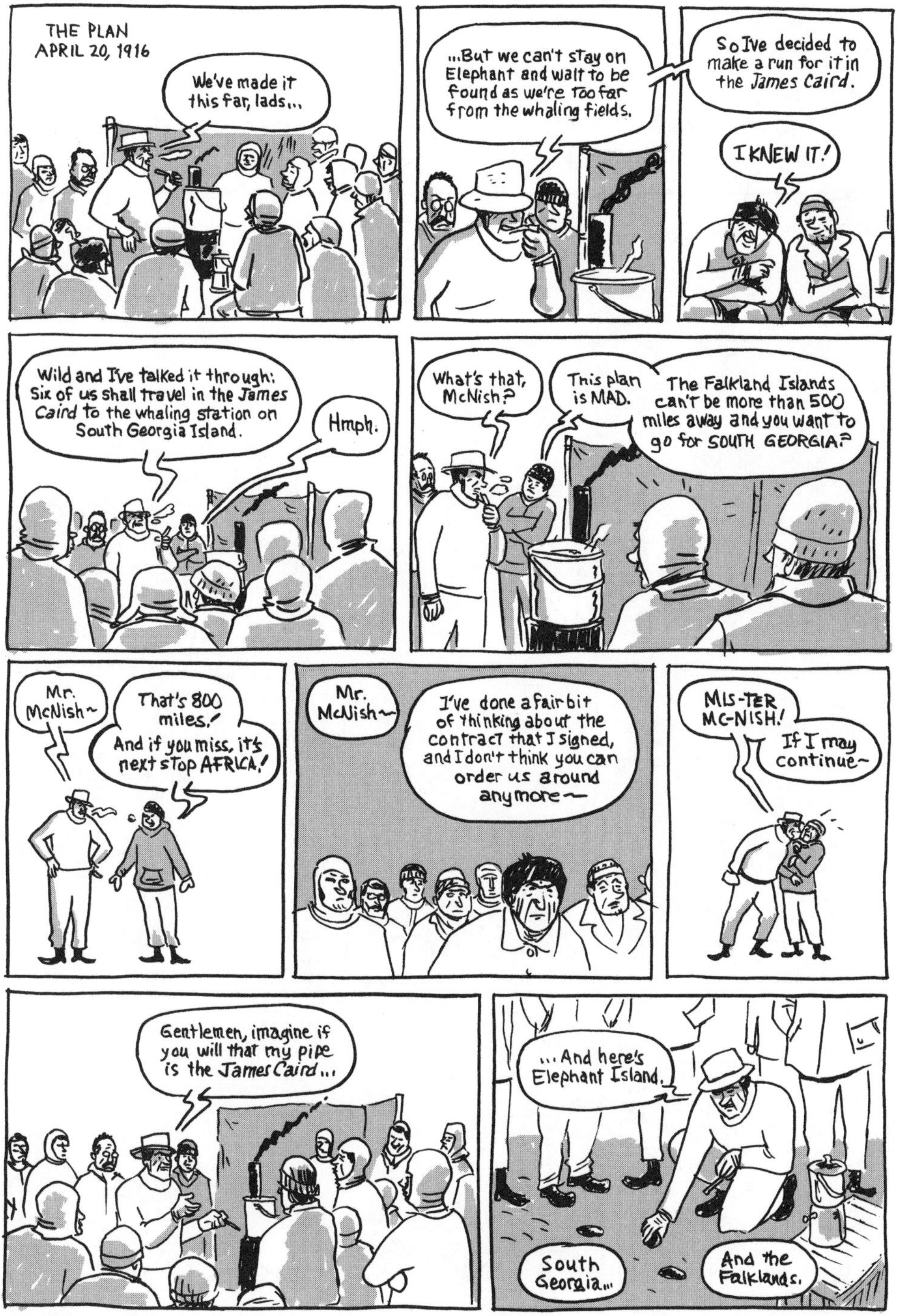
THE PLAN
APRIL 20, 1916
We've made it this far, lads...
...But we can't stay on Elephant and wait to be found as we're too far from the whaling fields.
So I've decided to make a run for it in the *James Caird*.
I KNEW IT!
Wild and I've talked it through: Six of us shall travel in the *James Caird* to the whaling station on South Georgia Island.
Hmph.
What's that, McNish?
This plan is MAD.
The Falkland Islands can't be more than 500 miles away and you want to go for SOUTH GEORGIA?
Mr. McNish~
That's 800 miles!
And if you miss, it's next stop AFRICA!
Mr. McNish~
I've done a fair bit of thinking about the contract that I signed, and I don't think you can order us around anymore~
MIS-TER MC-NISH!
If I may continue~
Gentlemen, imagine if you will that my pipe is the *James Caird*...
...And here's Elephant Island.
South Georgia...
And the Falklands.

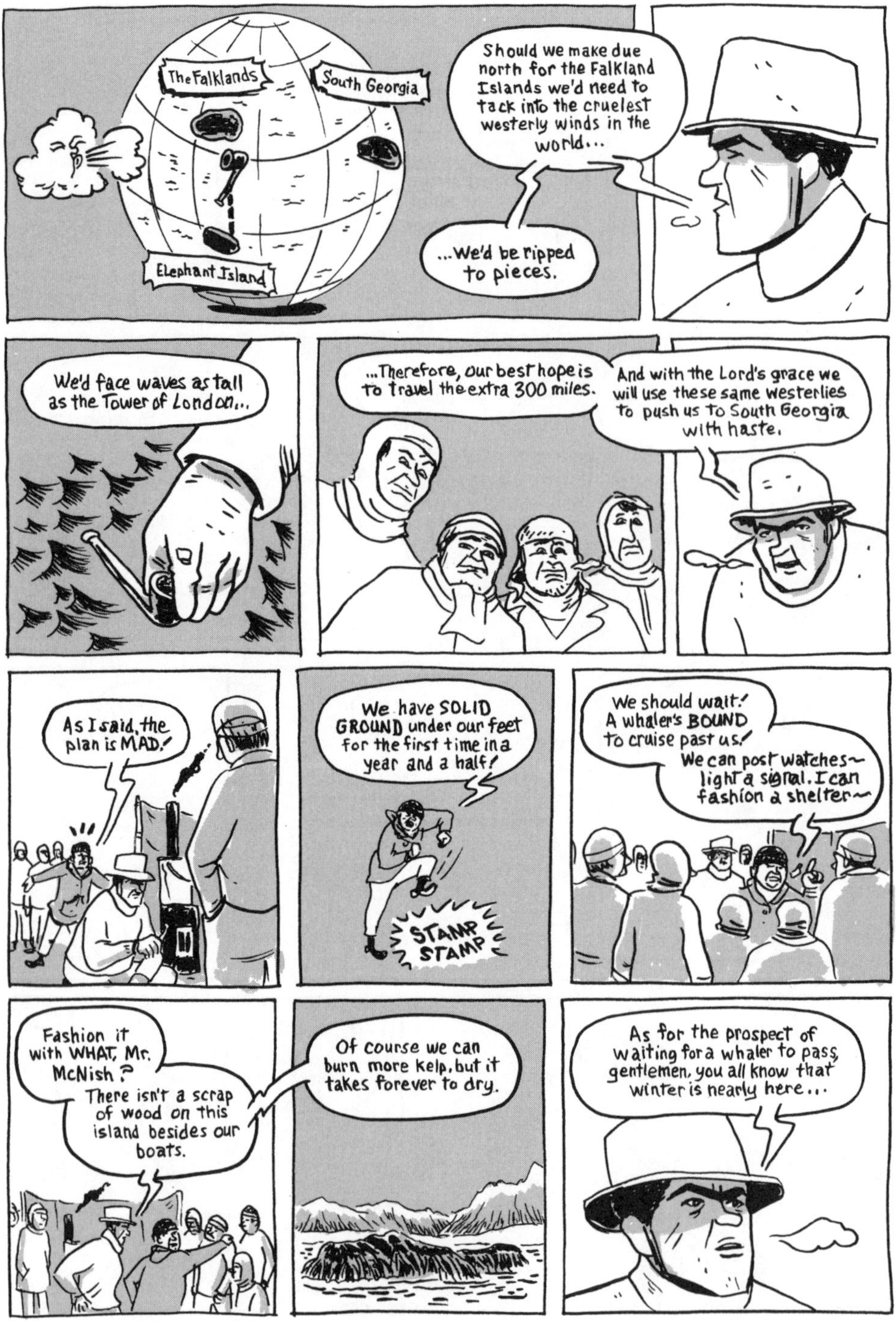
The Falklands
South Georgia
Elephant Island
Should we make due north for the Falkland Islands we'd need to tack into the cruelest westerly winds in the world...
...We'd be ripped to pieces.
We'd face waves as tall as the Tower of London...
...Therefore, our best hope is to travel the extra 300 miles.
And with the Lord's grace we will use these same westerlies to push us to South Georgia with haste.
As I said, the plan is MAD!
We have SOLID GROUND under our feet for the first time in a year and a half!
STAMP STAMP
We should wait! A whaler's BOUND to cruise past us!
We can post watches~ light a signal. I can fashion a shelter~
Fashion it with WHAT, Mr. McNish?
There isn't a scrap of wood on this island besides our boats.
Of course we can burn more kelp, but it takes forever to dry.
As for the prospect of waiting for a whaler to pass, gentlemen, you all know that winter is nearly here...

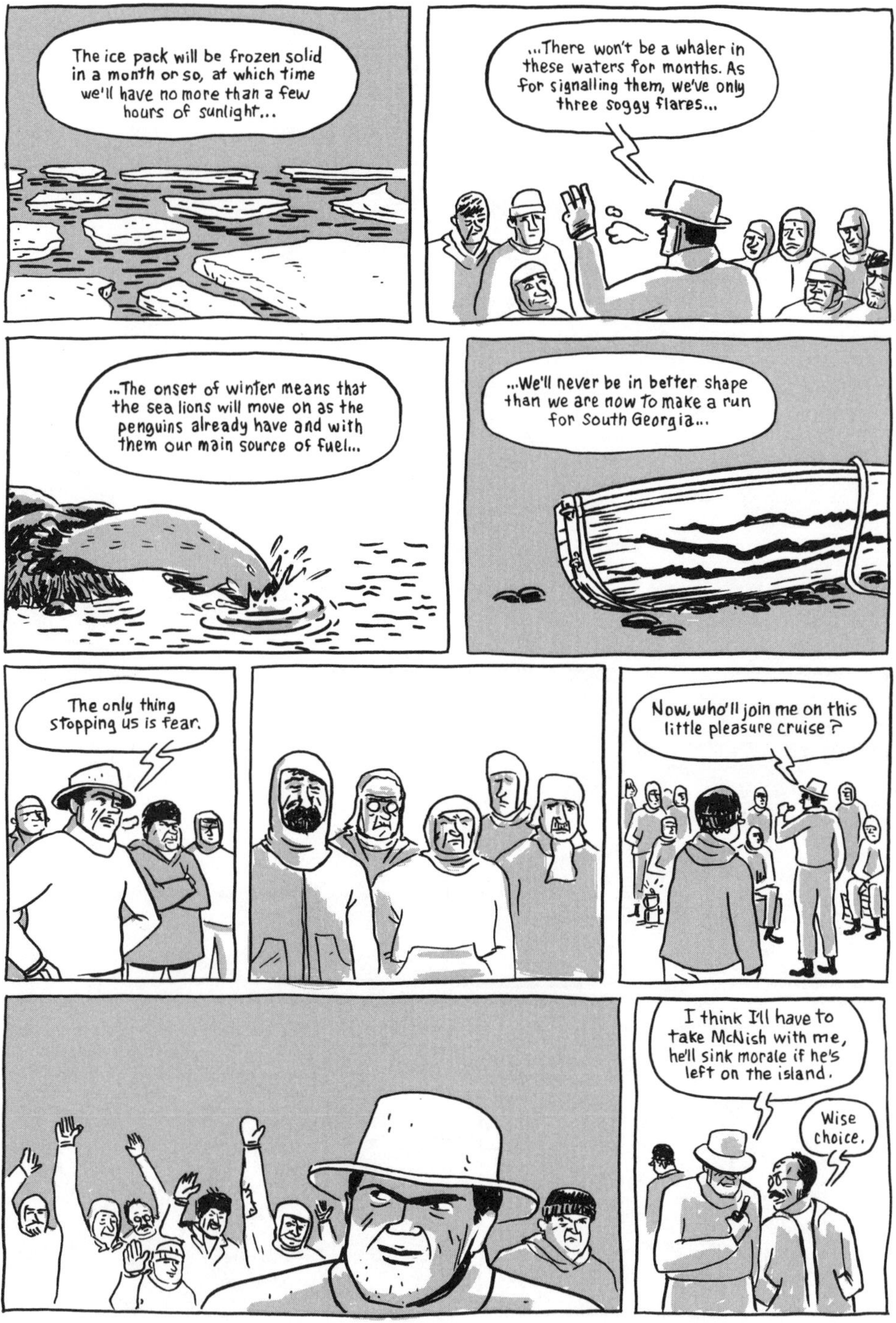
The ice pack will be frozen solid in a month or so, at which time we'll have no more than a few hours of sunlight...
...There won't be a whaler in these waters for months. As for signalling them, we've only three soggy flares...
...The onset of winter means that the sea lions will move on as the penguins already have and with them our main source of fuel...
...We'll never be in better shape than we are now to make a run for South Georgia...
The only thing stopping us is fear.
Now, who'll join me on this little pleasure cruise?
I think I'll have to take McNish with me, he'll sink morale if he's left on the island.
Wise choice.

THE VOYAGE OF
THE *JAMES CAIRD*
APRIL 24, 1916

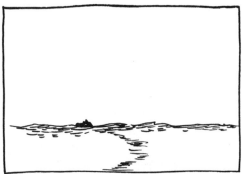

That's it
then...

...Only 799 more
miles to go!

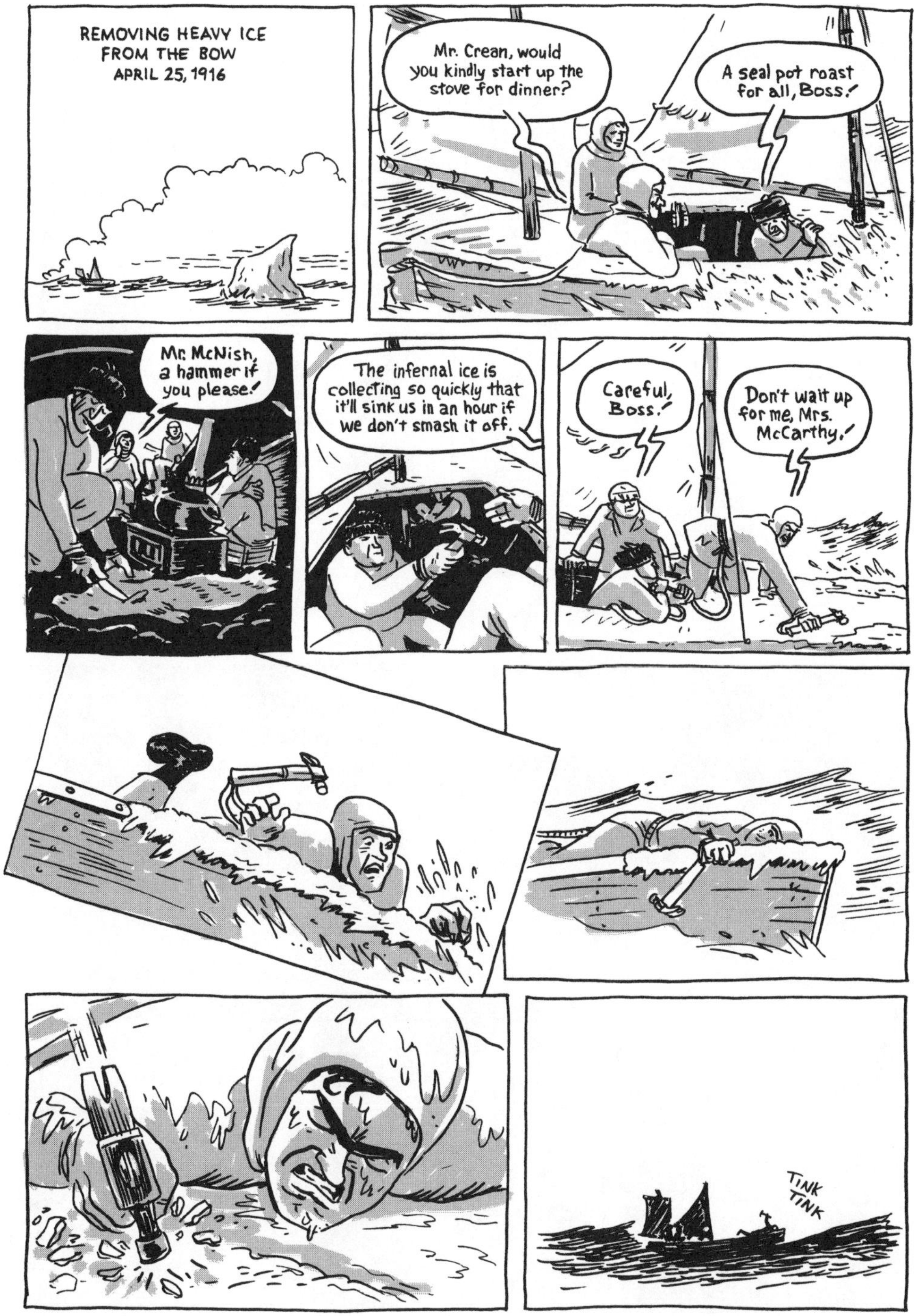
REMOVING HEAVY ICE
FROM THE BOW
APRIL 25, 1916
Mr. Crean, would you kindly start up the stove for dinner?
A seal pot roast for all, Boss.!
Mr. McNish, a hammer if you please.!
The infernal ice is collecting so quickly that it'll sink us in an hour if we don't smash it off.
Careful, Boss.!
Don't wait up for me, Mrs. McCarthy.!
TINK TINK

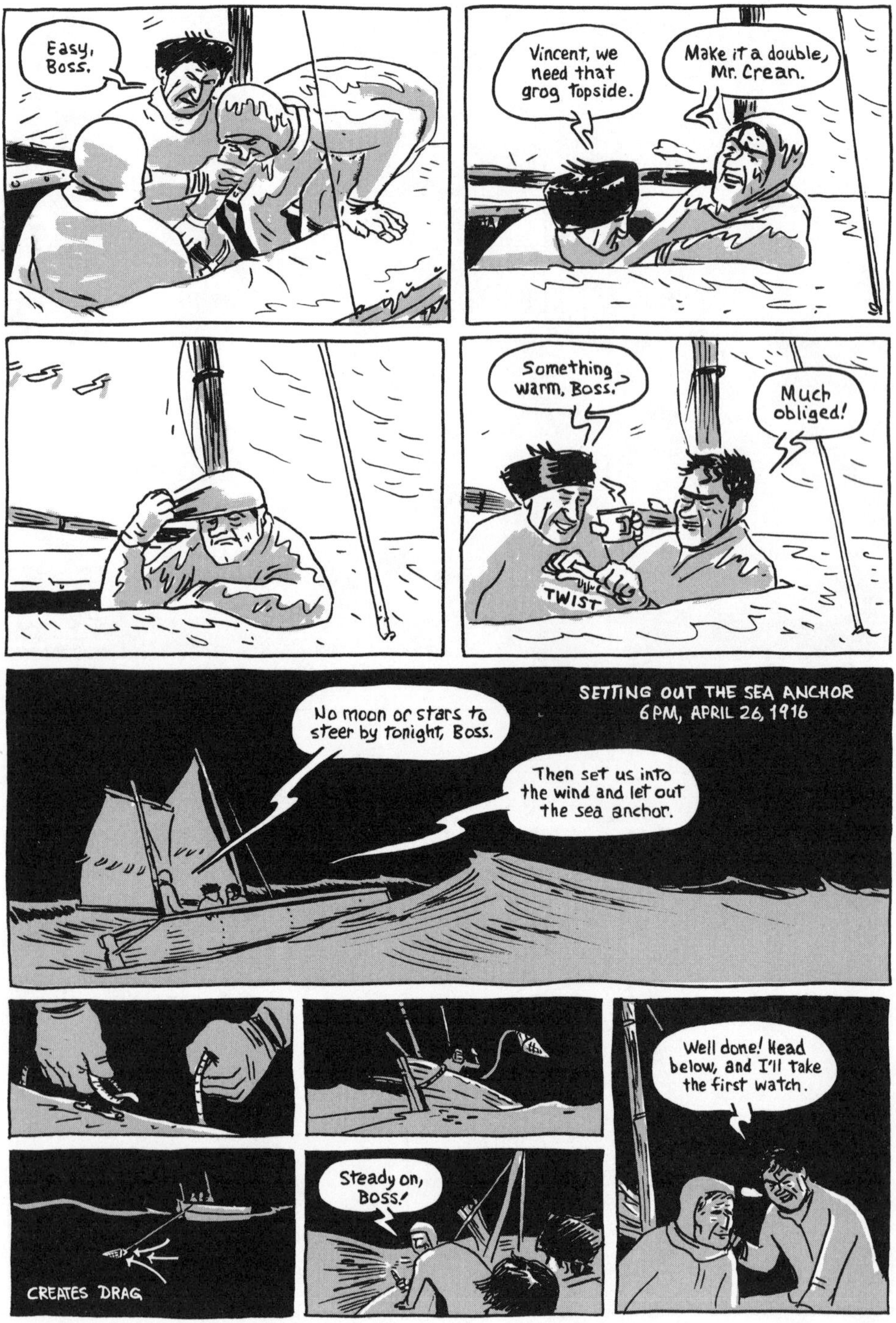

Easy, Boss.
Vincent, we need that grog topside.
Make it a double, Mr. Crean.
Something warm, Boss.
Much obliged!
TWIST
SETTING OUT THE SEA ANCHOR
6PM, APRIL 26, 1916
No moon or stars to steer by tonight, Boss.
Then set us into the wind and let out the sea anchor.
CREATES DRAG
Steady on, Boss!
Well done! Head below, and I'll take the first watch.

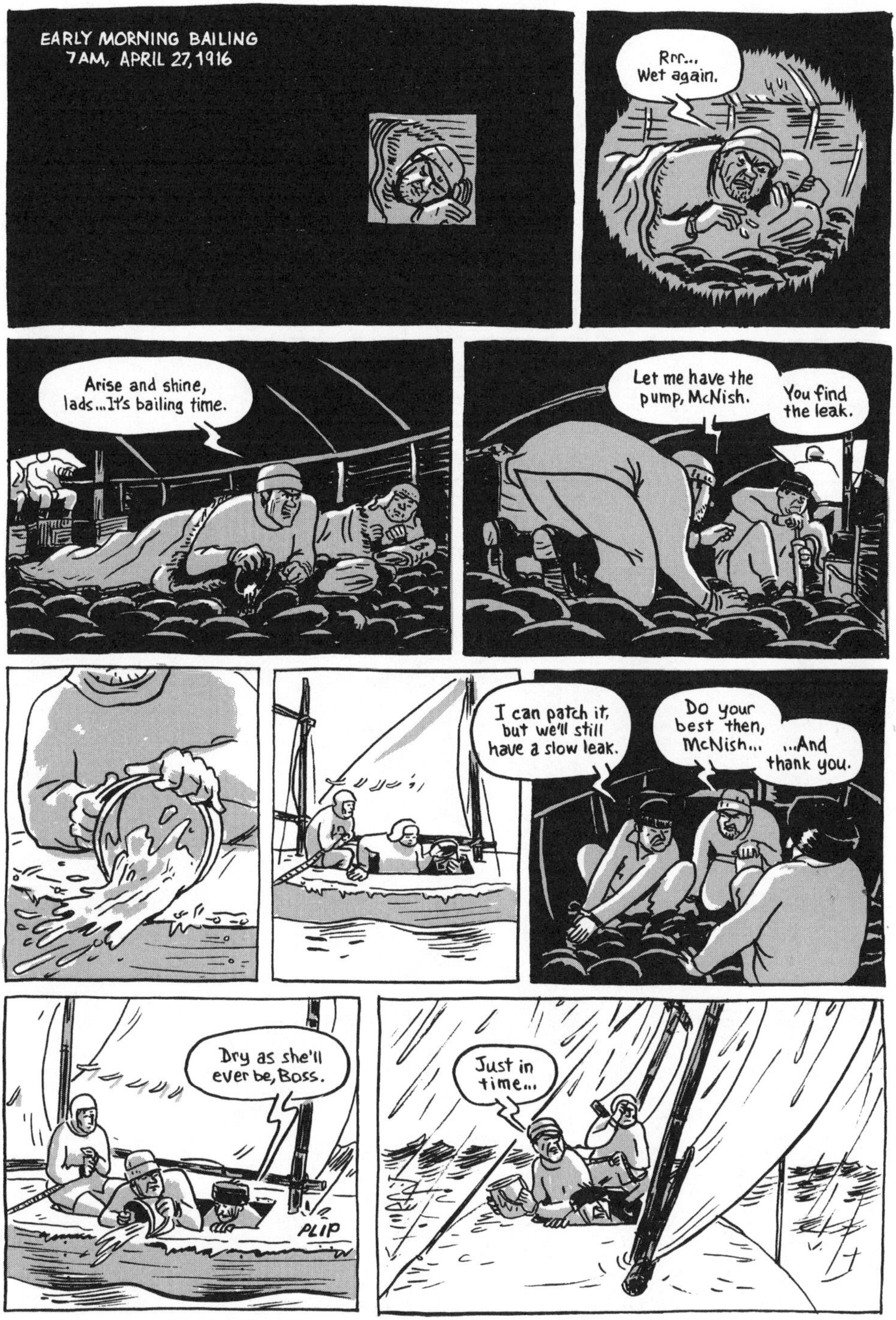
EARLY MORNING BAILING
7AM, APRIL 27, 1916
Rrr... Wet again.
Arise and shine, lads... It's bailing time.
Let me have the pump, McNish.
You find the leak.
I can patch it, but we'll still have a slow leak.
Do your best then, McNish...
...And thank you.
Dry as she'll ever be, Boss.
PLIP
Just in time...

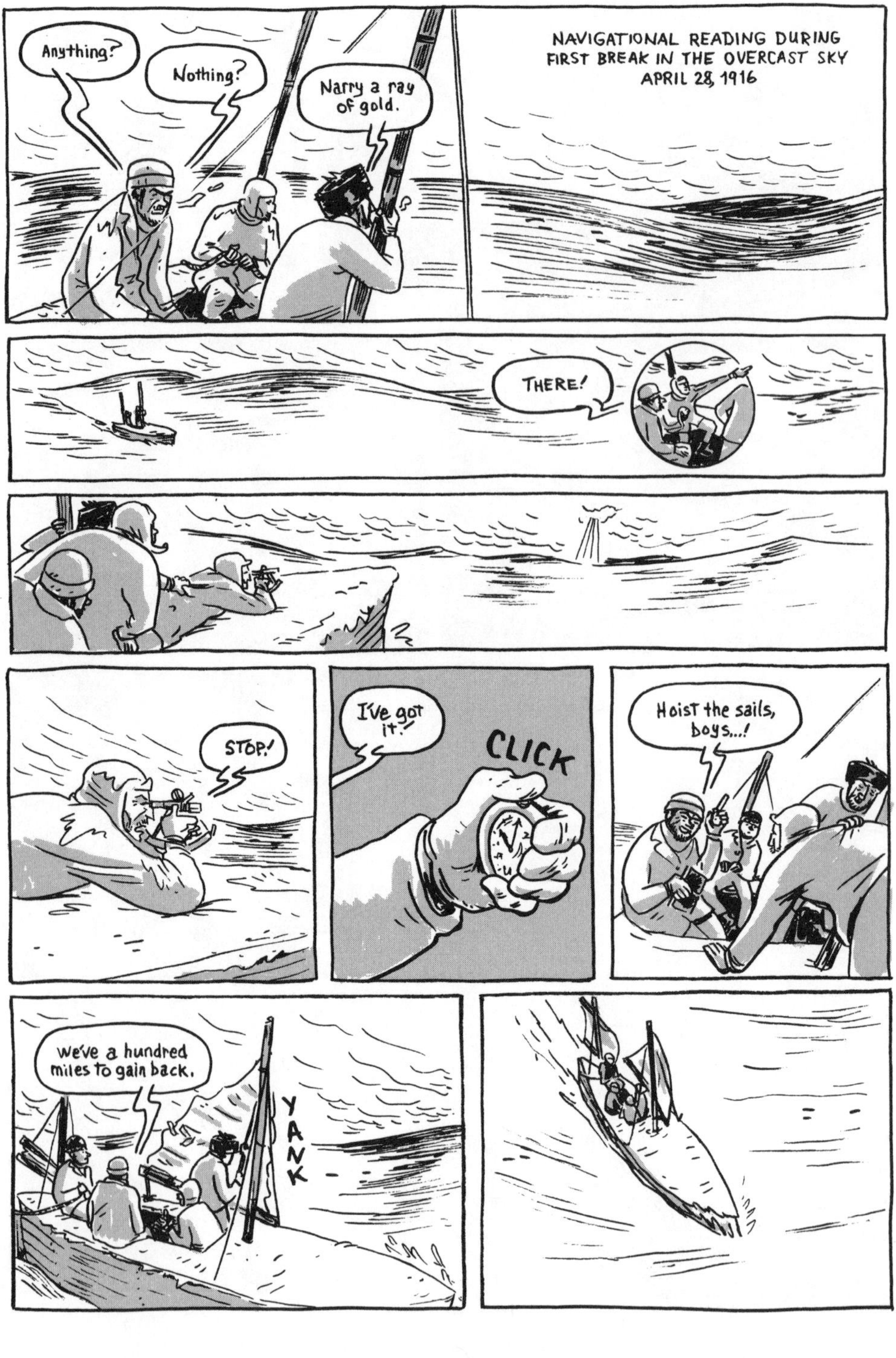
Anything?
Nothing?
Narry a ray of gold.
NAVIGATIONAL READING DURING FIRST BREAK IN THE OVERCAST SKY APRIL 28, 1916
THERE!
STOP!
I've got it.
CLICK
Hoist the sails, boys...!
We've a hundred miles to gain back.
YANK

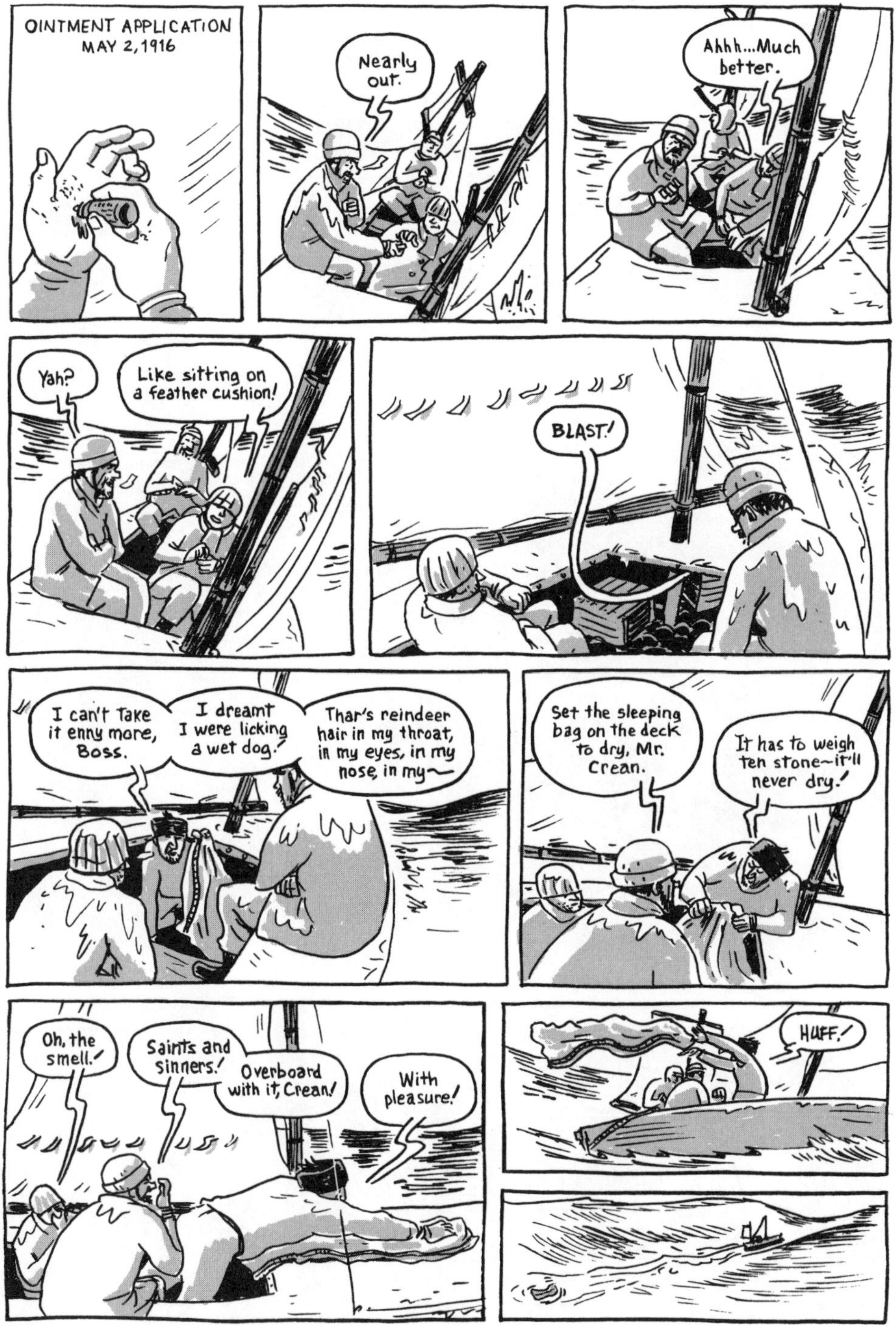
OINTMENT APPLICATION
MAY 2, 1916
Nearly out.
Ahhh...Much better.
Yah?
Like sitting on a feather cushion!
BLAST!
I can't take it enny more, Boss.
I dreamt I were licking a wet dog!
Thar's reindeer hair in my throat, in my eyes, in my nose, in my~
Set the sleeping bag on the deck to dry, Mr. Crean.
It has to weigh ten stone~it'll never dry!
Oh, the smell!
Saints and sinners!
Overboard with it, Crean!
With pleasure!
HUFF!

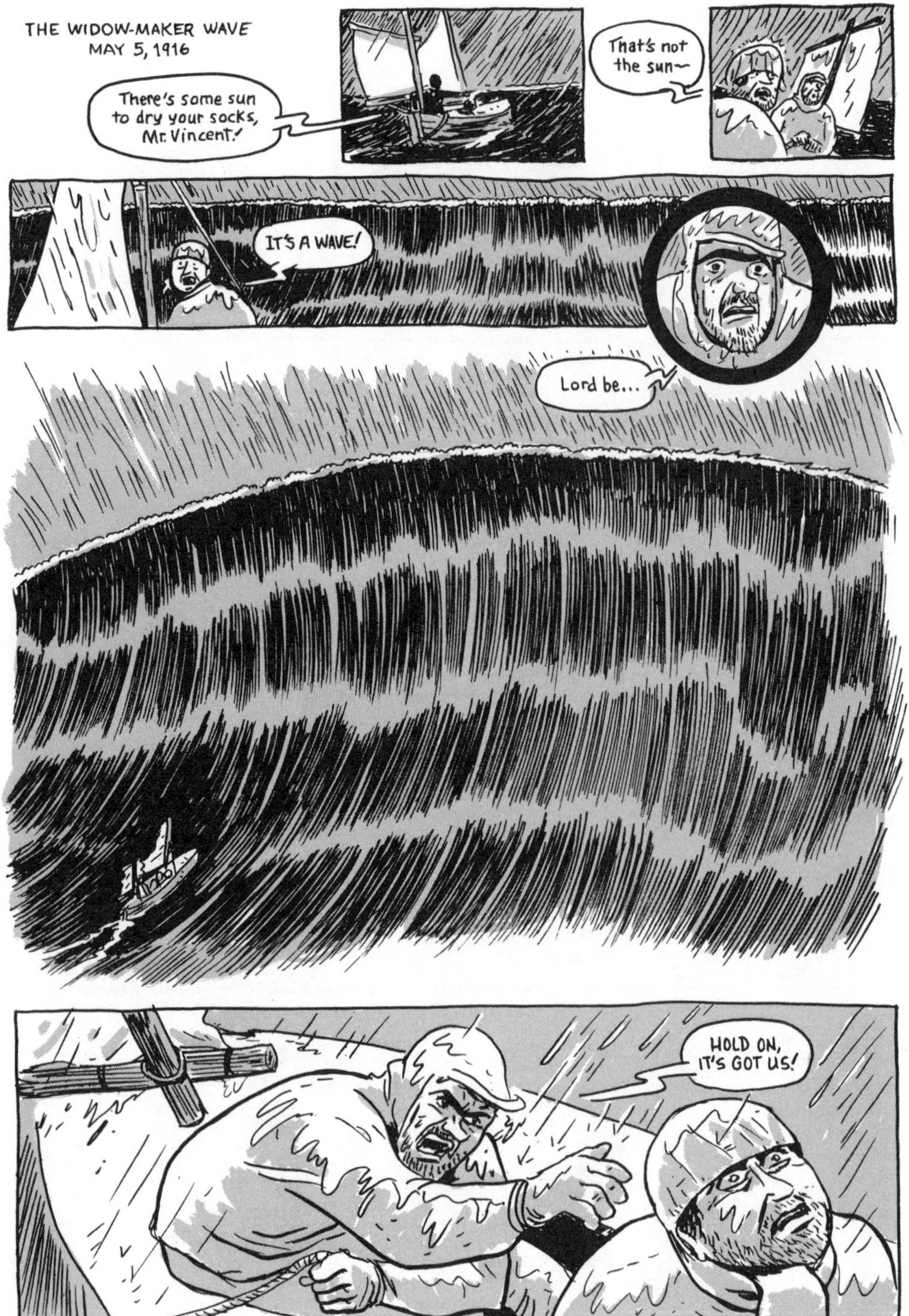
THE WIDOW-MAKER WAVE
MAY 5, 1916
There's some sun to dry your socks, Mr. Vincent!
That's not the sun~
IT'S A WAVE!
Lord be...
HOLD ON, IT'S GOT US!

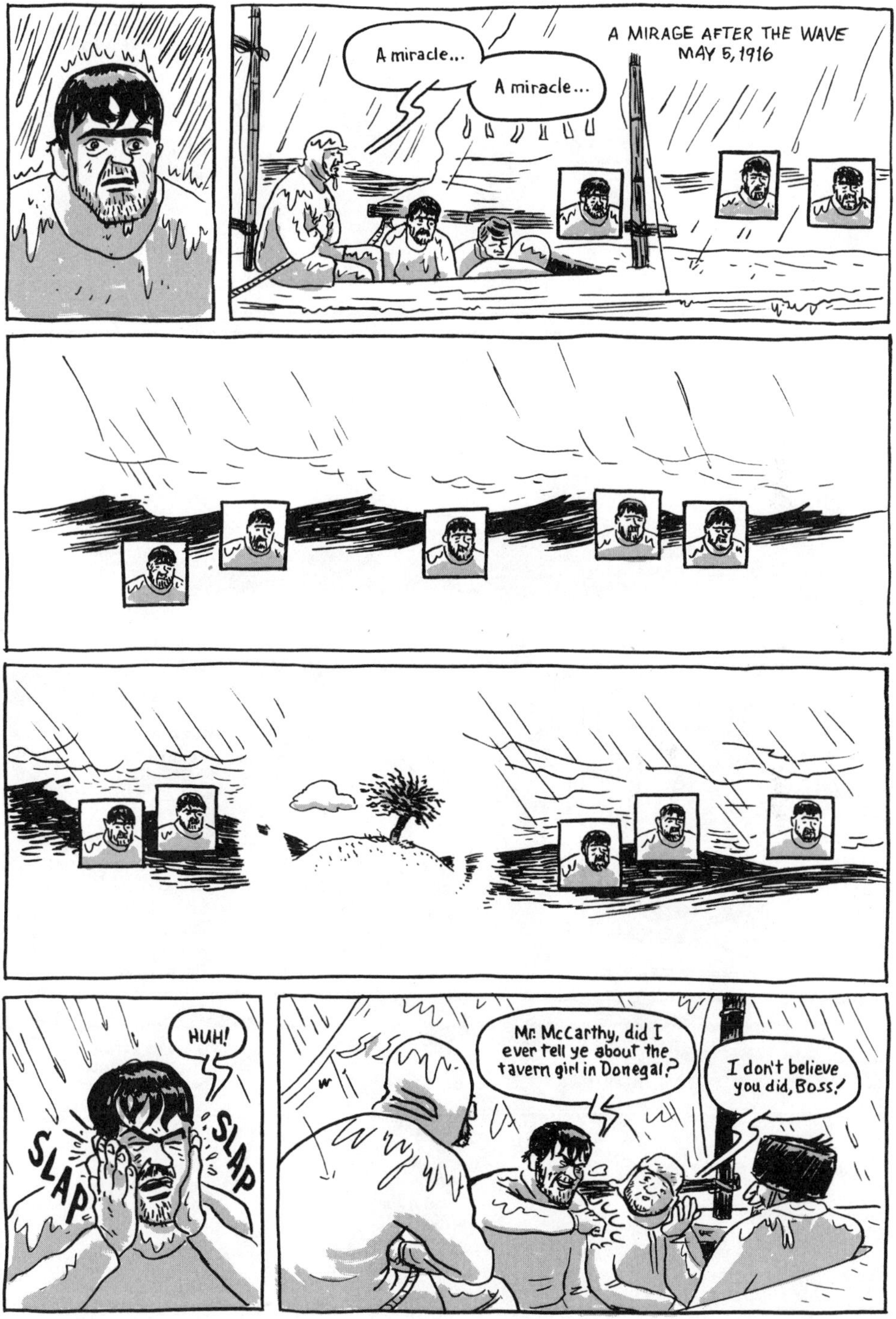
A MIRAGE AFTER THE WAVE
MAY 5, 1916
A miracle...
A miracle...
HUH!
SLAP
SLAP
Mr. McCarthy, did I ever tell ye about the tavern girl in Donegal?
I don't believe you did, Boss!

WATER CASK CONTAMINATED
BY SEA WATER
MAY 7, 1916

Ugh.

Not bad.

Come now, Worsley, you can't sit at the tiller forever!

I'm afraid I can't move, Boss...

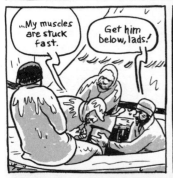

...My muscles are stuck fast.

Get him below, lads!

No more double shifts for you, Worsley.

We pooled our milk ration for you, Wuzzles.

Thank you, no. No need!

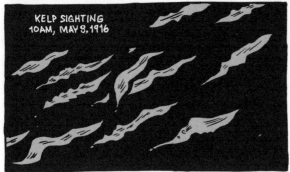

KELP SIGHTING
10AM, MAY 8, 1916

We're surely near land now!

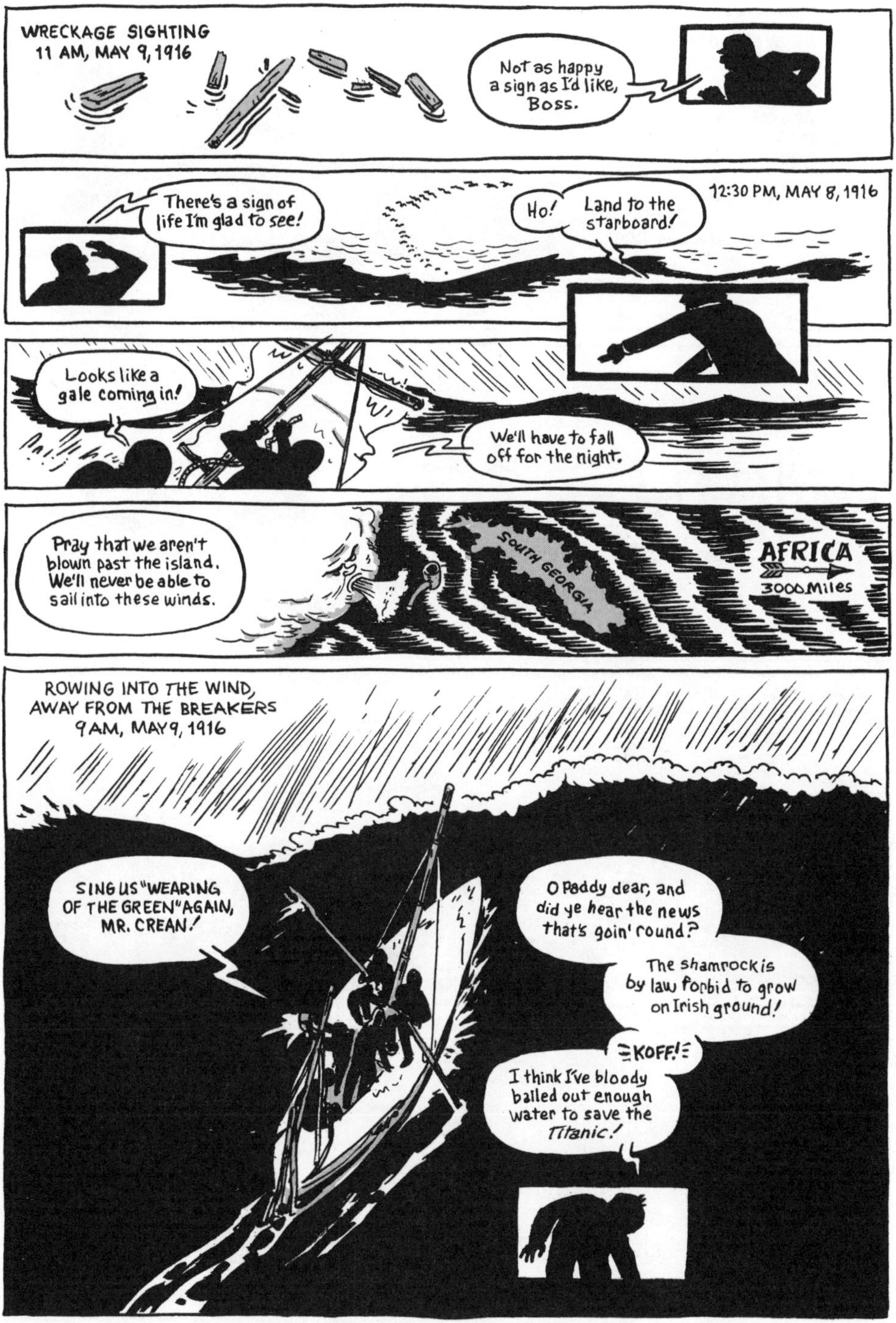
WRECKAGE SIGHTING
11 AM, MAY 9, 1916
Not as happy a sign as I'd like, Boss.
12:30 PM, MAY 8, 1916
There's a sign of life I'm glad to see!
Ho!
Land to the starboard!
Looks like a gale coming in!
We'll have to fall off for the night.
Pray that we aren't blown past the island. We'll never be able to sail into these winds.
SOUTH GEORGIA
AFRICA
3000 Miles
ROWING INTO THE WIND,
AWAY FROM THE BREAKERS
9 AM, MAY 9, 1916
SING US "WEARING OF THE GREEN" AGAIN, MR. CREAN!
O Paddy dear, and did ye hear the news that's goin' round?
The shamrock is by law forbid to grow on Irish ground!
KOFF!
I think I've bloody bailed out enough water to save the *Titanic*!

ROWING TO STAY OFF THE CLIFF
2 PM, MAY 9, 1916
THE WAVES ARE BREAKING ON THAT BLOODY CLIFF TO 40 FEET!
They must be filled with magnets, I've been rowing as hard as I can!
GALE DISSIPATES
5 PM, MAY 9, 1916
We were dead, lads... and now we're alive.
LOOKING FOR AN OPENING IN THE "KRAKEN'S TEETH" OF THE REEF
4 PM, MAY 10, 1916
Damned reefs!
Can't you see we're dying of thirst!
SEARCHING FOR A BEACH IN THE UNINHABITED KING HAAKON BAY
DAWN, MAY 10, 1916

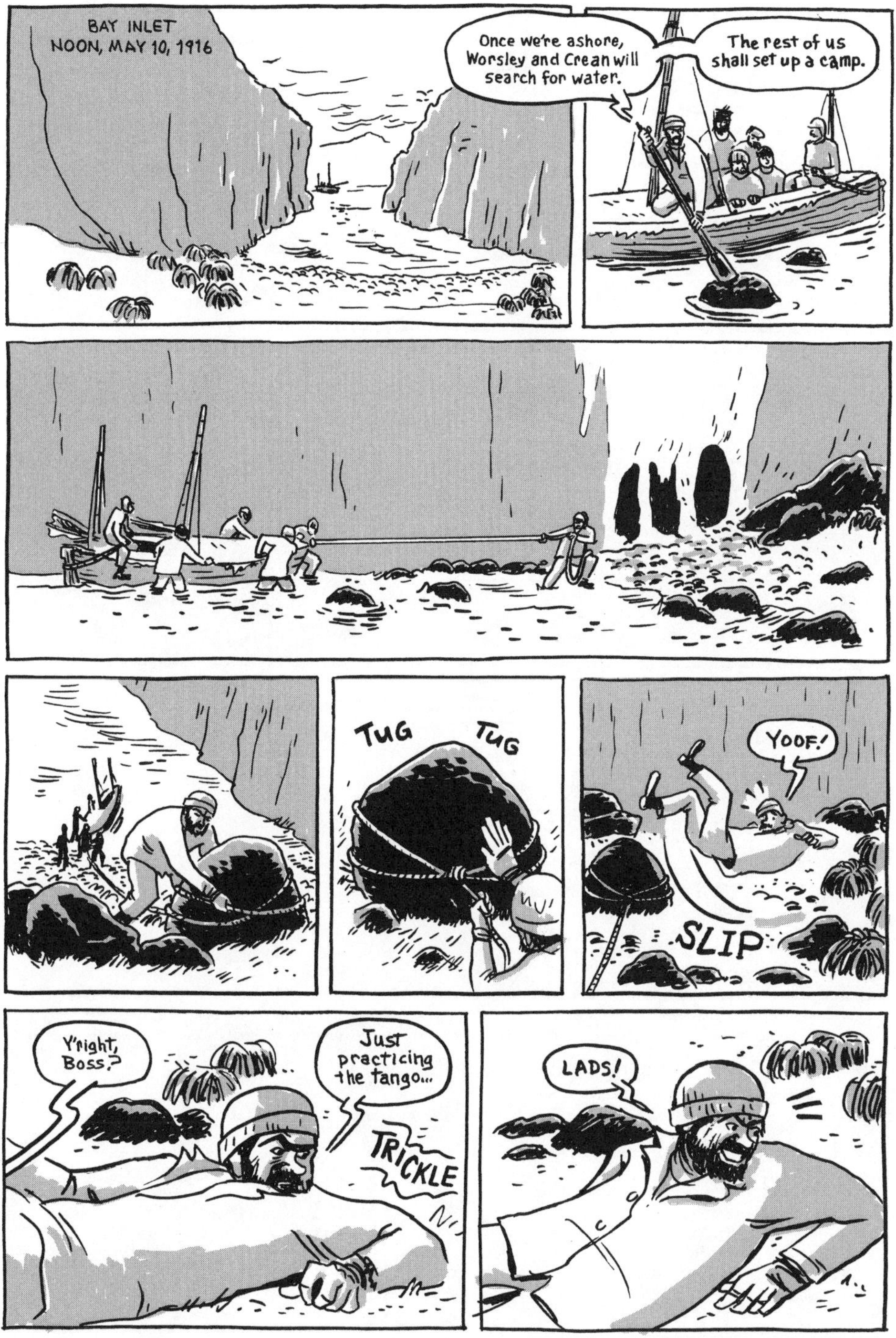
BAY INLET
NOON, MAY 10, 1916
Once we're ashore, Worsley and Crean will search for water.
The rest of us shall set up a camp.
TUG
TUG
YOOF!
SLIP
Y'right, Boss?
Just practicing the tango...
TRICKLE
LADS!

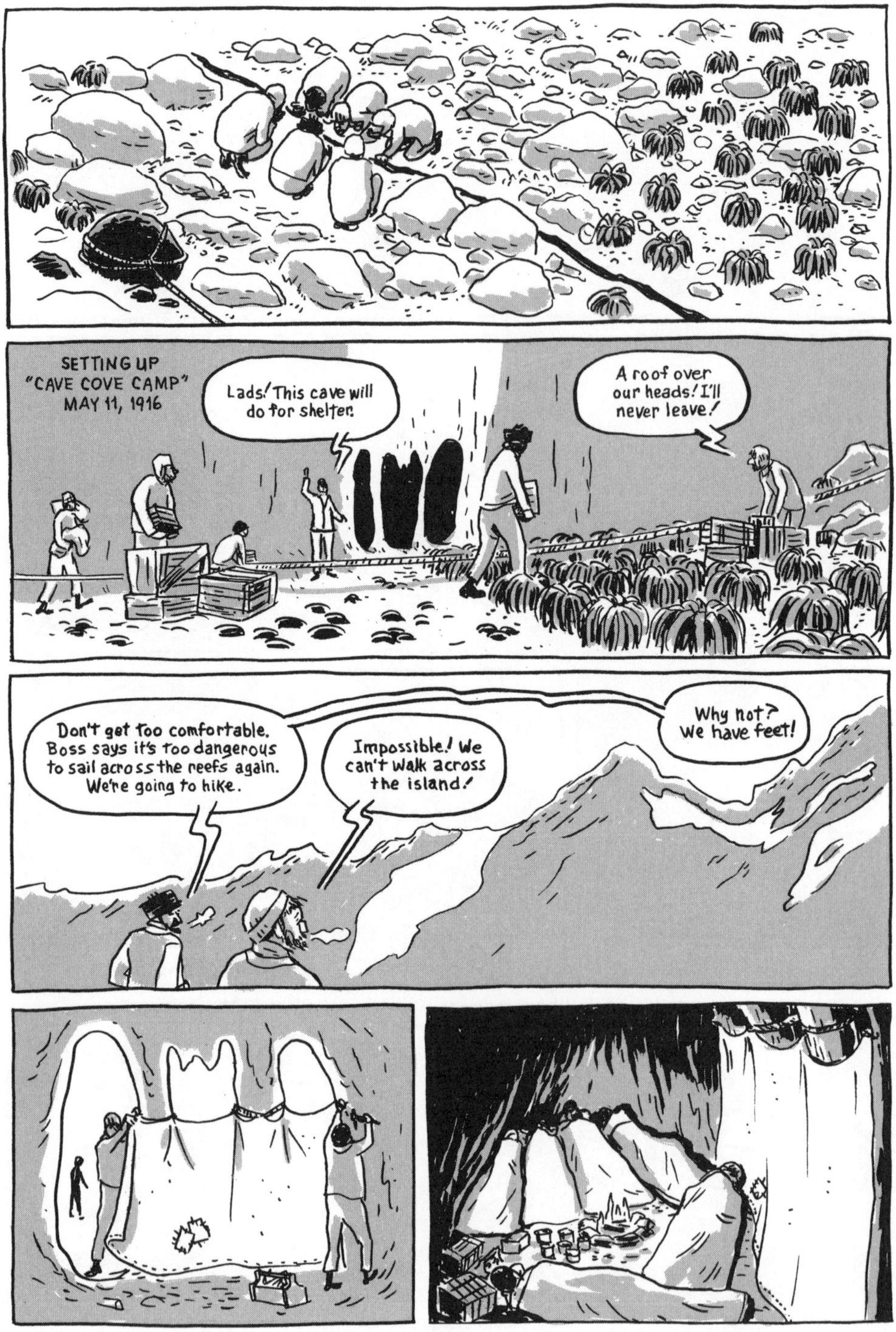

SETTING UP "CAVE COVE CAMP" MAY 11, 1916
Lads! This cave will do for shelter.
A roof over our heads! I'll never leave!
Don't get too comfortable. Boss says it's too dangerous to sail across the reefs again. We're going to hike.
Impossible! We can't walk across the island!
Why not? We have feet!

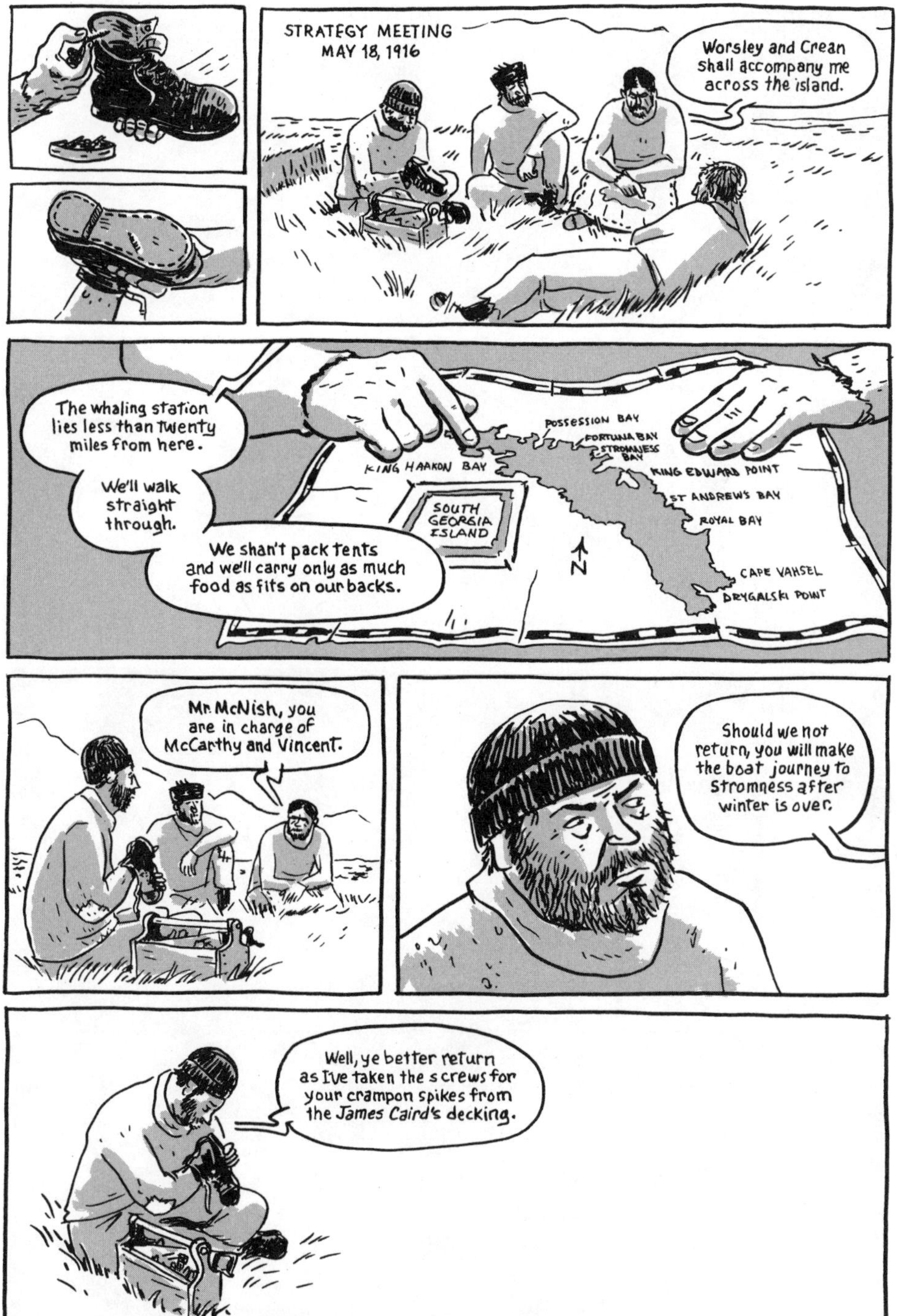
STRATEGY MEETING
MAY 18, 1916
Worsley and Crean shall accompany me across the island.
The whaling station lies less than twenty miles from here.
We'll walk straight through.
We shan't pack tents and we'll carry only as much food as fits on our backs.
POSSESSION BAY
FORTUNA BAY
STROMNESS BAY
KING HAAKON BAY
KING EDWARD POINT
ST ANDREWS BAY
ROYAL BAY
SOUTH GEORGIA ISLAND
N
CAPE VAHSEL
DRYGALSKI POINT
Mr. McNish, you are in charge of McCarthy and Vincent.
Should we not return, you will make the boat journey to Stromness after winter is over.
Well, ye better return as I've taken the screws for your crampon spikes from the *James Caird's* decking.

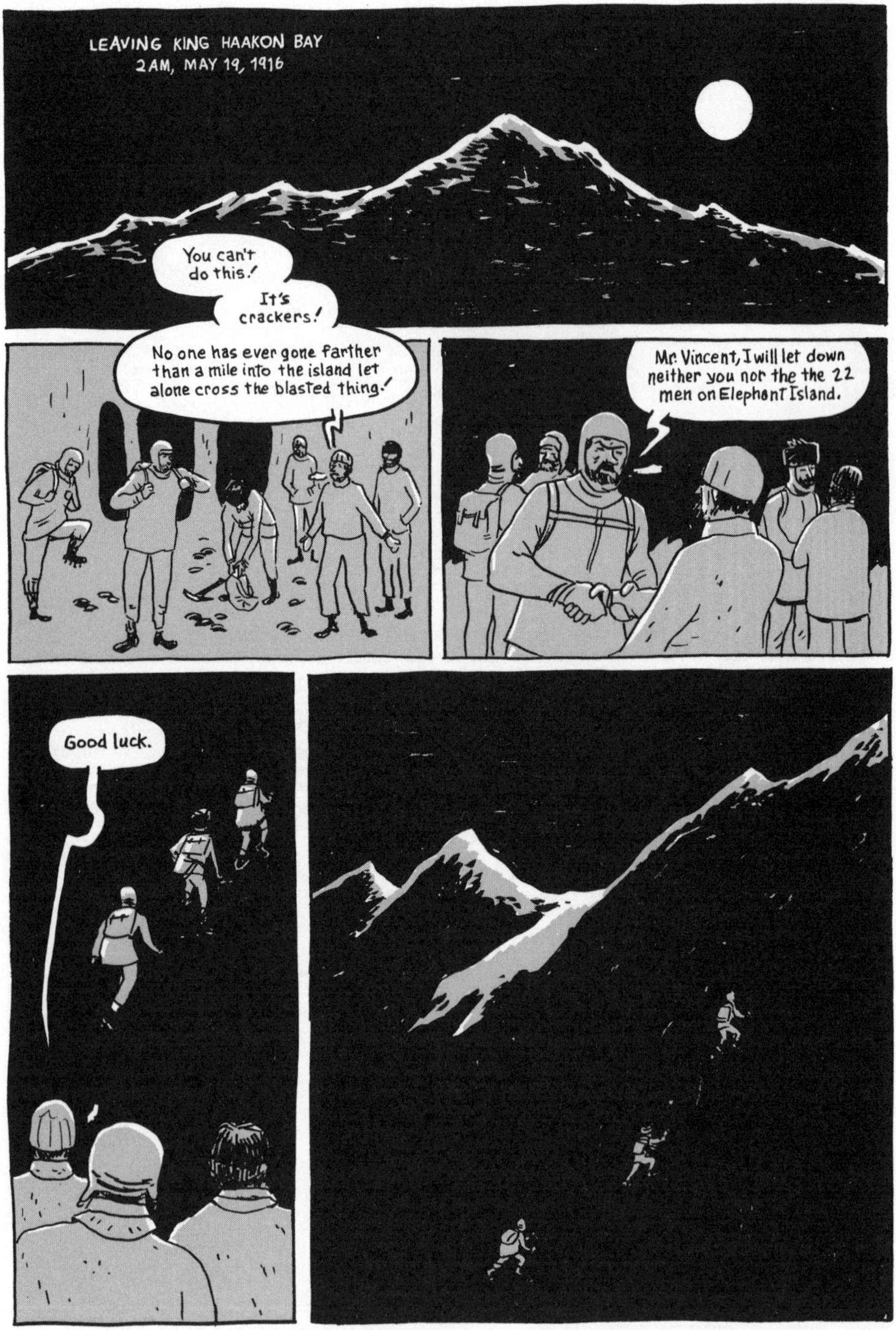
LEAVING KING HAAKON BAY
2AM, MAY 19, 1916
You can't do this!
It's crackers!
No one has ever gone farther than a mile into the island let alone cross the blasted thing!
Mr. Vincent, I will let down neither you nor the the 22 men on Elephant Island.
Good luck.

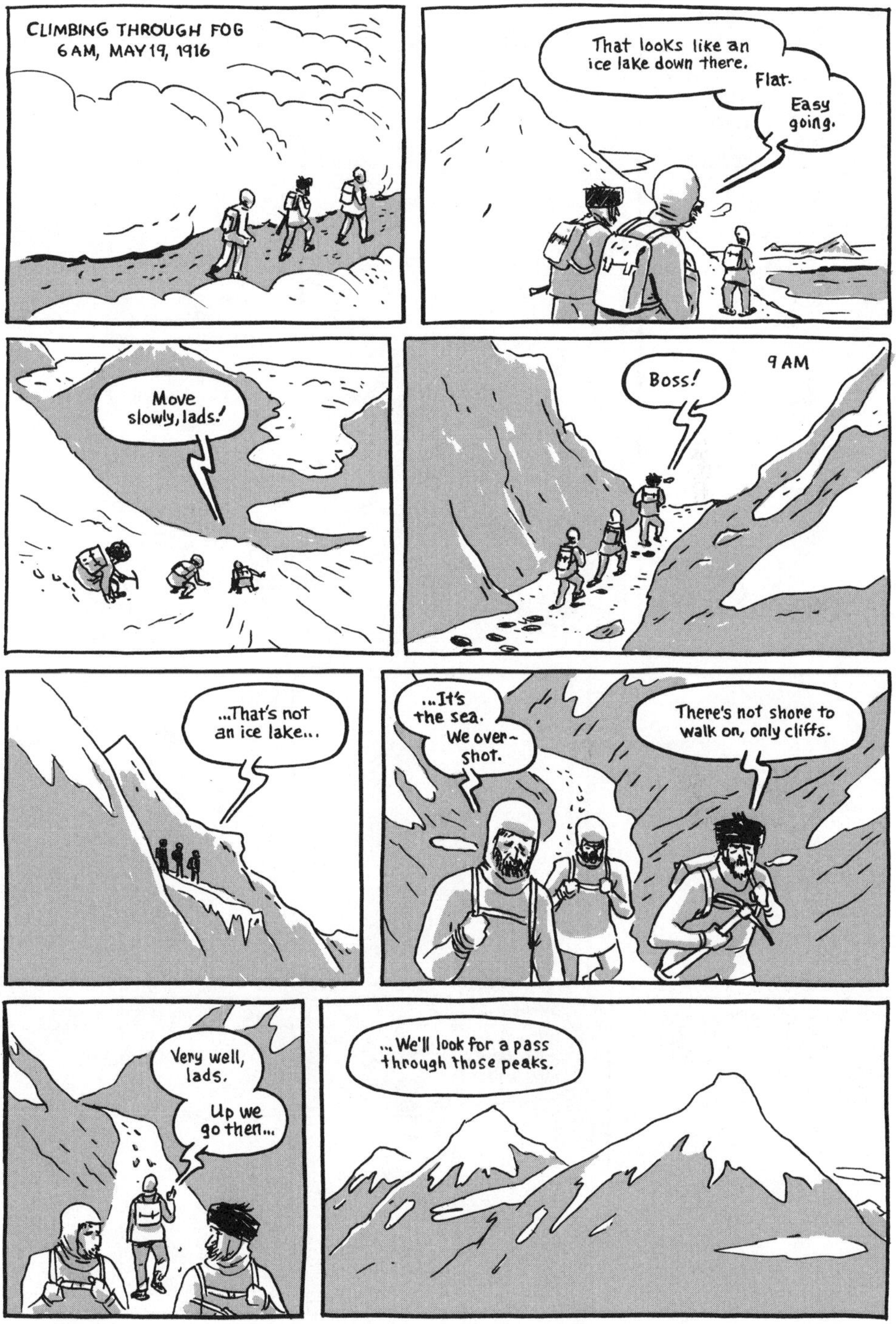
CLIMBING THROUGH FOG
6 AM, MAY 19, 1916
That looks like an ice lake down there.
Flat.
Easy going.
Move slowly, lads!
9 AM
Boss!
...That's not an ice lake...
...It's the sea. We over-shot.
There's not shore to walk on, only cliffs.
Very well, lads.
Up we go then...
... We'll look for a pass through those peaks.

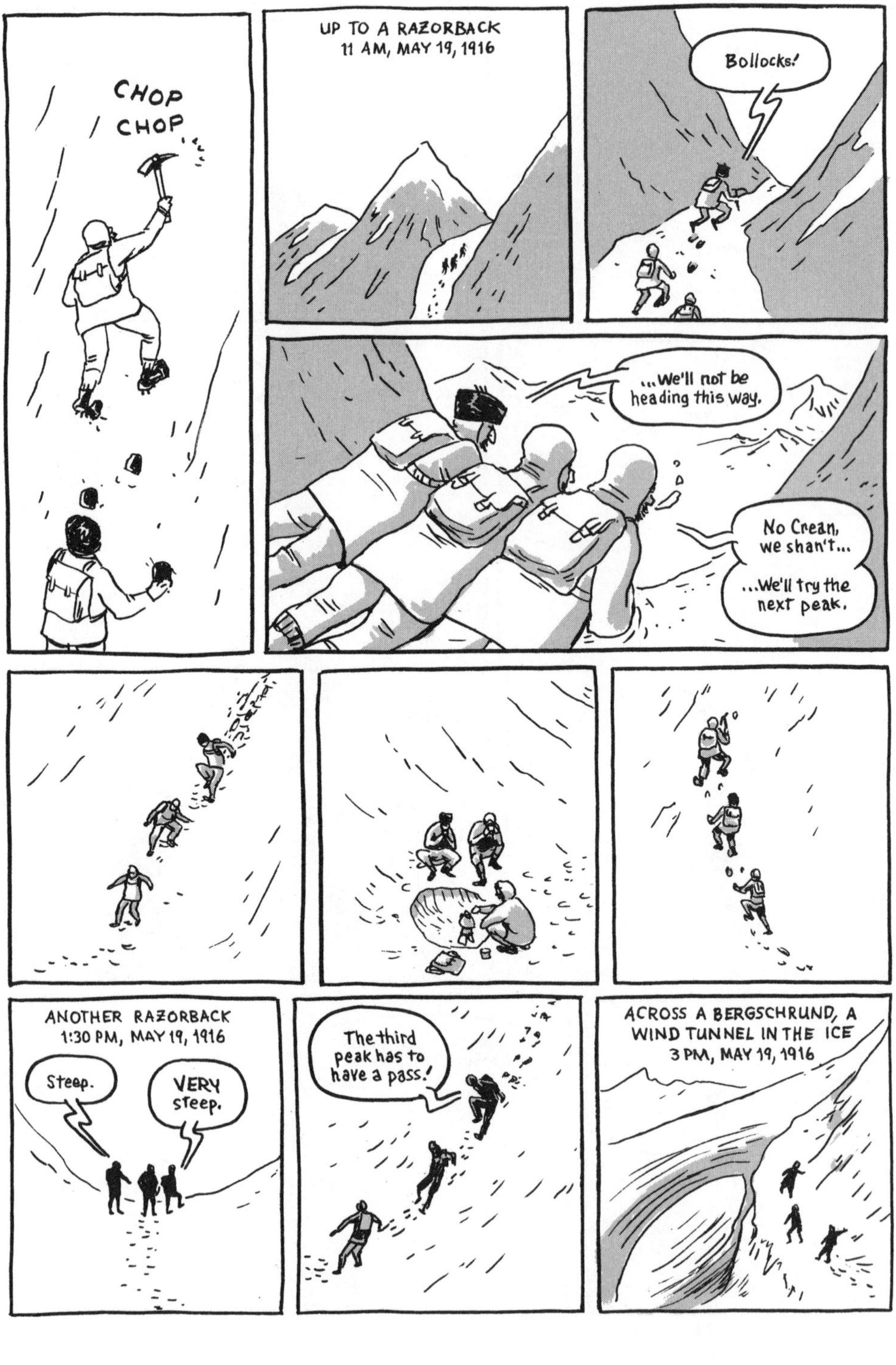
CHOP
CHOP
UP TO A RAZORBACK
11 AM, MAY 19, 1916
Bollocks!
...We'll not be heading this way.
No Crean, we shan't...
...We'll try the next peak.
ANOTHER RAZORBACK
1:30 PM, MAY 19, 1916
Steep.
VERY steep.
The third peak has to have a pass!
ACROSS A BERGSCHRUND, A WIND TUNNEL IN THE ICE
3 PM, MAY 19, 1916

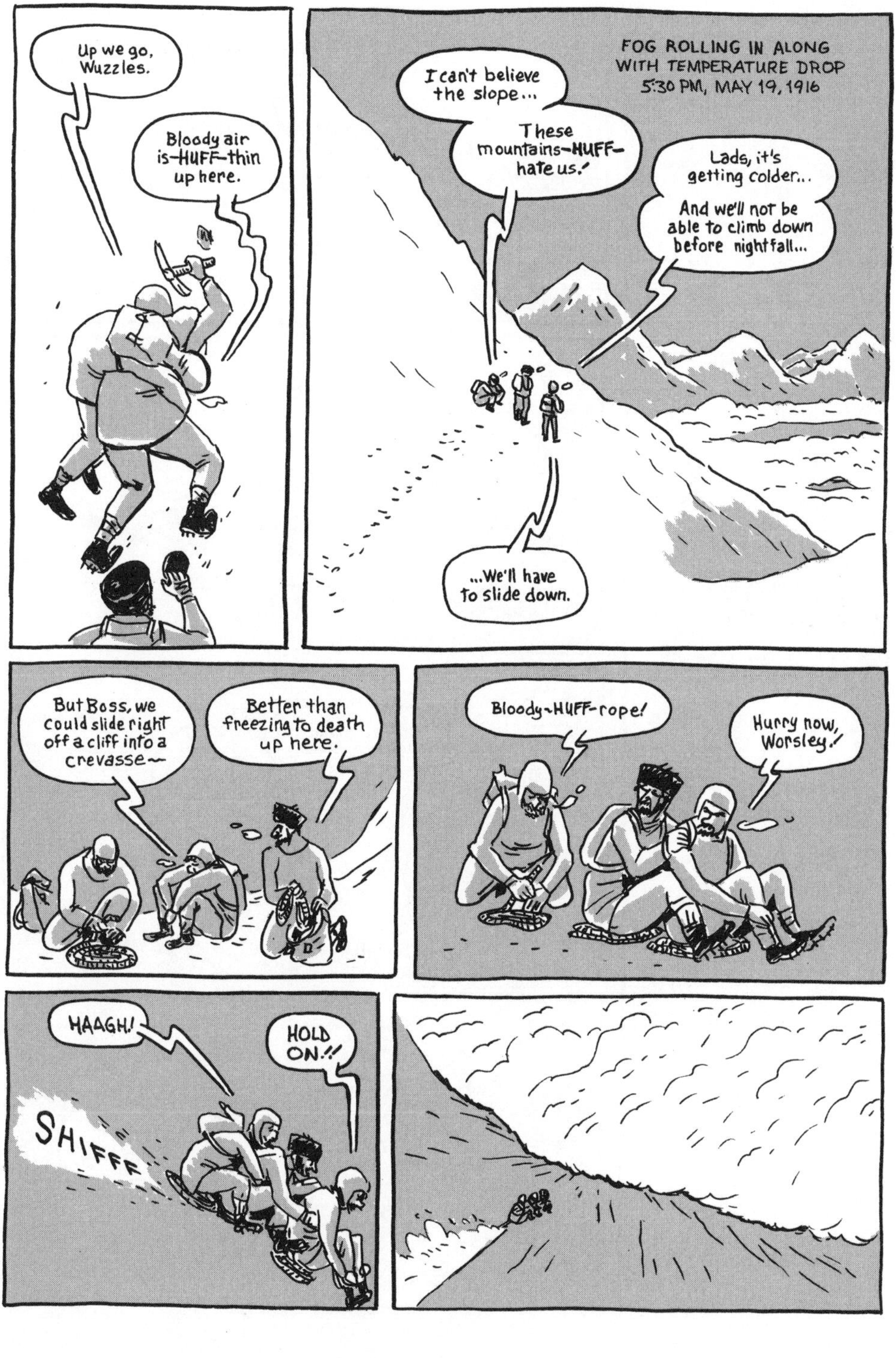
Up we go, Wuzzles.
Bloody air is—HUFF—thin up here.
FOG ROLLING IN ALONG WITH TEMPERATURE DROP 5:30 PM, MAY 19, 1916
I can't believe the slope...
These mountains—HUFF—hate us.!
Lads, it's getting colder...
And we'll not be able to climb down before nightfall...
...We'll have to slide down.
But Boss, we could slide right off a cliff into a crevasse—
Better than freezing to death up here.
Bloody—HUFF—rope!
Hurry now, Worsley.!
HAAGH!
HOLD ON!!
SHIFFF

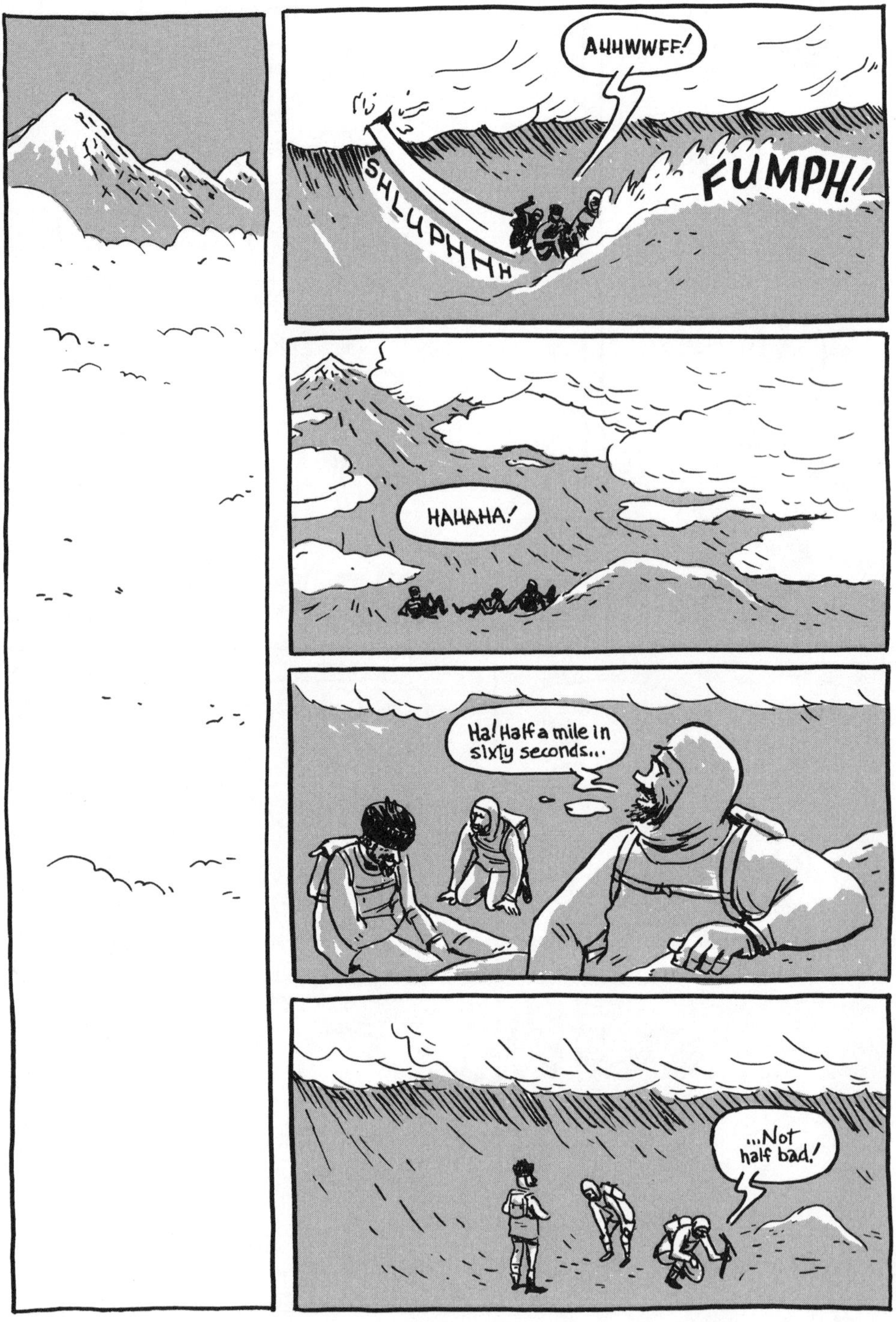
AHHWWFF!
SHLUPHHHH
FUMPH!
HAHAHA!
Ha! Half a mile in sixty seconds...
...Not half bad!

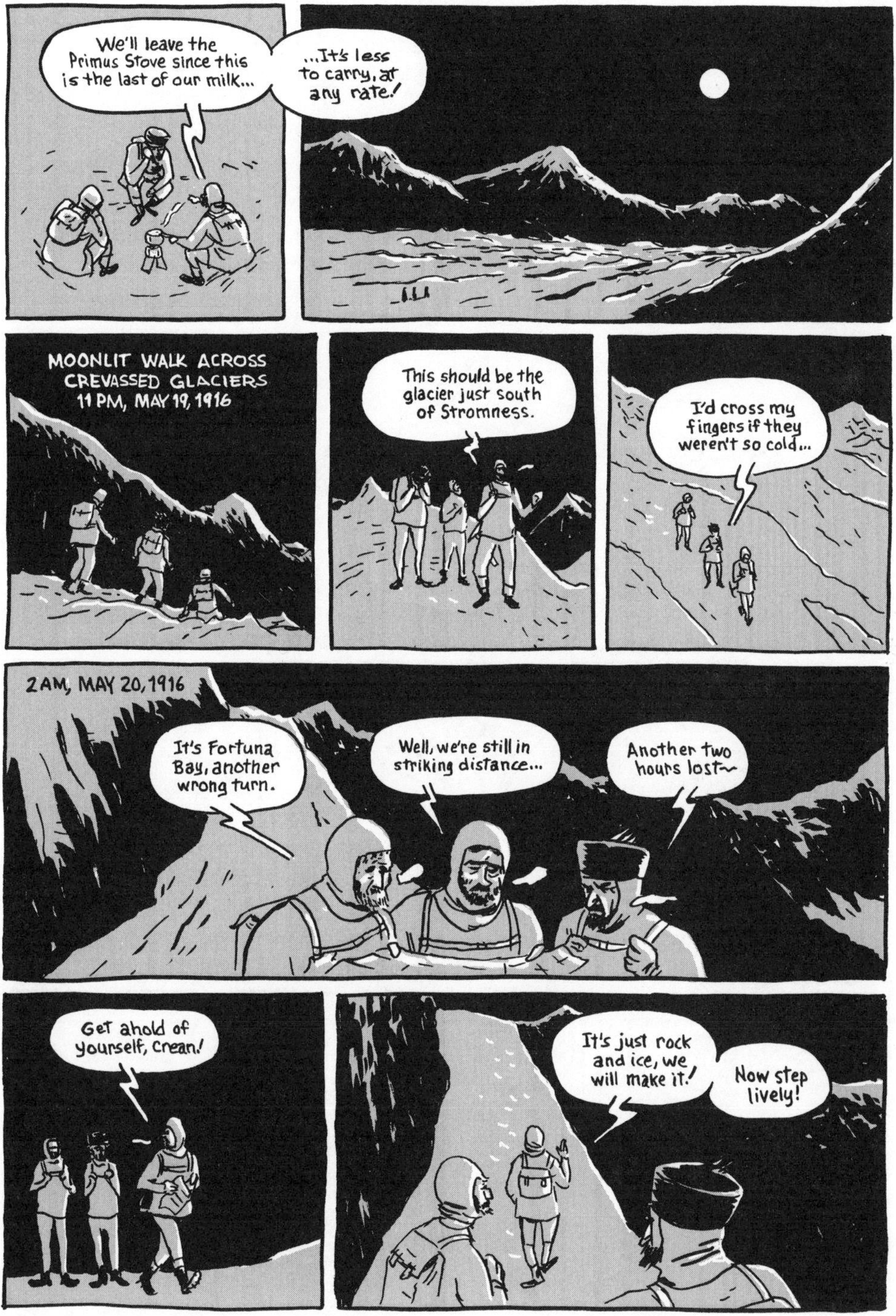
We'll leave the Primus Stove since this is the last of our milk...
...It's less to carry, at any rate!
MOONLIT WALK ACROSS CREVASSED GLACIERS 11 PM, MAY 19, 1916
This should be the glacier just south of Stromness.
I'd cross my fingers if they weren't so cold...
2AM, MAY 20, 1916
It's Fortuna Bay, another wrong turn.
Well, we're still in striking distance...
Another two hours lost~
Get ahold of yourself, Crean!
It's just rock and ice, we will make it!
Now step lively!

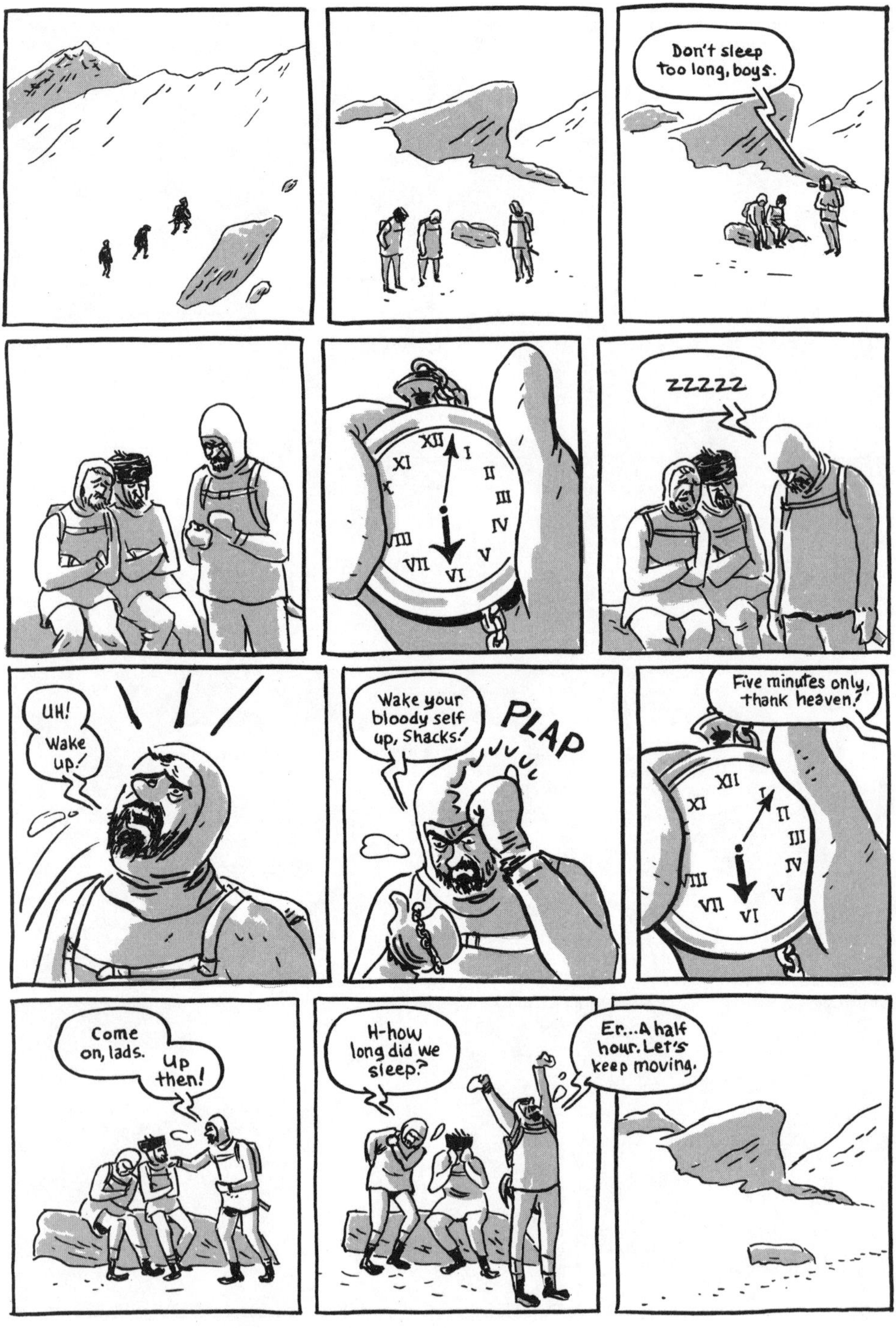
Don't sleep too long, boys.
ZZZZZ
UH!
Wake up!
Wake your bloody self up, Shacks!
PLAP
Five minutes only, thank heaven!
Come on, lads.
Up then!
H-how long did we sleep?
Er...A half hour. Let's keep moving.

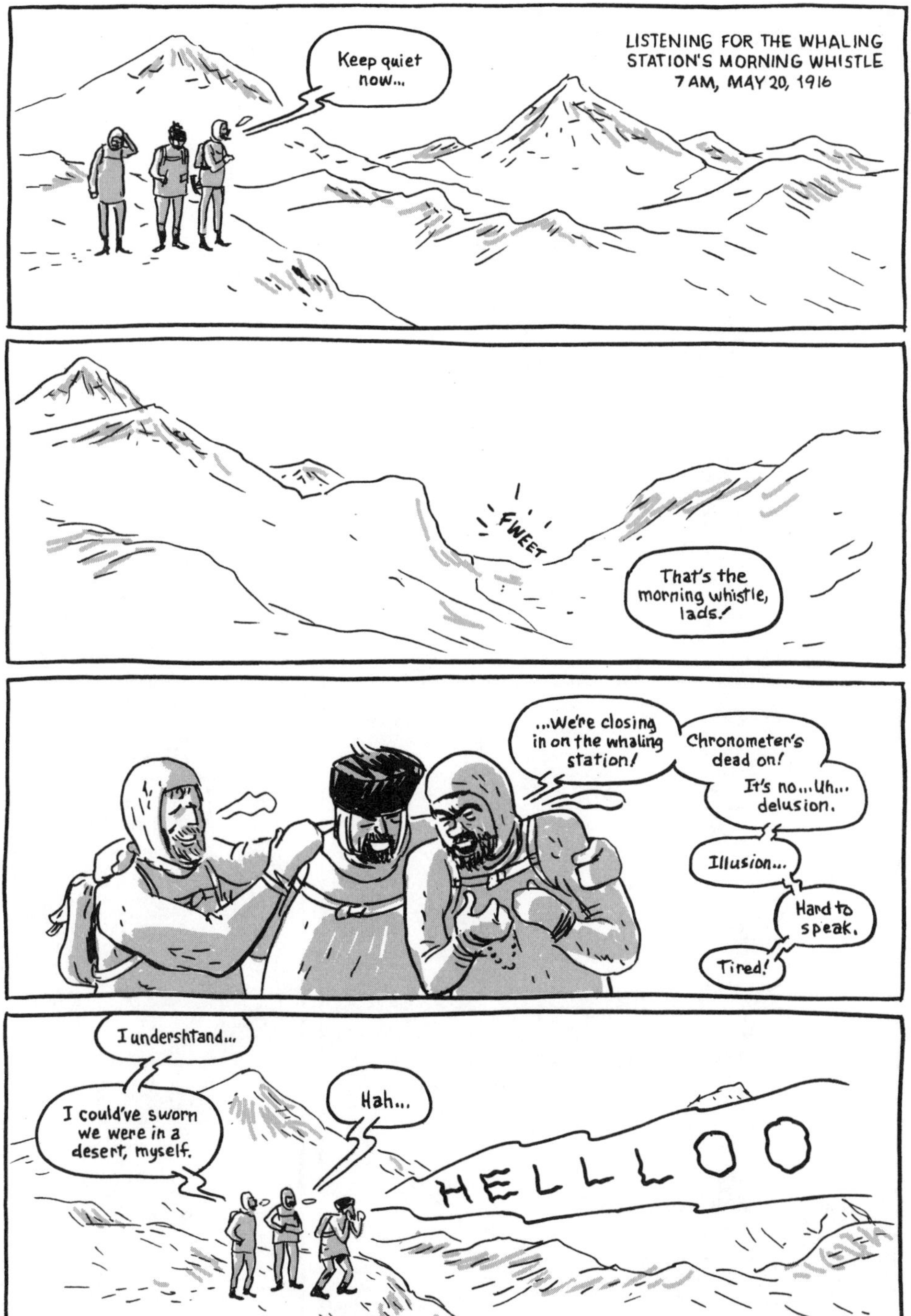
LISTENING FOR THE WHALING STATION'S MORNING WHISTLE 7 AM, MAY 20, 1916
Keep quiet now...
FWEET
That's the morning whistle, lads!
...We're closing in on the whaling station!
Chronometer's dead on!
It's no...Uh... delusion.
Illusion...
Hard to speak.
Tired!
I undershtand...
I could've sworn we were in a desert, myself.
Hah...
HELLLOO

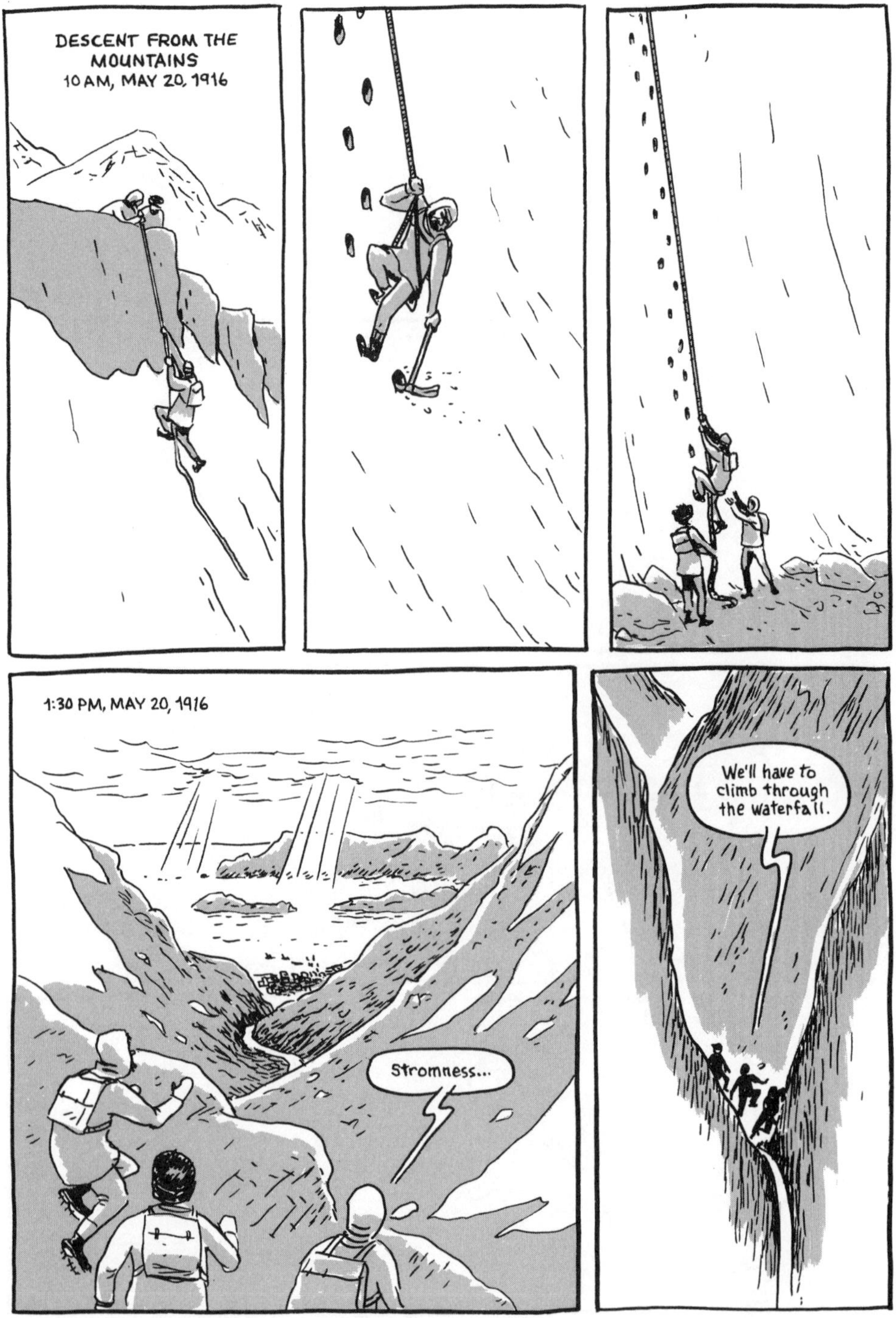
DESCENT FROM THE MOUNTAINS
10 AM, MAY 20, 1916
1:30 PM, MAY 20, 1916
Stromness...
We'll have to climb through the waterfall.

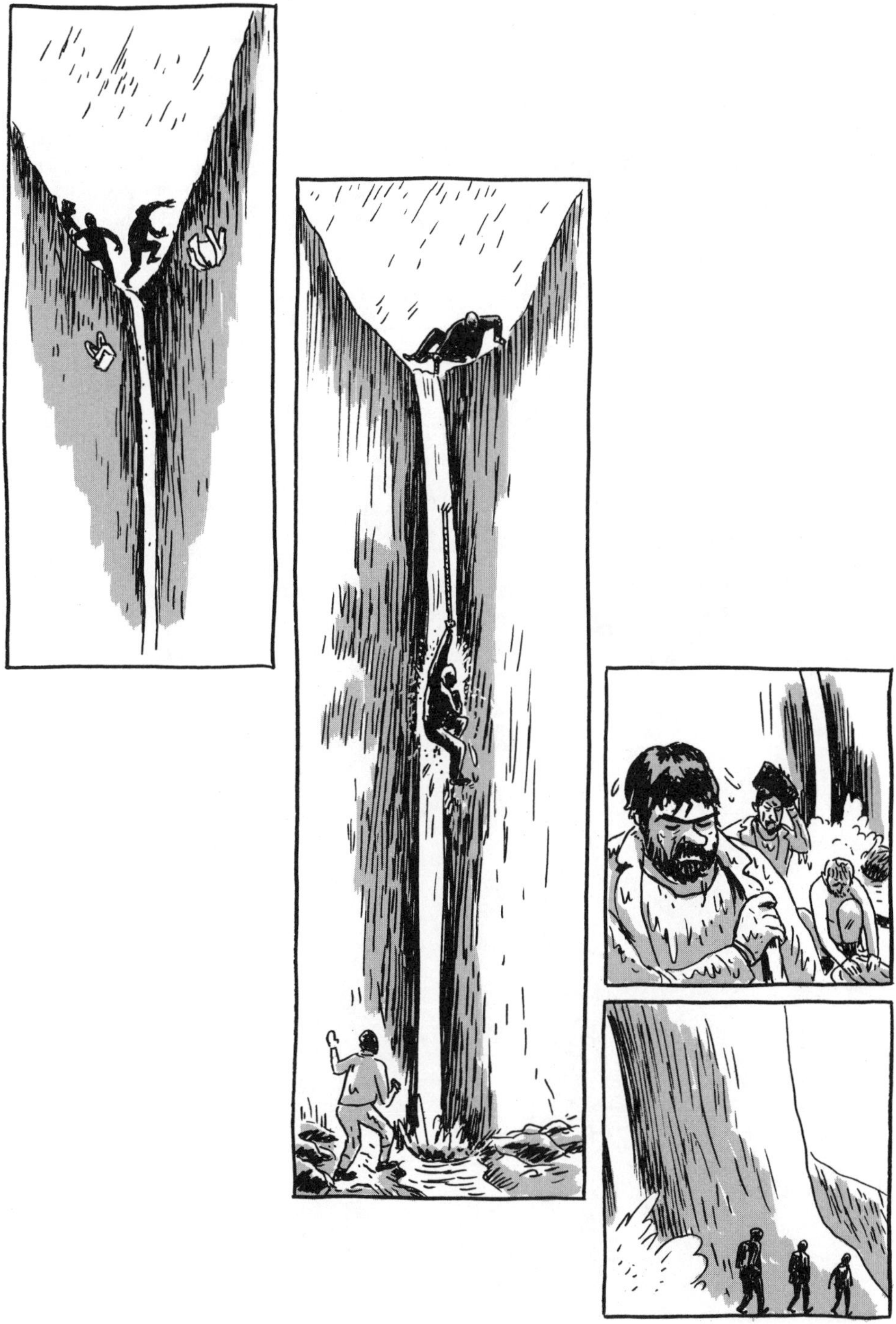

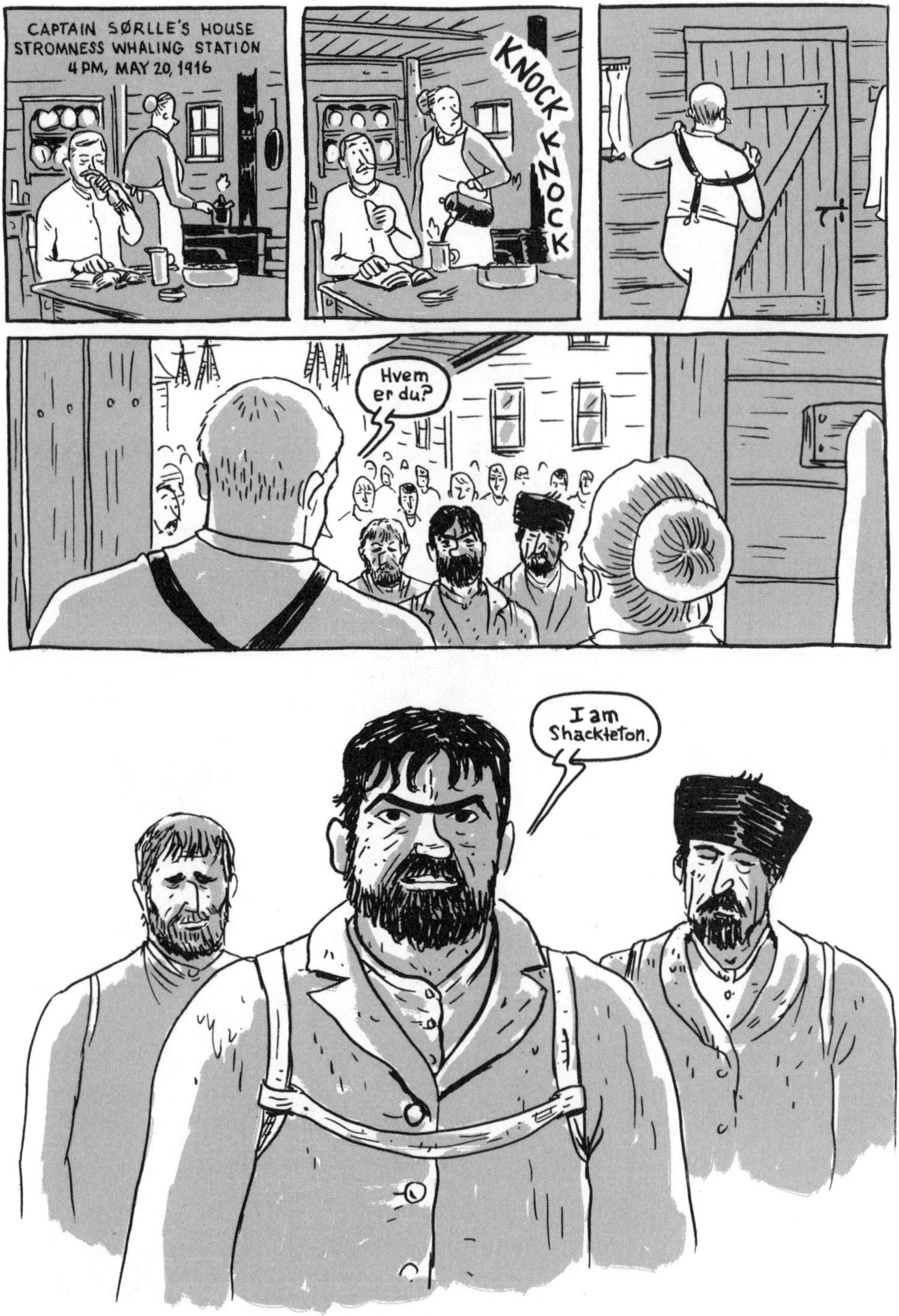
CAPTAIN SØRLLE'S HOUSE
STROMNESS WHALING STATION
4 PM, MAY 20, 1916
KNOCK KNOCK
Hvem er du?
I am Shackleton.

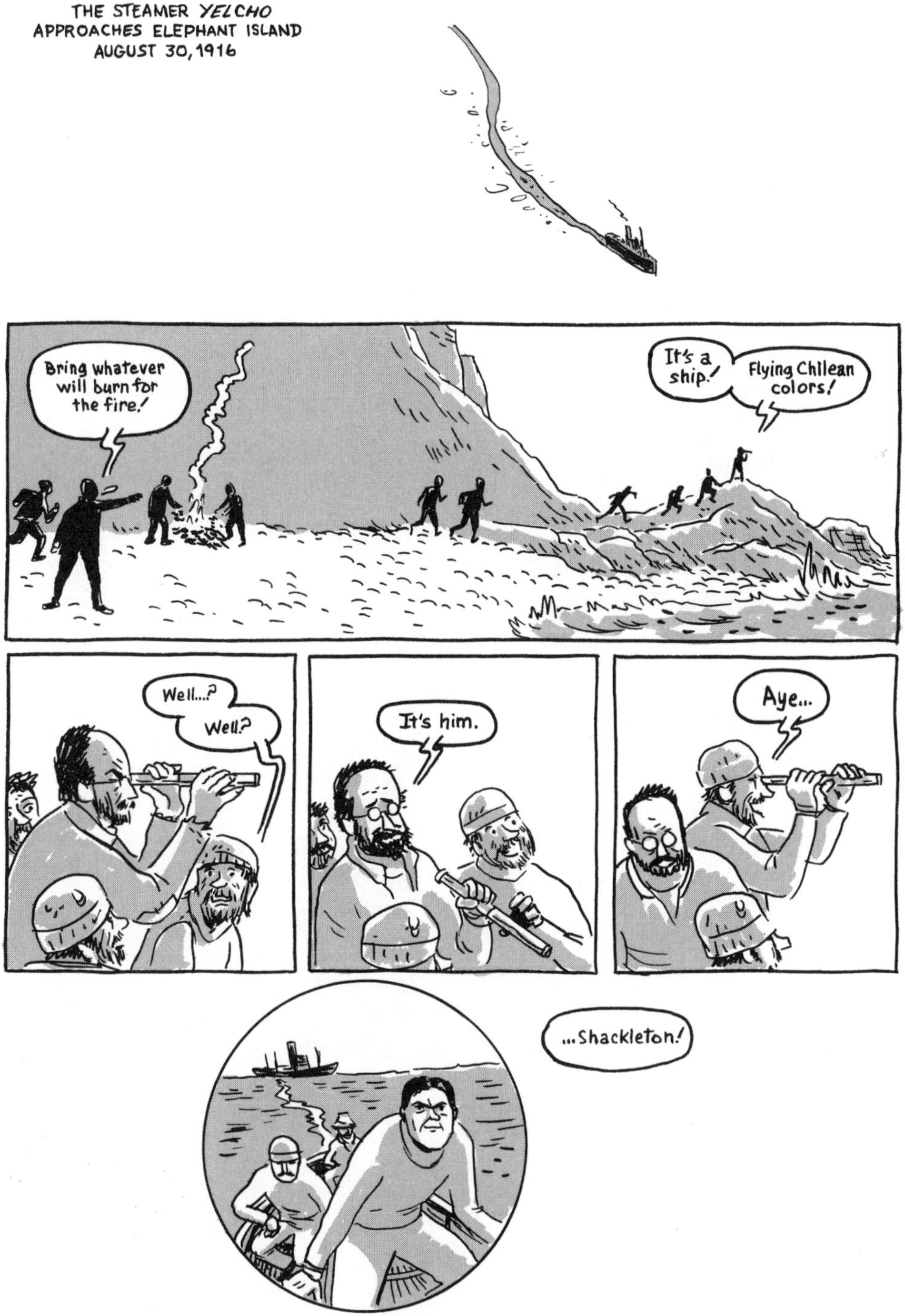
THE STEAMER *YELCHO*
APPROACHES ELEPHANT ISLAND
AUGUST 30, 1916
Bring whatever will burn for the fire!
It's a ship!
Flying Chilean colors!
Well...?
Well?
It's him.
Aye...
...Shackleton!

AFTERWORD

The twenty-two men left on Elephant Island were all saved. The crew of the relief ship *Aurora* succeeded in their mission to lay in supplies for the cross-continental team. They too were caught in ice, and though their ship was not crushed, it was carried away from land for months. The skeleton crew on the ship sailed back to shore once the ice broke up. During the separation, Captain Aeneas Mackintosh and Victor Hayward were lost as they attempted to walk across ice to their base camp. Their deaths followed that of Arnold Spencer-Smith who perished from scurvy as the team lay in supplies. Many of the members of the corps of *Discovery* went on to serve in the British military during WWI. Shackleton himself served in a diplomatic posting as well as a military officer in northern Russia. The majority of the expedition went on to serve in the war, several of the men were killed or severely wounded.

After the war, Shackleton returned to England, lecturing for several years until returning on a final expedition to the Antarctic. He died en route and is buried on South Georgia Island.

SOURCES

PUBLICATIONS

ALEXANDER, CAROLINE. *The Endurance: Shackleton's Legendary Antarctic Expedition.* Alfred A. Knopf: New York, 2001.

HEACOX, KIM. *Shackleton: The Antarctic Challenge.* National Geographic: Washington, D.C., 1999.

LANSING, ALFRED. *Endurance: Shackleton's Incredible Voyage.* Carroll & Graf Publishers, Inc.: New York, 1959.

SHACKLETON, JONATHAN & JOHN MACKENNA. *Shackleton: An Irishman In Antarctica.* The University of Wisconsin Press: Madison, Wisconsin, 2002.

SHACKLETON, SIR ERNEST C.V.O. *South.* Birlinn Limited: Edinburgh, 1919.

WORSLEY, FRANK ARTHUR. *Endurance: An Epic Of Polar Adventure.* W.W. Norton & Company: New York, 1931.

WORSLEY, FRANK ARTHUR. *Shackleton's Boat Journey: The Narrative From The Captain Of The Endurance.* Pimilco: London, 1940.

MUSEUM

HERRESHOFF MARINE MUSEUM/AMERICA'S CUP HALL OF FAME, Bristol, Rhode Island: herreshoff.org/

WEBSITES

AUSTRALIAN NATIONAL MARITIME MUSEUM: anmm.gov.au/site/page.cfm?u=1920

BRAINPICKINGS, "A Rare Look at Antarctica": brainpickings.org/index.php/2011/04/13/australian-antarctica-expedition-1911

LINDA HALL LIBRARY, "23. Dumont d'Urville, Jules Sébastien César (1790-1842)": lindahall.org/events_exhib/exhibit/exhibits/ice/23_dumont.shtml

MODEL SHIP WORLD: modelshipworld.com

NATIONAL GEOGRAPHIC: nationalgeographic.com

NEW YORK PUBLIC LIBRARY ONLINE GALLERY: digitalgallery.nypl.org/nypldigital/index.cfm

ROYAL GEOGRAPHICAL SOCIETY: rgs.org

SCOTT POLAR RESEARCH INSTITUTE: spri.cam.ac.uk

SHACKLETON MUSEUM: shackletonmuseum.com

Thank you to Kim Chaloner, David Mazzucchelli, Mickey Duzyj, the Bertozzi Family, Ted Chaloner & Lydia Walshin, Gregory Benton, Sebastian Coulthard FRGS, Bob & Saul Fingerman, First Second, Dean Haspiel, Seth Kushner, Jason Little, Bob Mecoy, Terry Peters & John Bryan, Charles Shackleton, Chris Sinderson

First Second
New York

Copyright © 2014 by Nicholas Bertozzi

Published by First Second
First Second is an imprint of Roaring Brook Press,
a division of Holtzbrinck Publishing Holdings Limited Partnership,
175 Fifth Avenue, New York, NY 10010

Cataloging-in-Publication Data is on file at the Library of Congress.

ISBN 978-1-59643-451-6

First Second books may be purchased for business or promotiona use. For information on bulk purchases please contact MacMillan Corporate and Premium Sales Department at (800) 221-7945 x5442 or by email at specialmarkets@macmillan.com.

Book design by Colleen AF Venable

First Edition 2014
Printed in the United States of America

10 9 8 7 6 5 4 3 2